checks
and
balances
The Alaska Pipeline Case

ALSO BY JETHRO K. LIEBERMAN

Privacy and the Law
Free Speech, Free Press, and the Law

checks and balances

The Alaska Pipeline Case

JETHRO K. LIEBERMAN

Lothrop, Lee & Shepard Books
New York

The summary of the provisions in the Alaska pipeline bill on pp. 63-66 has been reprinted from the *Congressional Quarterly Almanac*, 1973, by permission of Congressional Quarterly Inc.

The pipeline chronology on pp. 84-87 has been reprinted from the *American University Law Review*, vol. 23, no. 2 (1973) by permission of the *American University Law Review*.

Copyright © 1981 by Jethro K. Lieberman. All rights reserved. No part of this book may be reproduced or utilized in any form or by any means, electronic or mechanical, including photocopying, recording or by any information storage and retrieval system, without permission in writing from the Publisher. Inquiries should be addressed to Lothrop, Lee & Shepard Books, a division of William Morrow & Company, Inc., 105 Madison Avenue, New York, New York 10016.
Printed in the United States of America.
First Edition
1 2 3 4 5 6 7 8 9 10

Library of Congress Cataloging in Publication Data

Lieberman, Jethro Koller.
  Checks and balances.

  Bibliography: p.
  Includes index.
  Summary: Illustrates the complex workings of the system of checks and balances by examining the building of the Alaska pipeline which involved the federal government, a state government, and the actions of private citizens.
  1. Alaska pipeline—Juvenile literature. 2. Petroleum—Pipe lines—Law and legislation—Alaska—Juvenile literature. 3. Petroleum—Pipe lines—Law and legislation—United States—Juvenile literature. 4. Alyeska Pipeline Service Company—Juvenile literature. 5. Wilderness Society—Juvenile literature. [1. Separation of powers. 2. United States—Politics and government. 3. Alaska pipeline. 4. Pipelines] I. Title.
KFA1503.5.Z9L53   343.73′093   81-4787
ISBN 0-688-00672-8   347.30393   AACR2
ISBN 0-688-00673-6 (lib. bdg.)

For Seth and Jessica

Contents

1   OIL AND THE PIPELINE   *1*
    The Discovery   *1*
    The Problem   *3*

2   CONTROLLING THE MAJORITY: THE SYSTEM OF CHECKS AND BALANCES   *7*
    Majority Rule!   *7*
    Separation of Powers   *9*

3   WHO OWNS THE LAND?   *17*
    The History of the Native Land Claims, 1867-1968   *18*
    Congress Finally Acts   *25*
    Checks and Balances: Federal vs. State   *27*

4   THE COURTS INTERVENE   *29*
    The Environmental Issues   *29*
    In the District Court   *37*
    In the Court of Appeals   *41*
    Checks and Balances: The Courts vs. the Executive   *51*

5   CONGRESS REACTS TO THE COURT'S DECISION   *52*
    How a Bill Becomes Law   *53*
    Moving the Pipeline Bill Along   *54*
    The Vice-President Steps In   *56*

    In the House   *58*
    Ironing Out the Senate and House Versions   *59*
    The President Signs   *61*
    Checks and Balances: Congress vs. the Courts   *62*
    Summary of the Provisions in the Alaska Pipeline Bill   *63*

6   WHO PAYS THE LAWYERS?   *67*
    The Cost of Suing   *67*
    Should the Loser Pay?   *68*
    How the Court Reasoned   *69*
    Why Alyeska Should Pay   *72*
    The Dissent   *72*
    Checks and Balances: Public vs. Private Interests   *74*

7   IN THE SUPREME COURT   *75*
    Final But Not Infallible   *75*
    The Supreme Court Reverses   *76*
    Checks and Balances: Courts vs. Courts   *79*

8   THE LAND AND THE PIPELINE   *80*

APPENDIX 1   ROUTE OF THE TRANS-ALASKAN PIPELINE   *83*

APPENDIX 2   PIPELINE CHRONOLOGY   *84*

APPENDIX 3   TEXT OF PUBLIC LAW 93-153   *88*

GLOSSARY   *112*

BIBLIOGRAPHY   *114*

INDEX   *115*

checks and balances
The Alaska Pipeline Case

Chapter 1
Oil and the Pipeline

THE DISCOVERY

In the far Alaskan north, above the Arctic Circle, the sun begins a winter hibernation on Christmas Eve. The next morning the sun does not come up, though for a few hours around noon there is a faint twilight, as if there were leftover light from below the horizon. For three weeks the land lies in darkness, and a chill wind sweeps across the frozen ground.

The winter is cold. It is hard to imagine how cold. On many days, the temperature can drop to as low as 75° F. below zero.

Even in the summer the land is frozen, though stubby plants burst briefly into bloom, but in these weeks of winter gloom it is inhospitable in the extreme. Not the kind of place you would expect to find people busily at work. Yet through the winter of 1967-68, men from "the lower 48" (as Alaskans term the continental United States) were sinking deep shafts in the frozen terrain.

The sun stays below the horizon until January 18. But when it reappears it does not linger long. A month later, on February 18, it is visible for only four hours. By three o'clock in the afternoon, it is already slipping below the horizon, the sunset a dimming band of light at the edge of the earth. A few minutes after three, on this day in 1968, a sudden shock of light—white, then yellow and orange—explodes upward from the earth in a column into the darkening sky.

It is oil. The place is a desolate region of Alaska called Prudhoe Bay, just miles from the Arctic Ocean.

At this particular site on February 18, 1968, men from the Atlantic Richfield Company (now known as Arco) have found what they came for. They have dug a hole 8,800 feet down through the ice and rocks—more than a mile and a half below the surface. On a signal, a valve built into the pipes that line the hole is opened. Natural gas rushes forward, and the pressure of its movement forces up the oil. When it reaches the surface through a series of pipes, which help scientists measure its rate of flow, it is vented to the air. Rather than let it drift through the work site, it is set aflame, both the gas and the oil. The dramatic colors confirm that the search has been worthwhile.

More than worthwhile—the find is astonishingly large. After further testing during the next several months, Arco and Humble Oil and Refining Company, a subsidiary of Exxon Corporation, which had invested money with Arco in the search, announced that the "proven reserves" (that is, the amount of oil that existed for sure beneath the ground) were between 5 and 10 billion barrels. A little while later, these companies and others that had rights to drill in surrounding areas fixed the figure at 9.6 billion barrels. These figures are said to be highly conservative; there may be as much as 30 or 40 billion barrels of oil in the Arctic region of Alaska. Ten billion barrels would have amounted to a 12- to 14-year supply of oil that Americans were currently importing to make up for the excess of what they consumed over what they produced of the gooey substance created by vast pressures in the earth some 225 million years ago. Extra consumption above domestic production was then running about 2 million barrels a day. (From one barrel, 42 gallons of gasoline can be extracted.)

Thus began the great Alaska oil boom. In the mid-1960s,

OIL AND THE PIPELINE 3

when Alaska leased hundreds of thousands of acres for oil exploration, oil companies paid around six dollars an acre. In 1969, when the state held an oil-lease auction after Arco found oil, the lease rights sold for an average of $2,182 per acre. Land near the Prudhoe Bay discovery was leased for more than 14 times that figure: $28,233 an acre, to be exact. All in all, the state took in some $900 million and in return gave 16 companies the right to extract oil from 412,453 acres.

The Problem

The problem that remained was how to move the oil. The Arctic Ocean spends most of the year frozen or clogged with ice; ship passage is difficult most of the time and impossible the rest. (Some companies thought that tankers could make the long journey through the frozen waters and even specially outfitted a ship to attempt it, but in the end the experiment did not work.) If the oil was to move by tanker, it would have to be brought to a port that is open year round. There is such a port in Alaska: Valdez, a small village virtually due south of Prudhoe Bay. In the southeast of the state, Valdez sits on a tiny inlet that opens into the Pacific Ocean. From the oil companies' perspective, it possesses one indispensable feature: its port is one of the few in the United States that can accommodate the giant "supertankers" that can haul hundreds of thousands of tons of oil on a single journey. Oil from Valdez could be shipped to Seattle, where plans were readied to build a sophisticated refinery to transform the crude oil into usable products in domestic—and perhaps foreign—markets.

To get the oil to Valdez, however, is another matter. The complicating factor is the size of the state of Alaska. Though everyone knows that Alaska is the largest state, just how big it is is often forgotten. It is one fifth the land mass of the rest of the United States but its coastline is longer: 6640 miles, compared to 4980 miles for the lower 48. Alaska stretches across four time zones. It is interesting to superimpose a map of Alaska over that of the continental United States. Doing so will show that it would span the entire continent. The tip of the panhandle (the section that runs along the west coast of Canada) would rest in Florida. The westernmost island in the Aleutian Island chain, which is part of the state, would stretch to southern California. (The Aleutians extend to a point 1500 miles west of Hawaii.) The northernmost spot, Point Barrow, would land in northern Minnesota. Another way of looking at its size is the joke Alaskans like to tell on Texans who have bragged a bit too much about the size of their state. If you don't watch out, the story goes, we'll chop ourselves in two and then Texas will be the *third* largest state.

The Alaskan distances meant that to get the oil from the Prudhoe wells to Valdez, it would have to be transported across 789 miles of frozen ground. The only known way to do this is through a pipeline. It would be an expensive undertaking. When Arco, British Petroleum, and Humble Oil pooled resources in June 1969 to form the Trans-Alaska Pipeline System (known as TAPS until it was reorganized a year and a half later), they reckoned it would cost some $900 million to build.

The north-south Alaska pipeline was not the only alternative. There were several possibilities for bringing the oil through Canada and linking into existing pipeline systems, to deposit the oil ultimately at various points in the midwestern United States. But for a variety of reasons, some still not fully explained, from the very first days of the discovery, the decision was made to pipe the oil through Alaska.

Some thought—and still think—that the intense desire to build the trans-Alaska pipeline stemmed from the profits to be made by selling the oil to Japan. At the time, although the United States was beginning to import more oil, there seemed to be adequate supplies on the West Coast. The Prudhoe Bay oil might well have been surplus. Because of a twist in the law regulating the use of ships, the oil companies might have made more money if they sold the oil to the Japanese, who are heavily dependent on imports. Under the law, goods shipped to American ports had to be carried in American ships, which employ higher-priced labor. Sales to the Japanese could have been made through ships registered in foreign nations, and transportation costs could have been reduced considerably. Thus, it may not have been coincidental that in 1969 TAPS ordered the huge steel pipes—48 inches in diameter—from three Japanese steel companies at a seemingly cheap price, much to the consternation of the American steel industry.

Though it was an expensive and expansive construction project, it did seem at the outset that it could be undertaken and completed fairly quickly. The oil companies wanted the oil flowing by 1971.

But this was not to be. Legal problems developed beyond the control of Alaska that involved every branch of the federal government. TAPS needed permission to bisect Alaska with 48-inch steel pipe, and the person who could give that permission did not reside in Juneau, the capital, but in Washington, D.C., some 4,000 miles away. Moreover, because of an obscure law it looked as though even that person, the Secretary of the Interior, was powerless to do so. It might take an act of the United States Congress to permit construction across areas of the U.S. that most Americans had never heard of. But none of this could come to pass until that same Congress disposed of a problem that had been unresolved for over a century: the rights of Alaskan Natives to their ancestral land. And no sooner had this question been raised than groups concerned about the earth's ecology became worried about the possible adverse effects of the pipeline on the delicate Alaskan tundra, and went to court to try to do something about it. What had seemed like merely a difficult engineering job turned into a tangled story of law and democracy in action. But before we continue with the story, let's first see how our government is set up to come to grips with a complex problem like the building of the Alaska pipeline.

Chapter 2

Controlling the Majority: The System of Checks and Balances

MAJORITY RULE!

This familiar phrase seems to sum up for Americans the way we go about making any kind of group decision. "Let's vote," we say, when we want to decide where to go on a class trip, who the captain of our team should be, or what rules to use in a backyard game of football.

How else could we decide? The owner of the football could refuse to let the others play unless they abide by his rules; the teacher could decide on the trip for the class; the coach could pick the team captain. But that isn't very democratic. A decision dictated by someone in authority, even if it is a very good decision, tends to make people resentful, and it can interfere with the work to be done, the game to be played. It is usually easier, and provokes fewer quarrels, to let the majority decide. Their decision may not always be the best, but those who voted will feel it to be the proper one, and more often than not they will honor it.

Just so, majority rule is the essence of democracy and government in the United States. Our government is not composed of kings and nobility who rule us by dictating laws that they think are good for us (or, more likely, that they think are good for them). Our leaders are representatives of the public, elected by the majority. The laws that they make are the result of their votes, and again, the majority rules. Only laws made in this manner are accepted in a free country.

Majority rule is thus an important principle of democratic government, but it is not the only one. If the minority does not like the rules voted on for a football game, they can refuse to play. The majority has an incentive, therefore, to take into account the minority's feelings or there may be no game at all. But even if the majority insists on its own way, those who disagree can usually go somewhere else and play by their own rules.

This option—to leave and go elsewhere—is not so easy for citizens of nations. When the majority in the legislature passes a law that a minority in the community dislikes and disagrees with, it is almost never sensible or practicable for them to pack up and leave. Besides, where could they go, except to another country where the same problem could arise?

This is an often uncomfortable fact of life. If majority rule were the only principle of government, a person could be as oppressed as if a king were to dictate all the laws. A majority can be no less tyrannical than an individual dictator. For freedom to exist and flourish, there must be some way of curbing the majority.

In the United States, there are a number of such ways. One is the rule of the Constitution. This document, drafted in 1787 and ratified in 1789, prohibits the majority from passing certain kinds of laws. (For example, it is unconstitutional to pass a law punishing someone for doing something that was legal at the time that he did it. Kings and parliaments in Europe used to pass these kinds of laws frequently.) Various amendments to the Constitution (there have been 25 as of 1981), including the first 10 (known as the Bill of Rights), place additional restraints on the government.

By itself, however, the Constitution is not enough to guarantee freedom from oppression. Laws can be broken. Banks are still robbed even though there are laws against stealing. Governments can also break laws, and the people's representatives can violate the Constitution. There must be something more than the Constitution itself to ensure its survival.

Separation of Powers

One of the most important "somethings" is the "separation of powers." This phrase cannot be found in the Constitution. Yet the Constitution created it by dividing the powers of government and parceling them out to separate governmental branches.

The Legislative Branch

The legislative power (the power to legislate, or make laws) was given to Congress. This national legislative body is itself divided. It has two parts: the Senate and the House of Representatives. All members of Congress are elected by the people in their states, but in different ways and for different periods of time. Each state sends two senators to Congress, so there are 100 senators in the Senate. There are many more representatives—435 to be exact. These are elected from districts within the states. Each member of the House represents a district of roughly the same number of people. Thus, Alaska, with fewer than half a million people, sends the same number of senators to Washington as does California, with more than 20 million inhabitants. But Alaska sends only one representative, whereas California sends 43.

Senators are elected for six-year terms, and only one third of the Senate seats are up for election in any election year. The Senate is therefore called a "continuing" body, since 66 or 67 of the senators who were in the previous session of the Senate are automatically members of the next one. This is not the case with the House of Representatives. Each member of Congress is elected to a two-year term, so the voters get a chance to elect the entire House of Representatives every two years. The House is not a continuing body, since it is possible (though it never happens) for every incumbent congressman to be defeated for reelection and for there to be an entirely new list of congressmen.

For a "bill" (a proposed law) to become an actual law, each house of Congress must pass it by majority vote. The legislative power is therefore divided in half, and each half must agree before a law can be made. One house of Congress serves as a *check* and *balance* against the other.

This power to check and balance is of fundamental importance to American democracy. It means that no single majority can always have its way, because no single majority has all the power. The House of Representatives consists of people elected by majorities in 435 separate Congressional districts. Each of these majorities is different—different people, different problems, different interests. Similarly, the Senate consists of people elected by majorities in 50 different states, and rarely are the two senators in the same state elected in the same year. The statewide electorate differs, in turn, from the various electorates in the Congressional districts within the states.

By voting against it, the Senate can veto a bill that the House of Representatives passes. Likewise, the House can kill a bill that a Senate majority wants. For any bill to emerge as a law from Congress, all sorts of compromises must be made among the various interests at stake, so that a truly national majority can support it.

And that is not the end of the line. That is really only the beginning, because the legislative power is only the first of three major governmental powers.

The Executive Branch

The second is the executive power. This is the power to carry out (or "execute") the laws that Congress enacts. The Chief Executive of the United States is the President. He has the power to "veto" any bill the Congress passes. The President (along with the Vice-President) is the only official elected by the entire country (he gets a four-year term), so his majority is different from that of either house of Congress. The President can check the actions of Congress by refusing to sign one of its bills into law.

If the President vetoes a bill, is it then automatically dead? The answer is, not necessarily. Congress has still one more chance to check the action of the President. Under the rules laid down in the Constitution, each house can override the President's veto by reenacting the bill, only this time by a two-thirds vote. If Congress overrides the veto in this manner, the bill automatically becomes law without the President's signature.

Nor is this the end of the line. Other executive branch officials might now get into the act. Many laws that Congress enacts are relatively vague and leave it up to a federal department or agency to issue specific rules. For example, an environmental law might "delegate" to the Secretary of the Interior, one of the 12 Cabinet officers, the power to decide whether federal lands can be used for either private or public purposes. Though the Secretary is only one person, and the decision need not be put to a vote, he is subject to the wishes of his boss, the President.

Independent agencies and executive departments are not

mentioned in the Constitution, and so are sometimes said to be the "fourth branch" of government. (We will come to the third branch shortly.) In recent years, this fourth branch has gained increasing power to help make laws, according to the rules set forth by Congress and the President. The people who staff the agencies and departments, however, are not elected by the voters. These administrators and their assistants constitute still another group of government officials with power to check and balance the actions of Congress or the President. But since they are creatures of Congress and the President, if they step too far out of line they can be slapped down by Congress, which can either withdraw the powers delegated to an agency or directly overturn any of the rules it issues, just as the President can often overrule the decisions of his Cabinet officers.

The Judicial Branch

The third separate governmental power is the judicial power. The Constitution placed this power in the third branch of government—the courts (or the "judiciary"). The judicial power is the power to hear cases between people claiming rights under the laws. When necessary, the courts may interpret the law in order to decide the cases. In the federal government, the judicial power exists within three layers of federal courts.

Most cases begin in the United States district courts. Private citizens and the government may "file" (bring) lawsuits in the district courts when a federal law has been violated, causing injury to the private citizen or to the public as a whole. The U.S. district judge (who is the trial judge) sits to hear the case and rules on legal questions. If there is a jury, it decides what the facts of the case are; if there is no jury, the trial judge also performs this function. The U.S. district judge has the power, in the appropriate case, to rule that the government itself has violated the law—or even that the law in question violated the Constitution. The district courts are another means of checking the power of government, since they can overturn the legislative and the executive branches when they stray beyond their authority.

There are 91 federal district courts in the United States. Each state has at least one district, and some have as many as four, depending on the population and the number of cases filed annually. No federal district court covers more than one state. Altogether, there are 507 U.S. district judges.

After a judgment or verdict is reached in the district court, it can be "appealed" (taken to) an "appellate" court, known as the U.S. Court of Appeals. Judges of these courts have the power to review the decisions of the district judges and to "reverse" them when the district judges have misinterpreted the law. Many decisions of federal executive agencies, such as those of the Federal Trade Commission and others, may also be appealed to the courts of appeals.

There are 12 separate courts of appeals, divided across the country by "circuits." The U.S. Court of Appeals for the First Circuit hears appeals from district courts in Massachusetts, Maine, Rhode Island, New Hampshire, and Puerto Rico. The U.S. Court of Appeals for the Second Circuit hears appeals from the district courts in New York, Connecticut, and Vermont. And so on. There are 132 judges on the courts of appeals.

Finally, some decisions of the courts of appeals may be further appealed to the U.S. Supreme Court. This court is the only one mentioned in the Constitution, and it also has the power to hear appeals from various state courts.

There is only one Supreme Court. It sits in Washington and consists of the Chief Justice of the United States and eight associate justices. In deciding appeals, the court of appeals judges usually sit in panels of three judges each. The Supreme Court always sits as a panel of nine, and each justice's vote, including the Chief Justice's, counts equally. As in other parts of the government, the majority rules.

Federal judges are not elected. They are appointed by the President, with the consent of the Senate. If a majority of senators disapproves the President's choice, the nominee is not confirmed and cannot take a seat on the "bench." Those who are confirmed hold office for life, the only government officials in the United States who do so. Because they sit for life and because the Constitution says their salaries cannot be lowered while they are in office, federal judges are personally independent of the other two branches of government and feel free, therefore, to scrutinize carefully the actions of Congress, the President, and the executive branch.

But the courts are not beyond the reach of the other branches of government. Congress has the power to decide where the particular district and appeals courts should sit, and can increase or decrease their number at will (though it can only reduce the number of judges actually serving on the courts by waiting until some retire or die and then eliminating the vacant positions). Congress can also decide what types of cases the federal courts can hear. For example, ordinarily automobile accident cases can only be heard in state courts. But when the victim and the person who caused the accident are citizens of different states, their case can be heard in federal courts. If Congress chooses to, it can abolish the power of the federal courts to hear such cases. (Bills to abolish these so-called diversity-of-citizenship cases were introduced in Congress in the 1970s, and the debate whether or not to do so continues on into the 1980s.) Congress can also overrule the courts directly by overturning the courts' interpretations of the laws. This it does by passing new laws. (Congress cannot reverse the courts' interpretations of the Constitution, however; this can only be done by later courts' reversing themselves or by constitutional amendment.)

This brief sketch shows how very much more complicated American democracy is than the simple slogan "majority rule" would lead us to believe. The separation of governmental powers into three major branches—legislative, executive, and judicial—means that each can be a check on the attempts of the other branches to make bad laws, to carry them out wrongly, or to misinterpret them. And within each branch, a system of checks and balances is also at work. Congress is divided into two houses, the decisions of trial courts are subject to review in higher courts, and the work of executive branch officials is frequently reviewed by higher authority.

Private Power

But as intricate as this system of checks and balances is, it is not enough to guarantee that our law will be fair and applied evenhandedly. Checks and balances within the government are essential, but so is the power of the people privately to contest what the government does. In addition to public checks, there must be private ones.

The most familiar example takes us to where we started: voting for our representatives. Private citizens may organize parties and work actively for the defeat of certain candidates and the election of others. They may field a slate of candidates pledged to pass certain laws and carry out certain policies.

But this is not the only way in which private citizens have the power to check the actions of government. Thanks to the First Amendment* everyone may talk about, protest, and

---

* For the story of the First Amendment and how it applies to our life today, see *Free Speech, Free Press, and the Law* (New York: Lothrop, Lee & Shepard Books, 1980) by the same author.

write about the activities of government. They may go straight to Congress and remonstrate against the President or one of the departments or agencies. They may also go to court on their own, without waiting for some official to bring a suit. Only if power is dispersed in all these ways—through the various organs of the government and among the millions of people who inhabit the land—can we hope to avoid the tyranny of a democratic majority.

It was through the interactions, decisions, and orders of these various branches of our government—in other words, through the system of checks and balances—that the knotty questions surrounding the building of the Alaska pipeline were eventually answered. The very first question broached was: Who owns exactly what parts of Alaska?

Chapter 3

Who Owns the Land?

If you wanted to build a stone footpath that runs from the street at the front of your yard to the edge of your neighbor's property at the back, you need only map out the path and lay down the stones. If you wanted to continue the path through your neighbor's yard, to lead you out to the street behind you, you would, of course, have to ask your neighbor's permission. If your neighbor was agreeable, the work could start right away. But suppose the identity of your neighbor was not clear. Suppose three different people claimed that they owned the property next to yours. That was the situation TAPS faced when it set about to build the trans-Alaska pipeline.

The vast expanse of Alaska, more than 586,000 square miles (or 375 million acres), had three sets of claimants. One was the state itself: it claimed title, under an act of Congress, to 102 million acres. Another group of claimants was the Native Alaskans, the Eskimos, Indians, and Aleuts who descended from the tribes who had inhabited the land for thousands of years, who constituted about one sixth of Alaska's population of some 300,000 (in 1970), and who still roamed vast spaces to hunt, fish, and gather crops. Their claims embraced more than 90 percent of the state. The third claimant was the United States of America, which held at the time of statehood in 1958 92.4 million acres in federal reserves.

The land to which these groups laid claim overlapped. Natives claimed much of the acreage held by the state. Although the state government was entitled to nearly one third of the total area of Alaska, precisely which acres had not been determined.

Complicating the situation still further, by the late 1960s the lands of Alaska were doubly frozen. Extreme cold made the tundra difficult enough to build on, but the federal government, through the U.S. Interior Department, had declared a "land freeze"—a prohibition against the sale of oil and mineral rights by the state even on land to which it laid claim. Nothing could be built or developed on state land until the Natives' land claims were settled.

Though the Natives' claims were not TAPS's responsibility, they became its worry. If it was going to get its pipeline constructed, it had to know which acres belonged to whom and to secure from each permission to build. That would require Congressional legislation to end a century of legal uncertainty. To understand the connection between ancient land claims and the modern desire to transport oil, we must journey back to the beginnings, in 1867.

The History of the Native Land Claims, 1867-1968

In that year, the United States purchased Alaska from Russia for the sum of $7 million, in a deal arranged by Secretary of State William H. Seward. Alaska, which lies only 50 miles from a protruding limb of Siberia, was too much for the Russians to manage, and it seemed to the Americans to have commercial possibilities in the seal trade.

But buying a huge parcel of land on which thousands of people live is not quite like buying an empty lot down the street. All that the Russians could sell was what they owned, and they did not own clear title to the Natives' land. At most, the Russians exercised governmental authority over the peoples of Alaska, and at most that is what the United States government acquired.

That this is what the United States thought it was purchasing seems clear from the treaty with Russia. Article 3 read:

> The inhabitants of the ceded territory, according to their choice, reserving their natural allegiance, may return to Russia within three years; but if they should prefer to remain in the ceded territory, they, with the exception of the uncivilized tribes, shall be admitted to the enjoyment of all the rights, advantages, and immunities of citizens of the United States and shall be maintained and protected in the free enjoyment of their liberty. property, and religion. The uncivilized tribes will be subject to such laws and regulations as the United States may, from time to time, adopt in regard to aboriginal tribes of that country.

The language of the treaty suggests that Congress could do whatever it pleased with the Indians. But Congress did not act directly toward the Alaskan Natives at that time. Instead, American policy toward the Natives was the same as that stated officially in the Northwest Ordinance of 1787: "The utmost good faith shall always be observed towards the Indians; their lands and property shall never be taken from them without their consent; and in their property rights and liberty they never shall be invaded or disturbed, unless in just and lawful wars authorized by Congress." This was rather more an ideal than a practice; few, if any, wars against the Indians were justified in the continental United States, and most of the government's energy during the nineteenth century in its dealings with the native tribes consisted of herding them into reservations.

In Alaska, the territory's government during its first 17 years under U.S. rule was the captain of the Navy ships that patrolled the waters. There were few whites from the mainland: in 1880, only 300. The Natives were for the most part free to carry on their traditional ways.

In 1884, Congress enacted the Organic Act. It established a territorial governor, to be appointed by the President, and created a body of laws, especially those dealing with mining. But the 1884 law also contained a provision dealing with the Natives. It provided "that the Indians or other persons in said district shall not be disturbed in the possession of any lands actually in their use or occupation or now claimed by them but the terms under which such persons may acquire title to such lands is reserved for future legislation by Congress."

For some 90 years, Congress refused to enact such legislation. The government's relationship to the Alaskan Natives was remote. For the most part, Congress ignored them. Thus, when Congress enacted the Indian Allotment Act in 1887 to encourage Indians to settle on farms, the Alaskan Natives were excluded from its terms. A body of land law developed applicable to white settlers and businessmen, such as the fishermen, canners, and miners, but this body of law did not apply to the Natives.

Congress Sidesteps the Issue

As the years wore on, the activities of the white settlers increasingly infringed on the traditional activities of the Natives. Hunting and fishing grounds were being taken over. Natives protested to the Secretary of the Interior in the 1880s, but he responded that the power to do something about the encroachment lay in the hands of Congress.

By 1900, a growing national consciousness that conservation was vital began to take hold in Congress. From time to time, large chunks of land were "reserved from" private hands. This first happened in 1902 when Congress created the Tongass National Forest, a 16-million-acre preserve that included some Native lands. Four years later, coal mining was prohibited in all coal fields. In 1907, Congress established the four and one-half million acre Chugach National Forest.

In 1908, to make it easier to conserve lands in their natural state, Congress delegated the authority to the President, who in turn vested the power in the Secretary of the Interior. More preserves were created, including Mount McKinley National Park in 1916. In 1923, the Naval Petroleum Reserve Number 4, a 23-million-acre piece of wilderness, was set aside in the Arctic.

Meantime, the form of Alaska government was changed. In 1912, the same year that Arizona and New Mexico became states, Congress declared Alaska to be a territory, entitling it to an elected legislature and a Congressional representative (though he could not vote). One question was whether Natives were entitled to vote in the territorial elections. This question was settled in 1924 when Congress extended citizenship to all Natives throughout the United States.

Beginning in the 1930s, conflicts between the Natives and commercial interests over land began to grow more intense. By the 1950s, it became increasingly urgent for some sort of settlement to be made. The ultimate power to resolve the conflict lay with Congress, but only once had it acted. In 1935, Congress gave the Tlingit Indians the right to sue in the U.S. Court of Claims for land taken from them when the Tongass National Forest was created 33 years earlier. These claims were not finally settled until 1968, when the Tlingits accepted $7.5 million (or a mere 40 cents an acre).

Congress could have resolved all the legal uncertainties when it finally granted Alaska statehood in 1958. But it did not. Instead, it sidestepped the politically tricky issue; indeed, in some ways it made the problem more difficult.

At the time of statehood, the federal government controlled 92.4 million acres of Alaskan land. This included national parks, forests, monuments, petroleum and power reserves, wildlife refuges, and reservations held in trust for the Indians. That left 271.8 million acres. Under the law making Alaska a state, Congress declared that Alaska could take 103 million acres. At the time, private individuals held only some 700,000 acres and claimed an additional 600,000. But what of the Native land claims? The Alaska Statehood Act of 1958 said:

> As a compact with the United States, [Alaska] and its people do agree and declare that they forever disclaim all right and title to any lands or other property not granted or confirmed to the state or its political subdivision by or under the authority of this act, the right or title to which is held by the United States or is subject to disposition by the United States and to any lands or other property (including fishing rights), the right or title to which may be held by Indians, Eskimos, or Aleuts . . . or is held by the United States in trust for said natives; that all such lands or other property (including fishing rights) the right or title to which may be held by the United States in trust for said natives, shall be and remain under the absolute jurisdiction and control of the United States until disposed of under its authority, except to such extent as the Congress has prescribed or may hereafter prescribe, and except when held by individual natives in fee without restrictions on alienation.

This, unfortunately, is a fair sample of Congressional prose. Its meaning is difficult to interpret. It seems to say that the state of Alaska could not thereafter claim rights to land held by the Natives. But at the same time, the law seems to indicate that these lands are under the control of the United States, not the Natives. In any event, the law left unclear how the state's claims to its 103 million acres could be reconciled with Native claims to the same land. Did the law give Alaska the right to pick out any 103 million acres? Or did Alaska have to choose from lands not claimed by the Natives? The answer was that nothing had been settled, and the only authority for doing so was Congress. In effect, Congress had sidestepped once again.

The problem was especially serious. Under the law, the state had ten years, or until 1969, to choose some of its 103 million acres, and 25 years, or until 1984, to choose the rest. The procedure was for the state to submit its selection to the Bureau of Land Management, which is part of the Department of the Interior. But every time the state did so, one of several Native groups submitted a counterclaim to the BLM. Often, these groups were encouraged to submit their counterclaims by the Bureau of Indian Affairs, which was also part of the Interior Department. By 1966, the state had title to about 25 million of its promised acreage. But the Natives by then had laid claim to 388,820,240 acres. This was more land than Alaska possessed. In order to sort out the conflicting claims, Interior Secretary Stuart L. Udall issued the "land freeze." Until the Natives' claims were approved or rejected, no state claims would be approved.

This was the state of affairs when oil was discovered at Prudhoe Bay. Thus, a century-old problem stood in the way of TAPS's desire to build the pipeline, for until all claims were settled it would prove impossible to secure the necessary permits to build. If construction was to go forward, the Natives would somehow have to be satisfied. The legal solution remained with Congress.

In late 1968, Richard M. Nixon, just elected President, chose Alaska Governor Walter J. Hickel to be the new Secretary of the Interior. The choice pleased neither the Natives nor the environmentalists, who were just coming into the picture, because Hickel had been pledged to prompt selection of the best land for the state and for the development of the oil fields. He favored the pipeline.

Now, however, the system of checks and balances took over. The President is entitled to name his Cabinet officers, but each must be confirmed by the Senate. The chairman of the

Senate Interior Committee was Henry Jackson, Democrat of Washington State, who had long had an interest in Alaskan affairs. In order to win Jackson's and the Committee's backing, Hickel had to promise not to lift the land freeze without first securing the Committee's approval. The House Interior Committee made the same deal. So what by law was delegated to the Secretary of the Interior would now be shared with two committees of Congress.

Just before he left office, Secretary Udall issued a still stronger regulation that put Alaskan land into "the deep freeze." His regulation stated that "[a]ll public lands in Alaska which are unreserved . . . are hereby withdrawn from all forms of appropriation and disposition under the public land laws." In effect, nothing could be done with or to any land not already firmly owned by the state until two committees of Congress consented. If the oil companies were to succeed, they would first have to come to the aid of the Alaskan Natives.

This fact became clear to TAPS in 1970 when two kinds of trouble arose. One kind arose in the House Interior Committee. In part because the Natives had spent much of their time courting senators and not congressmen, the House committee was piqued and not in a rush to speed through land claims settlement legislation. Committee members would listen to the oil companies, however. So in an unlikely team, oil lobbyists united with lobbyists for the Natives. The oil lobbyists pressed hard for a bill that would satisfy the Natives. A weak bill might have led to lawsuits later on that could have held off pipeline construction indefinitely.

The fear of lawsuits was not a remote one. The second kind of trouble TAPS faced in 1970 was a lawsuit that was already pending in federal court in Washington, D.C. Five Native villages protested that the Secretary of the Interior had no authority to allow TAPS to use federal land to build the pipeline because in reality the land belonged to the Natives, not to the government. On April 1, 1970, U.S. District Judge George Hart agreed with the Natives and issued an order prohibiting any construction on pipeline or roadways until the legal questions could be settled.

Congress Finally Acts

The struggle to find an acceptable compromise between the Natives and the state occupied several committees of Congress for three years. The Alaska Federation of Natives, a statewide organization that sometimes uneasily represented most of the Native groups in the state, hired former U.S. Supreme Court Justice Arthur Goldberg (whose son was in law practice in Anchorage) to speak in its behalf. Goldberg proposed that the Natives receive 40 million acres and an outright payment of half a billion dollars. This was a sharp contrast to the original offer of a paltry $7 million and no land at all.

For three years the land and dollar figures waxed and waned in committee. Some congressmen pushed hard to settle the matter promptly; others kept putting off meetings to avoid it.

Finally, in the fall of 1971, a 29-page bill emerged from Congress. It granted the Natives the 40 million acres, and it provided for a total payment of $962.5 million, nearly twice what had been proposed only three years earlier. But this was the final settlement. Now, by law, no more "aboriginal" claims could be raised. They were said to be "extinguished." Moreover, the land that Alaska had already selected was confirmed as state land, and the "land freeze" was at last thawed out. Work on the pipeline could begin, Congress was saying, at least insofar as the Native land claims were concerned.

Why had the settlement taken so long? It had taken a century because until there was incentive to drill and market the vast reserves of oil, the dwindling numbers of Eskimos and

Indians had nothing for which they could bargain. Once oil was discovered, however, they could "offer" the state and the oil companies endless political battles and lawsuits. It would be delay versus land.

Once it became clear that a settlement was necessary, the fight still consumed three years in active prodding and arguing and compromising in Congress, because finding the proper mechanism for distributing the land and money to the Natives was a tricky business. It was finally resolved as follows:

> The largely unsurveyed map of Alaska was divided into squares, called townships, six miles on a side (36 square miles or 23,040 acres). The 220 Native villages with 25 or more inhabitants were allowed to select from three to seven of these townships, depending on population, so far as possible near their own locations. (National parks and of course any private land were out of bounds.) The villages would receive title to the surface rights in the land they chose, up to a total of 22 million acres, and from this, in turn, individual residents would get title to their homes or campsites; since the amount of land would not in most places be enough for subsistence—hunting, fishing, gathering—the villages were encouraged to form profit-making corporations that would find business uses for their land. Timber and mining rights (including oil) in the village lands were distributed among twelve regional corporations, along with surface and subsurface rights in another 16 million acres: that is, the state was divided into twelve regions corresponding to the Native organizations formed (or revived) in order to claim land; and a profit-making corporation was to be set up within each of these geographic units, receiving land from the total in proportion to its area. The regional corporations also got an additional 2 million acres in cemeteries and other historic sites, resolving another sensitive issue and making up the required total of 40 million acres.*

* Robert Douglas Mead, *Journeys Down the Line: Building the Trans-Alaska Pipeline* (Garden City: Doubleday & Co., 1978), pp. 137-38.

WHO OWNS THE LAND?

The money was distributed according to an equally complex formula. The regional corporations were granted $462.5 million to be allocated in proportion to their population over an 11-year period. The balance of $500 million would come from a 2-percent royalty to be paid whenever the state received money for leasing mineral lands. The royalty would not come from land already leased, however, and this meant that Prudhoe Bay land was exempt.

Now at last the Natives had their land, and the state was secure in the title to its land. The Secretary of the Interior, moreover, was directed to set aside 80 million acres to preserve the wilderness—national parks, forests, wildlife refuges, and scenic rivers would be carved out to prevent any state or private attempts to use the land for gain.

When President Nixon signed the Alaska Native Claims Settlement Act on December 18, 1971, it might have seemed that the way was clear at last to get on with the pipeline. And it would have been, but for another lawsuit that was pending at that very moment in a federal court in Washington, D.C.

CHECKS AND BALANCES: FEDERAL *vs.* STATE

The Alaskan Natives were an impoverished minority with relatively few modern skills. They lived on the land and from the land; without it their way of life would perish. For a century the settlers who arrived in Alaska from the lower 48 lived in a rough sort of balance with the Natives. Their coexistence was not always happy, but each population survived. The discovery of vast oil deposits threatened the Natives' very existence, however. But how, as a minority, could they come to prevail against the much wealthier and more sophisticated companies supported by much of the white majority?

The answer they found was to seek shelter in court and with the executive against the direct expression of the majority's desire in the legislature. The Natives had certain rights guaranteed to them by law. To protect these legal rights, they looked to the courts, aided by lawyers with whom the Natives could work and whose services they could manage to afford. Over the years, the Natives' claims also became the object of concern in the U.S. Interior Department, which reacted by freezing the land so no one could use it for different purposes. The federal law thus blocked the state government from allowing oil exploitation to begin.

The courts and the Interior Department could halt construction. They could not, however, sort out the conflicting interests. That had to be done by Congress. Oil, Native, and environmental interests engaged in a three-way struggle—testifying, pleading, arguing, cajoling, and buttonholing legislators—to persuade Congress to vote the way each wanted. In the end, Congress compromised, as it almost always will do. The Natives took title to land and money for development. The environmentalists got public parks, wild preserves. The oil companies got the right to drill and market oil. If no one was fully satisfied, each was nevertheless able to live with the Congressional solution. The power of each group, acting through the government, had checked the power of the other.

Chapter 4
The Courts Intervene

THE ENVIRONMENTAL ISSUES

In addition to the Natives, the oil companies, and the state of Alaska, there was one other group that was greatly concerned about the budding Alaskan oil industry: the environmentalists. For some time, certain individuals had begun to worry about pollution of the air, water, and land. During the early 1960s, Congress began to act selectively, passing laws requiring controls on the dumping of pollutants into rivers and the air. But "environmentalism" as a general concept was not well known and did not become a significant political force until quite late in the 1960s. Although there had always been conservationists, they had never been able to stop a major industrial project. But this time different winds were blowing.

Three environmental groups took a keen interest in the proposed pipeline: the Wilderness Society, Friends of the Earth, and the Environmental Defense Fund. For varying reasons, they were against the construction of the pipeline, at least in the manner in which it was first proposed. Their opposition stemmed from the fear that the pipeline would grievously upset the ecology of the Alaskan wilderness. (Some of the environmentalists were prepared to have the pipeline built if it could be done so safely; others were determined to see the Alaskan wilderness preserved intact, without human handiwork cutting across it.)

The fear was not based on pure emotionalism. There was at least one well-publicized incident that suggested the dangers. In the summer of 1968, after the discovery of oil was confirmed, the oil companies found it difficult to send their trucks and supplies to Prudhoe Bay. They could ship them either by barge through possibly frozen waters or by rail. In either case, it would have been an expensive undertaking. They needed a road. Governor Hickel was determined to build one. In the past, winter trails made out of firmly packed snow were of good enough quality to permit trucks to go slowly north to Prudhoe. Hickel's idea was different: he wanted a permanent, year-round road along the anticipated path of the pipeline. To do this, the state stripped away the plant life—stumps, roots, mosses—that covered the ground. Unfortunately, the vegetation that normally protected the ground in the summer against overheating was now gone. When the snow melted, the bare earth was exposed and the sun turned the road into a boggy and unusable mess that could not easily be repaired, if at all. (Shortly afterward, when Governor Hickel was summoned to Washington as Secretary of the Interior, the new governor cut new trails where the old road was impassable and named the road the Walter J. Hickel Highway.)

Against such despoliation of the land, the environmental groups decided to act. In 1969, the Wilderness Society asked James Moorman, a young lawyer who had recently joined the newly established Center for Law and Social Policy in Washington, to consider legal ways of preventing the Secretary of the Interior from issuing construction permits.

The Center for Law and Social Policy and the suit that Moorman proposed to bring were both new to the American legal scene. The Center was one of the first of the so-called public-interest law firms, an association of lawyers who seek out clients who cannot normally pay for legal services and who represent a broad public concern that is not normally represented in court. Though the suit would be brought in the name of the three environmental groups, they were in effect serving to represent all Americans with an interest in preserving the environment to the fullest extent possible.

Moorman went to the law library to research the case. He needed to find some law that prohibited the issuance of a construction permit. Whether it was wise or foolhardy to construct the pipeline would not be a court's concern. Congress could stop a pipeline on the grounds that construction posed serious dangers; so could the Secretary of the Interior. But a court could act only if a law said it must act.

Moorman came up with two laws. One that he considered relatively minor was a provision in the Mineral Leasing Act of 1920 that seemed to restrict the width of a "right-of-way" over federal land. The second, and by far the more important, Moorman thought, was the National Environmental Policy Act of 1969 (NEPA) that had just taken effect on January 1, 1970. Let us examine each of these laws briefly in turn.

The Mineral Leasing Act of 1920

The Mineral Leasing Act grew out of the federal government's historical experience with land grabs by private industry. The best-known example was that of the railroads. During the years just prior to the Civil War, the U.S. gave up 25 million acres in the Mississippi Valley to the states, which in turn deeded the land to the railroads. The railroad lines needed rights-of-way across public property to lay their track and operate their equipment. The pace of land grants accelerated in the 1860s. For nine years, from 1862 to 1871, the federal government deeded 140 million acres to the railroads. Unfortunately, much of the land was fraudulently transfered on the word of inspectors who were bribed to say that construction was completed (as required by law) when, in fact, often it had not even been started. And a good deal of the land the railroads obtained they did not need.

In the late nineteenth century, as pipelines began to be built to transport oil and natural gas, questions arose concerning how much public land private companies should be allowed to use. Congress passed various laws regulating the manner by which the government could grant pipeline companies rights-of-way over federal lands. Beginning in 1914 and for a period of six years, Congress debated national policy toward the disposition of federal lands containing minerals.

One seemingly minor provision governed the width of the rights-of-way. In the original legislation, Congress imposed a ten-foot restriction. Under this law, the government could not grant a right-of-way any wider than ten feet on each side of the pipeline to be constructed. By 1920, at the insistence of Representative Mondell of Wyoming, who feared that any shorter width would make pipeline development impossible, Congress changed the allowable width to 25 feet on either side of the pipeline. "If we secure the development of oil on the public lands," Mondell said, " . . . long pipelines will have to be built, and they will have to be built over a rough country [he was speaking of Wyoming]. In many cases they will have to be carried on trestles and at elevations that will require a great spread of the trestle at the base. In many cases they will have to be built along sloping hillsides and mountainsides, and the width of 50 feet is none too great."

Mondell and his colleague, Representative Taylor of Colorado, a state with terrain similar to Wyoming's, successfully fought an attempt to reduce the right-of-way back to ten feet. Said Taylor: "In a mountainous or rough and broken or hilly country, pipelines are sometimes buried on side hills or gulches, sometimes on high trestles, and on all kinds of ground, and people have to go up and down the lines to mend breaks in and repair the pipeline, and for various reasons, and you cannot drive teams or haul material on a ten-foot strip of ground through that kind of country."

Those who objected to so much land being used for pipeline construction reminded proponents that the railroads had been greedy. Here is an extract of House debate in 1920:

> MR. NORTON. [D]oes not the gentleman know, as a matter of fact, that the width of the right-of-way granted to the railroads has been found by practical experience to be altogether too great in the Western States?
>
> MR. TAYLOR. The 400-foot right-of-way granted to the Union Pacific was more than was necessary, especially on level ground for nearly a thousand miles; but in no place where there is rough ground has the 100-foot right-of-way been too wide or been curtailed.
>
> MR. NORTON. I am sure it is the consensus of opinion of the people in the Central West that the right-of-way of 100 feet on each side granted to the Northern Pacific and the Great Northern Railway through Minnesota, North Dakota, and Montana is altogether too wide.
>
> MR. TAYLOR. On level farm land I think that is true. I think those railroads got a large amount of good land that they did not need and had no right to; but we are not asking for any good land or any land that we do not need.

In the end, Congress refused to reduce the right-of-way provision and left the figure at 25 feet.

As we shall see shortly, this figure posed an uncomfortable problem for the builders of the trans-Alaska pipeline, because it limited any right-of-way that the Secretary could grant to 54 feet (25 feet on either side of the pipeline plus the 4 feet taken up by the metal pipe itself). The builders needed much more land. The environmental litigants said the Secretary could not legally give it to them.

The National Environmental Policy Act of 1969

The second legal problem was new. The National Environmental Policy Act had only just gone into effect and its provisions were untested in the courts. NEPA was the first great success of the environmental movement. Congress intended it as a way of regulating the activities of the entire federal government. NEPA declares that every government department, bureau, and agency must "create and maintain conditions under which man and nature can exist in productive harmony." To do this, the government must attempt to assure "safe, healthful, productive and esthetically and culturally pleasing surroundings," and "attain the widest range of beneficial uses of the environment without degradation."

Saying all this is easier than doing it, of course. NEPA, therefore, spells out a complex set of requirements for government agencies to follow to ensure that they will take account of the impact on the environment in carrying out their duties.

One specific requirement created a significant change in how the federal government does its business. Before taking any "major federal action," each agency must predict how its proposal will affect the environment and then write down that prediction in a report to be circulated to interested parties. This prediction has become known as the "environmental impact statement" (EIS).

NEPA does not tell the government what plans it can or cannot implement. It merely says the government must first

THE COURTS INTERVENE

consider the environmental impact of those plans. After it considers them, it is free to carry out its proposals, no matter what the environmental impact actually is.

It is not easy to determine what the environmental impact will be, however. NEPA says that the EIS must set forth all the adverse effects that will be unavoidable if an agency carries out its plans. The EIS must set forth alternatives to the proposed action. It must discuss the "relationship between local short-term uses of man's environment and the maintenance and enhancement of long-term productivity." The EIS must also note any "irreversible and irretrievable commitments of resources which would be involved in the proposed action should it be implemented."

There is no easy road to figuring out alternatives, predicting environmental harms, and weighing the benefits of the proposed government action. Preparing an EIS can therefore take a long time. Whether the Interior Department spent sufficient time and considered all the implications of issuing a right-of-way permit that would authorize the building of a 789-mile pipeline through the Alaskan tundra would have to be considered in court.

Notice that neither NEPA nor the Mineral Leasing Act is aimed at private companies. These laws provide restrictions on what the government may do. They became the legal underpinnings of the environmentalists' lawsuit because TAPS needed permission to use federal lands. The only person who could give that permission was the Secretary of the Interior. So to ban the pipeline, the environmentalists had to sue the Secretary to stop him from issuing the permit.

By early 1970, TAPS had completed its preliminary plans and had asked the Secretary formally for rights-of-way across federal preserves in Alaska. TAPS's plan was to bury all but 45 miles of the pipeline in the ground from Prudhoe to Valdez.

But to accomplish this immense engineering feat, the contractors would need considerably more than a 54-foot strip of land. In the past, pipeline builders had frequently ignored the Mineral Leasing Act's 25-foot restriction; they used whatever land they needed to build the pipeline and then, when they were finished, they managed to stay within the law by assuring that the completed pipeline took up no more room than 50 feet plus the width of the pipe. But TAPS's scheme called for much more land: "the 361-mile-construction road north of the Yukon, permanent access roads for maintenance all along the route, sites for airfields, camps, a microwave communications system, eventually a dozen pump stations each occupying the area of a small town, besides the pipeline itself."*

To get around the Mineral Leasing Act, TAPS sought three different rights-of-way. One was for the 54 feet allowed by law. A second was for 200 feet for a "haul road" on which pipe and other materials could be brought to the work sites. A third was for 46 feet for construction and access to the pipeline. Only the 54-foot slice of ground was labeled a "right-of-way." The other applications were for something called "special land use permits" (SLUPs). In February 1970, Secretary Hickel issued the first such permit—for a "transportation corridor," or road.

By that time, of course, NEPA had become law, and the Secretary was required to prepare an environmental impact statement. There was very little time, however; TAPS wanted to begin building immediately in order to finish the pipeline by July 1971 and to keep its cost within a $900 million budget. Since there were no guidelines on how to prepare an EIS (the Council on Environmental Quality, established by NEPA, would not issue guidelines until fall 1973), the Interior Department hastily prepared and released an eight-page state-

---

* Robert Douglas Mead, *Journeys Down the Line*, p. 151.

ment. It discussed only the proposed haul road. There was not even a mention of the pipeline.

The stage was now set for the environmentalists to go to court.

In the District Court

On March 26, Moorman filed his suit in U.S. District Court in Washington. Filing a lawsuit in federal court is easy. The lawyer needs only submit a document called a "complaint" that lists the particular ways in which the client is legally aggrieved. The complaint is often one of the shortest documents in the case. Stacks of paper begin to build up once the defendant has answered the complaint (in a document called the "answer") and each side begins to gather evidence.

The case was assigned to Judge Hart, who, 17 days earlier, had been handed the suit by the 5 Native villages who claimed the pipeline would trespass over their land (see page 24). On April 1, Judge Hart issued his first ruling in the case, temporarily stopping the Secretary from issuing a construction permit in view of the Natives' claims. On April 13, lawyers for the government, the environmentalists, the oil companies, and the Natives assembled before Judge Hart in court to hear "argument," as the lawyers called an oral presentation, on the issues that Moorman raised.

Moorman said that the eight-page EIS just completed was inadequate. It discussed none of the real environmental hazards. "It's an attempt to paper over the problems by ignoring them," he asserted. Moorman also argued that the Mineral Leasing Act did not allow the Secretary to grant the permits TAPS had requested.

Answering Moorman was a Justice Department lawyer, Herbert Pittle. Although dozens of lawyers work for each federal department and agency, they are rarely allowed to represent their agency in court. Instead, the Justice Department sends in its lawyers to represent the various branches of government when they are summoned to court as defendants (those who are sued) or when they themselves file suits as plaintiffs.

Pittle's argument was brief. Under questioning by the judge, he conceded that the sole reason for the road was to construct the pipeline and that it had not been mentioned in the EIS. He asserted that the SLUPs were not rights-of-way and were not governed, therefore, by the Mineral Leasing Act. Judge Hart asked rhetorically: "What was the sense of Congress making this law if you can give them ten miles by giving them rights-of-way alongside one another? You can't violate the law just by spending a billion dollars to do it."*

On April 1, when the Natives came to court, Judge Hart had suggested that they and the government meet to try to settle their problems separately. He could not make a similar suggestion to Secretary Hickel, the environmental groups, and TAPS. If the Secretary of the Interior did not have the legal authority to grant the construction permits, then there was no way for the litigants to settle the case privately. Moorman asked the judge to issue a "preliminary injunction"—a judicial order prohibiting the Secretary from issuing the permits until the case could be fully tried after all the evidence was gathered.

Two weeks after the case was argued, on April 28, 1970, Judge Hart granted Moorman's request in a brief signed order. He ruled that the three separate applications for permission to use the land "are, in effect, a single application for a pipeline right-of-way" and that, as such, it violated the law. He also ruled that the Secretary "has not fully complied with the

---

* Moorman and Pittle are quoted in Mary Clay Berry, *The Alaska Pipeline: The Politics of Oil and Native Land Claims* (Bloomington: Indiana University Press, 1975), p. 120.

requirements of NEPA." The pipeline was temporarily stopped.

Although none of the parties knew it at the time, the preliminary injunction would stand for more than two years. During that time, the Department of the Interior began to study the environmental problems in depth. So did the oil companies. This was not easy work. From the very beginning of the lawsuit, it became clear that what TAPS had planned initially was not well thought out. Indeed, at the hearing before Judge Hart in April 1970, a memorandum from the head of the U.S. Geological Survey just the month before stated that "TAPS has not demonstrated acceptable fundamental design criteria for below-ground construction in permafrost of a hot-oil pipeline that would be reasonably safe from failure." One of the dangers in the underground design was that the oil, which had to be kept heated at around 160° F., would melt the permafrost, causing the ground to sag and the pipe to break, and the oil to spill out over the ground.

For the next two years, the Interior Department and the oil companies wrestled with the question of environmental impact. During the course of 1970, TAPS was disbanded. As a joint oil company venture it had been too loose an arrangement to work smoothly. So the companies formed the Alyeska Pipeline Service Company, which would take over TAPS's functions but perform them better (it would still be owned by the oil companies). In December of 1970, the government sent Alyeska a draft of a new EIS for comment. But at that very time, President Nixon fired Secretary Hickel for his outspoken criticism of the Administration's policies. The President appointed Rogers C.B. Morton, a congressman. Morton continued the land freeze and said that pipeline construction would not begin in 1971. The Interior Department held hearings on the proposals. One two-day session in Washington produced a transcript 10,000 pages long.

Alyeska was busy rethinking the project. By 1971, when it had originally hoped to have the line built, Alyeska had downgraded the amount of pipe to be buried beneath the permafrost from 95 percent to 52 percent. The route and techniques for constructing it were also changing. So was the estimated cost, which climbed from the original $900 million to $2 billion—and threatened to continue to rise.

In August, Alyeska sent the Interior Department a detailed description of its plans. These were contained in 29 volumes. Their existence forced the Department to plow through this thick stack of paper in order to redo its EIS. The questions that needed answering were numerous. For example, how would the oil temperature affect the permafrost? How would the pipeline affect the migratory and feeding habits of the Alaskan wild game? What would the impact on ocean and shore life be of oil-tanker traffic steaming in and out of the port at Valdez? What alternatives existed to the route through Alaska?

After many ups and downs (see chronology in Appendix 2, p. 84), the Department issued its final environmental impact statement. It was nine volumes long. Secretary Morton asked for comments from interested persons within 45 days. Lawyers at the Center for Law and Social Policy (Moorman had left by then to take a job with the Sierra Club and a lawyer named Dennis Flannery had taken over) divided up the EIS into small segments and shipped them to experts around the country. On May 4, 1972, the Center submitted a 1000-page comment attacking the Department's EIS as inadequate. For example, they said, there was no consideration of a pipeline that would have to be built to carry the natural gas also found at Prudhoe Bay to the Midwest and that would have to cross Canada. Since there would have to be a pipeline through Canada anyway, a similar route for oil should have been considered.

But Secretary Morton decided that the time had come to let construction proceed. One week later, on May 11, he announced that he would grant the necessary permits. "I am convinced," he said, "that it is in our best national interest to avoid all further delays and uncertainties in planning the development of the Alaska North Slope reserves by having a secure pipeline located under the total jurisdiction and for the exclusive use of the United States."

Only the temporary injunction that Judge Hart had granted two years earlier now seemed to stand in the way. On August 15, after all the time to submit legal papers had expired and the lawyers were all reassembled in his court, Judge Hart agreed to dissolve the injunction. The EIS was adequate, he ruled. He also concluded that the Mineral Leasing Act no longer barred the permit. Alyeska had withdrawn its request for rights-of-way for the haul road and struck a deal with the state of Alaska, and the state separately applied for a permit to build. Judge Hart was satisfied with this and other arrangements—and was tired of the case. He saw no practical way by which any pipeline could be built within the 50 feet allowed by law and decided that there had to be flexibility. Alyeska and the government seemed to have cleared the legal hurdles.

IN THE COURT OF APPEALS

The environmentalists, however, had the right to appeal to a higher court. The ruling that dissolved the injunction was "stayed" (stopped from taking effect) while the appeal was pending in the U.S. Court of Appeals for the District of Columbia Circuit.

The judges of this court work in the same building as the judges of the district court in Washington. Their courtrooms are smaller, and there is no space for a jury. An appellate court sits to review rulings that trial judges make. These rulings concern the meaning of the law. Appellate judges do not review the finding of facts announced by juries (or, if there has been no jury, by the trial judges). It is much quieter in the U.S. Court of Appeals. There is appeal to reason and logic, not to the emotions and passions that may sway a jury.

Ordinarily, a case on appeal is assigned to a panel of three judges, picked at random from the nine judges that constitute the District of Columbia Circuit. The pipeline case, when it was finally ready to be argued, was assigned to the entire court because of its importance (and also because of the need for speed; the decision of a panel of the court can sometimes later be appealed to the entire court, and the parties wanted to avoid this extra step). Ordinarily, also, when a case is taken up on appeal, the record of the proceedings in the lower court is prepared (transcripts of testimony are typed up, many of the papers delivered to the district judge are gathered together), and a separate set of arguments is written out for the judges to read. These are called "briefs," though they are frequently hundreds of pages long. Again, because of the need for speed, the parties dispensed with new briefs and the circuit judges agreed to review the briefs already submitted to Judge Hart. What might have been a year-long wait between the lower-court ruling and the day of oral argument in the Court of Appeals was held to 51 days.

On October 6, 1972, with the lawyers and spectators already present in the courtroom, seven of the nine circuit judges entered through a side door. As custom dictates, everyone stood until the judges took their seats. The Chief Judge, the senior member of the bench,* called the case. He said it

---

* Seniority is determined by length of service on the court. When a Chief Judge reaches 70 years of age, he or she automatically steps down as Chief Judge and becomes a Senior Judge, and the next senior judge under 70 becomes Chief Judge. The other two judges on the District of Columbia Circuit disqualified themselves for reasons not stated.

concerned Alaska Airlines. That was, of course, a mistake. Collecting his wits, Dennis Flannery, the environmentalists' lawyer, rose and said: "Your Honor, while this case deals with everything under the sun, it does not deal with Alaska Airlines." The argument began.

Oral argument is an ancient tradition in the law. No matter how many documents have been prepared, no matter how many briefs have been filed, nor how lengthy they are, lawyers and judges believe that the opportunity to present the case in an open court and to respond to questions of the judges is essential to the judicial process. Oral argument allows judges to focus on the critical questions and to discover where the weakness of each side lies.

The lawyer stands at a lectern facing a long bench at which the judges sit. The lawyer begins to "state the case," to tell the judges what the case is all about. But in most appellate courts, no lawyer will be left alone to speak his mind for very long. Almost immediately, he will be interrupted and peppered with questions. The judges have read the briefs and they want the lawyer to explain the argument more clearly. Though it is quieter than a trial and though it is much quicker (normally oral argument lasts 30 minutes to an hour and it can be as short as 5 minutes), it is a taxing ordeal. The lawyer must be mentally alert at every instant he is at that lectern.

The argument was finished in a few hours on October 6. The Justice Department contended on behalf of Secretary Morton that the EIS had been prepared adequately and that the SLUPs were not rights-of-way and were not governed therefore by the Mineral Leasing Act. The environmental lawyers pressed the opposite conclusions.

Now it was in the hands of the court. There is no timetable to which the federal courts must adhere in making their decisions. The judges can "rule from the bench," announcing a decision as soon as the oral argument is completed, or they can retire to their "chambers" (offices) to mull over the case at their leisure. How long it takes to rule depends on the complexity of the case, differences in opinion among the judges, and the number of other cases also awaiting decision. As it turned out, the Court of Appeals did not rule until February 9, 1973, more than four months after the argument. On that day, in a 48-page written opinion by Judge J. Skelly Wright, the court announced its decision.

The Decision of the Appeals Court

Judge Wright began by considering the special land use permit that Alyeska wanted the Interior Department to grant for pipeline construction. In its final form, the permit granted by the Secretary was not fixed in feet, but it stated rather that Alyeska could use as much land "as may be reasonably necessary for construction" of the pipeline. It was conceded that the amount of land required would be more than 54 feet. Judge Wright described the construction process:

> [P]rior to construction a centerline is surveyed and marked. A construction zone is cleared and graded, and the ditch for the pipe is dug. The pipe, valves, fittings and coating materials are then transported to the job site and the pipe is strung along the open ditch. Frequently it is necessary to bend the pipe by machine at the site to fit the alignment and contour of the ditch. Strings of pipe are then aligned, clamped, and welded together. Joined sections of pipe are lowered into the ditch by heavy sideboom tractors. These sections are then joined to the pipe already in place and the pipe receives its final coatings. The ditch is then backfilled and compacted. . . . The modern method of pipeline construction requires use of bulky and heavy equipment designed to operate from one side of the pipe only. It is essential to provide adequate vehicle passing space along the entire length of the proposed route since pipe sections must constantly be trucked to the head of the

construction area, and sideboom tractors which have finished lifting and lowering sections of pipe must pass ahead of others still engaged in such operations to take up new positions as construction of the line advances. Space is needed for the transport of men and equipment, and safety margins must be provided to avoid collisions.

Thus, unless the special land use permits were granted, there would not be sufficient room to maneuver the trucks or lay the pipe.

The Interior Department argued that the SLUP the Secretary granted did not violate the Mineral Leasing Act because it was not a permanent right-of-way. Instead, it was only a "revocable permit," a temporary license to use the land that would expire when the pipeline construction was completed. The Department also argued that the SLUP was permissible because the land in question would not be used for "pipeline purposes" or for "the transportation of oil," forbidden by the Mineral Leasing Act.

Judge Wright rejected these arguments. A right-of-way does not have to be permanent; it merely has to be permission to use land. The special land use permit clearly conveyed an interest in federal land to the construction company. As for the purpose of the SLUP, "it simply makes no sense to insist on the one hand, as all parties do, that use of this land is absolutely necessary if the pipeline is to be built and oil to be transported, and to claim on the other hand that the land will not be used for pipeline purposes or for the transportation of oil."

But could the width limitation be ignored? Could Congress really have intended to limit construction in such a manner? To see what the Act really meant, Judge Wright surveyed the "legislative history" of the law. He looked to the debates in Congress (excerpts from which we have already examined, page 33). The legislative history is not always conclusive; frequently it can be made up by a few congressmen who are dissatisfied with the language of the bill they are about to vote on and want to place on record a different meaning of the bill. But in this case, Judge Wright noted, although "we deal with a debate that engaged but a few members of one house of Congress, a Congress that was not even the one that eventually passed the Mineral Leasing Act of 1920," there is no reason to reject the obvious implication of the debate. "This is not a case where opponents and proponents characterized the provisions of the act differently. They disagreed as to what was a proper width limitation, but they all agreed that the width limitation applied to the construction area."

Does the court's conclusion make a lot of sense? Shouldn't the court have ruled that Congress must have intended some leeway in constructing large pipelines? To these questions, Judge Wright gave the following answer:

> One might have expected the Congress of the United States to exercise foresight in a situation in which it was expressly warned that the statute it was enacting was then, or might in the future become, ineffective. But such foresight was notably lacking. Foresight no doubt would have been the wisest choice in this instance, since after the passage of the Mineral Leasing Act pipeline technology developed to permit construction of larger pipelines needing greater amounts of construction space. It might fairly be said that Congress overreacted to the prior excesses of railroad rights-of-way. But it is not our function, when we pass on either the constitutionality of statutes or their interpretation, to substitute our opinion as to what is wise for that of Congress. . . . Congress chose not to be foresightful; it chose to retain control of the width of the pipeline rights-of-way over public land itself, and that decision and its consequences must stand until Congress chooses otherwise.

Judge Wright went on to consider other arguments pressed on the court. The Interior Department contended, for example, that for years regulations of the Bureau of Land Management had permitted construction to use land outside the statutory rights-of-way and that other federal agencies for decades had permitted private companies to use federal land for similar purposes. The courts should accord great weight to such federal regulations and practices, the Interior Department argued. Judge Wright wrote that normally it is true that the practices of federal agencies should be respected, but not where the practice violates a specific enactment of Congress.

Moreover, Judge Wright noted, the Secretary's grant of the SLUP violated the Bureau of Land Management's own regulations, which say that special permits can be made only when the purposes for which they are sought are not already governed by federal law. (In addition, the Bureau's regulations state that a special land use permit must be revocable at any time in the discretion of the responsible federal official. But the conditions of the Alaska pipeline were such that once the huge gravel road was built and the pipeline laid, it would be impossible as a practical matter for the Department to revoke its permit, because then there would be no way to maintain the pipeline and the road would have to be torn apart. The government would never want the pipeline to be left untended nor would it desire a gaping hole left for hundreds of miles along the Alaskan tundra.)

So much for the special land use permits. But these were not the only rights-of-way sought. The Secretary of the Interior also granted permits to Alyeska to construct pumping stations and communications facilities and to the state of Alaska to build highways and airports. The environmentalists argued that these requests were identical to those for the construction rights-of-way and that they should be rejected on the same reasoning. This time the court disagreed. Permission could be granted to use land for the pumping station, because the pumps are necessary to move the oil through the pipeline and the stations must therefore be considered part and parcel of the pipeline itself. A separate provision of law permits land to be used for communications facilities. So land permits for these uses are not barred by the Mineral Leasing Act.

Similarly, other land laws, not related to the Mineral Leasing Act, permit the Secretary to allow states to use federal land to build highways and airports. The environmentalists charged that the highways and airports were not genuinely public ones (and therefore did not come within the terms of the laws) because they were intended for the private use of the pipeline companies only. Judge Wright rejected these contentions, saying that it was not the court's business to inquire into the motives of other branches of government and that, in any event, it appeared likely that the state intended to open the road to public traffic eventually and the airports to public business as soon as they were built.

After considering all these matters, Judge Wright finally turned to the National Environmental Policy Act. In addition to the specific provision of the Mineral Leasing Act, the environmentalists had launched a broadside attack on the adequacy of the government's assessment of the land permits' environmental impact. But the court decided not to decide these issues. The issues, Judge Wright declared, were complex and important. Trying to answer them would not "affect the real outcome" of the case, however. Why? The answer was to be found in what the court had already done. By ruling that the special land use permits for constructing the pipeline violated the Mineral Leasing Act, no pipeline could be built unless Congress acted to change the law. Nobody knew whether Congress would act or how long it would take to act. By the time the law was changed, environmental considerations might well have changed also. If so, a whole new environmental impact statement would need to be prepared, and anything that the court said about the EIS prepared in 1972 would be out of date. Thus, said Judge Wright, the NEPA issues were not "ripe for adjudication at the present time."

So the Alaska pipeline case was at an end. Issues of great importance and interests of great magnitude were at stake, in the court's words: " . . . billions of gallons of oil at a time when the nation faces an energy crisis of serious proportions; hundreds of millions of dollars in revenue for the state of Alaska at a time when financial support for important social programs is badly needed; industrial development and pollution of one of the last major unblemished wilderness areas in the world, at a time when we are all becoming increasingly aware of the delicate balance between man and his natural environment." And all these issues and interests turned on some simple language in an act of Congress that the court felt powerless to do anything about.

The companies wanted more land than the law allowed. The Interior Department was prepared to give it to them. But the court said no. As Judge Wright summed up:

> Congress intended to maintain control over pipeline rights-of-way and to force the industry to come back to Congress if the amount of land granted was insufficient for its purposes. Whether this restriction made sense then, or now, is not the business of the courts. And whether the width limitation should be discarded, enlarged, or placed in the discretion of an administrative agency, is a matter for Congress, not for this court.
>
> In the last analysis, it is an abiding function of the courts, in the course of decision of cases and controversies, to require the Executive to abide by the limitations prescribed by the Legislature. The scrupulous vindication of that basic principle of law, implicit in our form of government, its three branches, and its checks and balances, looms more important in the

abiding public interest than the embarkation on any immediate or specific project, however desirable in and of itself, in contravention of that principle.

The Dissenting Opinion

Of the seven judges who participated in the decision of the case, three agreed completely with the reasons and conclusions of Judge Wright. Two others dissented in part. They concurred in the opinion that the Mineral Leasing Act prohibited the Secretary from issuing the SLUP for the reasons given by the majority, but they disagreed with the conclusion concerning NEPA. They felt that the environmental impact statement prepared by the Interior Department was sufficient to meet the requirements of the law. A third judge, Judge MacKinnon, agreed with the dissenters on the last point but disagreed with all the others concerning the reasons for ruling on the Mineral Leasing Act. In a separate 19-page opinion, he traced the origins and history of the Mineral Leasing Act and concluded that the majority's recitation of the legislative history was faulty. Judge MacKinnon felt that the special land use permits were legal if they were truly temporary and revocable. But he agreed with the majority, after a detailed analysis, that they could not, in fact, be revoked, and therefore he sided with the majority in concluding that the particular permits could not be allowed under the law.

All seven judges thus agreed that the Mineral Leasing Act had been violated, and four of the seven concluded that the NEPA issues need not be discussed. As a result of its decision, the court "remanded" (sent back) the case to the district court with instructions to enjoin the issuance of special land use permits for the construction right-of-way but to declare the other right-of-way permits valid.

The pipeline had been stopped.

CHECKS AND BALANCES: THE COURTS vs. THE EXECUTIVE

The fight over the pipeline shifted from land claims. Now the battle was over the interpretation of environmental laws. Did the law give the Secretary of the Interior leeway to grant rights in excess of the statutory maximum? Did the government in its environmental impact statement comply with the requirements of the new environmental laws?

Congress had passed these laws, and it was up to the courts to interpret them—if anyone cared to come before the judges by filing a lawsuit. (Judges cannot make rulings based on what they read in the newspapers; they must wait until disputants appear before them.) Since a federal judge has the power to prohibit officials in the executive branch from taking actions contrary to law, the environmentalists sought the writ of a court to stop the Secretary of the Interior from giving the green light to the pipeline builders.

After a temporary victory in the trial court, the environmentalists lost—though not without having caused a number of changes to be made in the original pipeline design. But a trial court, too, is subject to checks and balances: A court of appeals stands ready to review the decision of the trial judge. This time the environmentalists won. The U.S. Court of Appeals ruled that a federal statute stood in the way of the pipeline. It could not be built unless the law was changed.

Chapter 5

Congress Reacts to the Court's Decision

The pipeline controversy moved to the Congressional stage in April of 1973, after the Supreme Court declined to review the decision of the Court of Appeals. Alyeska had hoped that the Supreme Court would agree to hear a further appeal, but the justices have the authority to pick and choose the cases they want to hear (except for a tiny number of cases that by law they must take up), and they did not want to hear this one. The Court of Appeals had ruled that the law prohibited the Secretary from granting permits for the use of federal land. Congress has the power to change that law, and President Nixon called on Congress to do so promptly. In a message to Congress on energy on April 18, 1973, the President asked for an end to "any further delay in order to restudy the advisability of building the pipeline through Canada. . . . At a time when we are importing growing quantities of oil at great detriment to our balance of payments . . . we clearly need the two million barrels a day which the North Slope could provide—a supply equal to fully one third of our present import levels."

The question was how the law ought to be changed. It would not do simply to write a law that said: "The decision of the Court of Appeals is reversed." Such a law would not settle very much, if anything. At most, it would permit the Secretary to grant the particular permits involved in the lawsuit, but it would not make clear his power to grant future permits nor would it resolve the environmental issues. Something more fundamental was required.

How a Bill Becomes Law

Any congressman or senator may "introduce" a bill—that is, offer it for approval by his colleagues. But getting it through Congress and signed into law is not a simple process. There are four major steps.

When it is introduced, the bill is assigned to a committee with jurisdiction over the subject matter. A bill to amend the Mineral Leasing Act, introduced in the Senate, for example, will be assigned to the Senate Interior and Insular Affairs Committee. That committee, in turn, will usually assign it to a subcommittee, which will hold hearings and allow proponents and opponents to comment and criticize the bill's purpose and proposed language. If a majority of the subcommittee votes for the bill, it will then be voted on by the full committee. If the full committee approves the bill, it will be "reported" (sent) to the "floor" of the Senate (if that is where the bill originated) and must be approved by a majority of the senators present on the day it is called up for a vote.

The bill can be defeated at any one of these three stages: subcommittee, full committee, floor vote. If it is passed by the house in which it originated, however, it must then repeat the same process in the other house. Since at any step along the way the bill can be amended in the other house, what usually happens is that the two houses of Congress will wind up with different versions of the same bill. In order to be presented to the President for signature, the same bill must pass each house. That means that either the original house to consider the bill must accept the other's amendments or both must compromise and agree on the same bill.

To accomplish this accommodation, a "conference committee" is appointed, consisting of members of both House and Senate. Members of each house are sent to the conference committee with instructions on what to save and what to yield. The committee members must strike a compromise that they can sell to their colleagues back in the House and Senate, for whatever changes they make in the bill must be voted on anew in both the House and Senate. If the bill passes each house again, and this time without any changes, then the bill is ready for the President—who may, if he chooses, veto it altogether if it contains provisions he finds undesirable or does not contain the provisions he wants.

At any point in this long and frequently tangled process, a variety of forces can be brought into play to force change and compromise—to check and to balance the desires of one faction or another.

Moving the Pipeline Bill Along

Congressional action on a bill to get the Alaska pipeline built began even before the Supreme Court declined to review the decision of the Court of Appeals. On March 9 and 27, and again on May 2 and 3, 1973, the full Senate Interior and Insular Affairs Committee held hearings. Oil company executives testified in favor of legislation that would let the construction begin immediately. Environmentalists, like George Alderson, legislative director of Friends of the Earth, insisted that there was "an almost total lack of information on the justification for haste." Two U.S. Senators, both from the Midwest, urged construction of a Canadian pipeline that would bring oil to Midwest refineries. But Committee Chairman Henry M. Jackson, from Washington State, spoke in favor of an amendment to the Mineral Leasing Act to permit a trans-Alaska pipeline; a Canadian pipeline would take too long, he said.

On June 12, the Committee reported a bill to the full Senate by a 12-0 vote. It would permit the Interior Secretary to grant rights-of-way for pipelines, electrical transmission systems, and transportation facilities, without imposing a maximum width. The bill also required the Secretary to issue regulations to prevent environmental damage through the use of any federal land over which he granted a right-of-way.

Two days later, Senator Mike Gravel of Alaska introduced an amendment to the reported bill. The Gravel amendment declared as a matter of Congressional policy that all actions taken by the federal government in connection with the trans-Alaska pipeline complied with NEPA. Such an amendment would immunize Alyeska from further attack in court. In effect, the amendment was a specific, one-time exception to the environmental law. "The main point," said Gravel in defending his amendment, "is that the urgency of the nation's energy crisis demands that the Congress apply its decision-making authority in this area. It would be much easier for us to do only what we have to do—clear up the technical right-of-way problems and let the court handle the rest. Circumstances demand that we not pass the buck."

A month later, on July 13, a substitute amendment offered by then senators Walter F. Mondale of Minnesota and Birch Bayh of Indiana, which would have delayed construction for at least a year while a Canadian alternative was studied, was defeated on a roll-call vote, 61-29. Four days later, the Gravel amendment came up for a vote. The issue was in doubt down to the end of the roll call. It finally passed by a one-vote margin, 49-48 (one senator was absent because of illness, one was absent on official business—and their two votes would probably have canceled each other—and the third, Senator Alan Cranston of California, arrived on the Senate floor just after the vote, having been delayed in California because of an illness in his family).

THE VICE-PRESIDENT STEPS IN

Under the Senate rules, at this point in the voting, a senator could change his vote, and so the outcome was not yet certain. There is a parliamentary device to make the vote binding, and that is the "motion to reconsider." Senator Gravel "moved to reconsider"—that is, put before his colleagues the request that the roll be called again. At that point, in accordance with the parliamentary custom, a motion to "table" the motion to reconsider was offered. This second motion asks, in effect, that the Senate refuse to reconsider its original vote. Under the rules, the motion to table is voted on first. With Senator Cranston now available to vote, the motion to table ended up in a dead heat: 49 senators in favor of tabling, 49 senators opposed.

Only one person could break the tie: the Vice-President of the United States. Under the Constitution, the Vice-President serves as President of the Senate. This is a largely ceremonial job, without real power. The Vice-President rarely presides over the Senate sessions; instead, various senators take turns sitting in the presiding officer's chair to make occasional rulings on disputed points of procedure. The Vice-President normally has no power to vote. In fact, the only time he can ever vote in the Senate is when a tie has resulted in a roll-call vote.

Now such a time had come to pass. Shortly before the roll call was completed, Vice-President Spiro M. Agnew took the presiding chair. When the senators had finished voting, Agnew announced the result and then cast the deciding vote himself:

"The Vice-President votes yea," he said; "the motion to table is agreed to." By that final vote, the Senate made binding its adoption of the Gravel amendment to override the National Environmental Policy Act. The rest was anticlimax. Now the entire bill came up for a vote, and the Senate passed it 77-20.

(This was the only time Agnew cast a decisive vote in the Senate. Once earlier he had voted when there was a tie, but on that occasion, the 50-50 vote on an amendment to a bill meant, under the Senate's parliamentary rules, that the amendment had failed, and therefore the tie-breaking vote was unnecessary. It was Agnew's last chance; in three months he would resign the vice-presidency in shame as a convicted tax evader who was shown to have taken bribes while in public office.)

In its final form, the Senate bill was not a simple piece of legislation. It had numerous provisions. They dealt with oil exports, price controls, standards for oil tankers, oil allocation among the states in the event of shortage, confirmation of the director of the federal Energy Policy Office and head of the Mining Enforcement and Safety Administration.

It also had two unrelated provisions. One was to allow the Federal Trade Commission to use its own lawyers in court in certain kinds of cases instead of Justice Department lawyers. The other provision exempted independent federal agencies (like the FTC) from the need to get permission from the federal Office of Management and Budget in order to collect information from private companies. Both of these provisions were highly political. The Democratic Congress was at odds with the Republican President over these matters, and the Senate decided that if it attached these "riders" (unrelated provisions) to a bill the President desperately wanted, he would have no choice but to sign it. (The President does not have the authority to strike out particular provisions; he must accept or reject the entire bill when it is passed by Congress.)

In the House

In the meantime, the Subcommittee on Public Lands of the House Interior and Insular Affairs Committee had been holding hearings on similar bills. The same arguments pro and con were pressed in April and May before the Subcommittee members, who reported a bill to the full Committee, which in turn, on July 28, 1973, 11 days after the Senate's action, reported the bill to the full House. This bill had a provision closely resembling the Senate's Gravel amendment. It directed the Secretary of the Interior to grant the necessary permits, declared that the pipeline as planned conformed to NEPA, and prohibited further judicial review of the environmental issues. A report of the Committee to the House members made this point:

> It is fitting and proper for Congress to make this decision. The issue is of national importance. The issue involves the use of the public lands, the control of which the Constitution expressly reserves to Congress. It is the responsibility of Congress to decide whether the pipeline should be authorized. It would be an abdication of congressional responsibility to say "let the secretary of the interior make this decision, and then let the courts decide whether the secretary has done *what Congress wants him to do*." Congress is able to say what it wants the secretary to do, and it should issue the proper directive.

The Committee bill also contained a number of other provisions. One said that whoever held the rights-of-way to build the pipeline would be financially responsible for any damages caused during construction, no matter how carefully the builders acted, and a similar provision imposed financial liability on the holder of the rights-of-way if oil carried in the pipeline spilled out of a tanker owned or leased or operated by the holder.

The major debate in the House centered on the environmental aspects of the bill. Dissenters bitterly attacked supporters for attempting to sweep serious environmental issues aside. Representative John Dellenback of Oregon offered an amendment on the House floor to delete the environmental clause in the bill. After vigorous debate, his amendment failed by a vote of 198-221.

Twenty-one other amendments came up for debate on that day; only six minor ones were approved. They dealt with such things as oil exports, labor clearances for foreign workers, and use of foreign-made materials in construction. After some ten hours of debate, the bill was ready for a vote. On that day, August 2, 1973, the House passed it by a 356-60 vote.

Ironing Out the Senate and House Versions

Now the Senate and House versions of the pipeline bill needed to be reconciled. A conference committee was appointed and began its work on September 12. On October 31, the committee filed its conference report on a compromise bill.

It contained the two essential features found in both the Senate and House versions, designed to speed pipeline construction. First, the rigid width limitation in the Mineral Leasing Act was softened. Although a general 50-foot width was retained, the Secretary was empowered to grant a broader right-of-way if necessary. In this case, the House language won out over the Senate language, which had abolished the 50-foot width limitation altogether. But the Senate language was retained for a related matter, allowing rights-of-way not just for oil and gas pipelines but also for many other types of uses, including transportation, electrical power, communications, and other types of pipelines.

The second major provision, allowing Alyeska to avoid the environmental laws, followed the House approach. The Senate bill had prohibited the courts from considering any further challenge to the pipeline. The House restricted the prohibition to challenges dealing with environmental issues.

And so on down the list, the conference committee borrowed language first from the House, then from the Senate, version of the bill, until the final bill incorporated all of the various provisions that had been debated throughout the spring and summer—financial liability, export controls, use of federal lands, right to sue, and others. (A summary of the bill's provisions is set forth in an appendix to this chapter and the full text of the Act is included in Appendix 3.)

Four unrelated provisions that the Senate insisted on remained in the conference bill, and they caused problems. The Nixon Administration opposed them because they were perceived as infringements on its power to administer the executive branch. In late October, 1973, Roy L. Ash, director of OMB, warned members of the conference committee and Republican House leaders that the President might veto the bill if it was passed with these provisions intact.

Few took these threats seriously. The President had been pushing for the bill since the spring. That summer, for the first time, an oil shortage developed across the United States. And by the fall, when the threats were made, Egypt and Syria had gone to war with Israel, prompting the oil-exporting countries, dominated by the Arab bloc, to embargo crude oil to the United States for the first time, causing long lines at the gas pumps. Since the oil from Alaska would help reduce American dependence on foreign oil, it was not likely that the Administration would wind up vetoing the bill.

Ultimately, parliamentary attempts to delete them failed. But a series of technical objections kept the bill from coming to a final vote while various groups like the Chamber of Commerce and General Motors Corporation lobbied intensively to knock out certain provisions, which, they felt, would adversely affect the business community.

Finally, however, time for delay ran out. On November 12, the House approved the conference report by a vote of 361-14, after defeating a motion to send the bill back to conference 162-213. The following day the Senate passed the same report by a vote of 80-5. Congress had enacted the pipeline bill. All that remained was the President's signature.

The President Signs

Three days later, on November 16, 1973, at a ceremony in the White House, President Nixon, who at that very time was in the thick of his Watergate problems (he had just fired Archibald Cox as special prosecutor and the first cries for his impeachment were being heard), signed the bill as expected. He hailed the bill as a whole, declaring that it was the first step on the road to American self-sufficiency in energy. (He predicted this would come to pass by 1980, a prediction that was sadly off the mark.)

Four pens were used in affixing his name to the bill. This is a common practice so that the ceremonial pens can be given to dignitaries or others attending the signing. Three pens went to Alaska's Congressional delegation, senators Mike Gravel and Ted Stevens and Representative Donald E. Young. The first pen had been offered to Senator Henry M. Jackson, chairman of the Senate Interior and Insular Affairs Committee, who had championed the bill, but Senator Jackson turned it down in favor of Mrs. William Pecora, the widow of an undersecretary of the Interior who had been intimately involved in the pipeline project.

The legal battle against construction of the trans-Alaska pipeline had ended. But it was not the end of the legal fight.

CHECKS AND BALANCES: CONGRESS vs. THE COURTS

A court's interpretation of a law is not binding for all time. The law can be changed. To be sure, there are tens of thousands of judicial rulings based on interpretations of statutes passed by the legislature. If the legislators had to consider every case, they would have no time left to do anything else. So Congress does not overturn a great many court decisions by passing new laws. But Congress certainly has the power to do so, and it exercises this power when a majority considers it important to change the direction of public policy.

That was indisputably true of the pipeline case. A court had stopped construction, and a majority—though a bare majority—wanted it built. The way to have it built was to amend the Mineral Leasing Act to allow the Secretary to grant permits when necessary. As an added precaution, to prevent the plaintiffs from going back to court, Congress declared that the pipeline conformed to the requirements of the National Environmental Policy Act. Such a provision is rare: Congress does not usually sit, in effect, as a court and judge whether a particular person or company or project has complied with a law. But congress wanted the oil to flow.

A new majority thus had formed to overturn the law as it stood. That does not mean the court was wrong. It acted properly, but a majority in a democracy can and will sooner or later make the changes it wants, at least in the broad outlines, even if it does not prevail on every point it seeks.

Summary of the Provisions in the Alaska Pipeline Bill

To give an idea of the diversity of provisions that can wind up in a single bill, what follows is a *Congressional Quarterly* summary of the provisions in S 1081, the number of the bill ultimately signed into law ("S" stands for Senate, where the bill was first introduced; the number means that it was the one-thousand-eighty-first bill introduced in that session). The complete text of the bill can be found in Appendix 3, p. 88.

- Required the secretary of interior to authorize construction of the trans-Alaskan pipeline.
- Provided that all actions necessary for completion of the pipeline be taken without further delay under the National Environmental Policy Act of 1969.
- Restricted judicial review 1) to the constitutionality of the act, 2) to actions taken under the act which violated constitutional rights, and 3) to actions which went beyond the authority granted by the act.
- Required that court challenges be brought within 60 days of enactment of the bill or within 60 days of any action which allegedly violated constitutional rights or went beyond the authority of the act.
- Provided that such challenges be filed in a U.S. district court, which would have exclusive jurisdiction.
- Required the court to give precedence to complaints brought against the act or against actions taken under the act over all other matters on its docket.
- Barred the court from granting injunctive relief against any action taken in connection with the pipeline except as part of its final decision.
- Provided that appeals of district court decisions be taken directly to the U.S. Supreme Court.

- Provided liability of up to $50,000,000 for each incident for damages resulting from pipeline construction or operations which affected the subsistence or income of Alaskan natives.
- Held the pipeline owners liable for the full costs of controlling and removing any pollution caused by the pipeline.
- Established liability without regard to fault of up to $100 million for each incident of oil spills from vessels carrying oil from the pipeline unless the oil spills were caused by acts of war or actions of the United States.
- Limited liability for oil spills to $14 million for owners of vessels transporting crude oil.
- Established a Trans-Alaskan Pipeline Liability Fund to meet claims of more than $14 million.
- Provided that oil companies using the pipeline pay into the fund five cents for each barrel loaded on vessels until the fund reached $100 million.
- Directed the President to use any statutory authority granted to him to ensure the equitable allocation of Alaskan North Slope crude oil among all regions of the United States.
- Authorized semi-annual advance payments of $5 million starting in fiscal 1976 for the Alaska Native Fund, pending delivery of North Slope oil to the pipeline, and limited total payments to $500 million.
- Authorized the President to negotiate with Canada concerning an alternative pipeline to carry North Slope oil across Canada to the midwestern United States.
- Prohibited any form of discrimination in any activity connected with construction and operation of the pipeline.
- Made the trans-Alaskan pipeline subject to the provisions of the Mineral Leasing Act of 1920, as amended by the bill, except for provisions of the 1920 act dealing with environmental standards and liability.

Other Rights-of-Way

- Authorized the interior secretary and other federal officials to authorize additional pipelines across federal lands

for the transportation of oil, natural gas, synthetic liquid or gaseous fuels, or refined products.
- Defined federal lands as all lands owned by the United States, except the National Park System, Indian lands, or lands on the outer continental shelf.
- Permitted the secretary to authorize rights-of-way wider than 50 feet, in addition to the ground occupied by pipelines and related facilities, if he found that wider rights-of-way were necessary.
- Required applicants for right-of-way permits to submit plans which would have to conform to regulations issued by the secretary incorporating environmental standards established by the act.
- Directed the secretary to issue regulations outlining the extent to which owners of a pipeline were liable to the United States or to third parties for damages or injuries resulting from pipeline operations.
- Provided that no domestically produced crude oil transported through any pipeline authorized under the act could be exported unless the President found and reported to Congress that such exports 1) would not diminish oil supplies in the United States and 2) would be in the national interest.
- Provided that such exports would be prohibited if Congress disapproved the President's findings by concurrent resolution within 60 days after receiving the report.

Miscellaneous Provisions

- Required Senate confirmation of the director of the White House Energy Policy Office and the head of the Interior Department's Mining Enforcement and Safety Administration, including the incumbents.
- Permitted the Federal Trade Commission (FTC) to go to court to enforce its own subpoenas and to seek temporary injunctions to avoid unfair competitive practices.
- Permitted the FTC to prosecute cases under its jurisdiction after consulting with the U.S. attorney general and giving

him 10 days in which to take the action proposed by the FTC.

• Increased from $5,000 to $10,000 the civil penalty for each violation of an order of the FTC.

• Transferred from the Office of Management and Budget to the General Accounting Office the authority to review regulatory agency requests for information from businesses and corporations.

• Directed the GAO to eliminate duplication of effort by agencies in gathering information and to minimize the compliance burden on businesses.

• Exempted from price controls under the Economic Stabilization Act of 1970 and from subsequent fuel allocation programs the sale of oil and natural gas liquids from wells producing no more than 10 barrels daily.

• Advanced the effective date of the Ports and Waterways Safety Act of 1972 with respect to U.S. vessels engaged in coastal trade to June 30, 1974, from January 1, 1976. (The 1972 act established construction standards for tankers to prevent pollution.)

• Specified that the rest of the act would not be affected if any provision were held invalid.*

---

* *Congressional Quarterly Almanac,* 1973, pp. 597-98.

Chapter 6

Who Pays the Lawyers?

THE COST OF SUING

The Alyeska Pipeline Service Company may be forgiven if it thought, at the end of 1973, that it had seen the last of the environmental lawyers. After all, the new legislation specifically directed the Secretary of the Interior to grant the necessary rights-of-way. Because the law removed the outmoded width limitation, there would be no way for the lawyers to renew their challenge to the pipeline on that ground. And the really substantial legal point, that the government failed adequately to consider the environmental impact, was also foreclosed by the act of Congress. What else was left?

Money. The lawyers wanted to be paid.

As public-interest lawyers, they had not charged their environmental clients legal fees. The Wilderness Society, the Friends of the Earth, and the Environmental Defense Fund had agreed to pay their expenses—duplicating costs, telephone bills, postage, and the like. Such costs added up to several thousands of dollars, but compared to the fees that a regular attorney would have charged, they were small.

Attorneys generally charge by the hour. The case before the Court of Appeals involved 4,500 hours of lawyers' time. In those days, a partner at a law firm in the Washington, D.C., area would have charged at least $50 an hour. That means that on the appeal alone—ignoring all the effort that went into developing the facts of the case and writing the briefs for the district court—the time expended was worth $225,000. But instead of receiving an hourly fee, the environmental lawyers were paid a low salary by the Center for Law and Social Policy, which was funded, in turn, by foundation grants. If the lawyers could be reimbursed for their time on an hourly basis, then they could make a significant contribution to the Center for which they worked, and both they and other such lawyers would have an incentive to bring other cases from which the public might derive some benefit.

But what theory would justify their collecting such a sum? Who would pay it?

Should the Loser Pay?

The normal fee rule in the United States—called the "American rule" to distinguish it from the opposite rule in the United Kingdom—holds that each party to a lawsuit must pay its own expenses and lawyers' fees. Ordinarily, a winning plaintiff must pay his own lawyers; he cannot ask a court to order the losing defendant to ante up for his lawyer, no matter how large the fee. Similarly, a winning defendant cannot collect a lawyer's fee from the losing plaintiff, no matter how much trouble the plaintiff put the defendant to in bringing the suit in the first place.

There are some exceptions to this American rule. If it can be shown that the plaintiff brought a meritless lawsuit in bad faith, maliciously, in order to harm the defendant, then a court has the power to order the plaintiff to pay all the defendant's legal costs. And in some kinds of cases, Congress or state legislatures by statute have declared that the winning plaintiff can recover lawyers' fees from the losing defendant—in federal antitrust and employment discrimination cases, for example. But none of the exceptions to the American rule seemed to apply in the pipeline case.

The environmental lawyers pursued a third theory. That was that the plaintiff had acted as a "private attorney general," suing as a private citizen to preserve the rights of all citizens generally. This was the essence of public-interest law: to seek in court the protection of public rights, especially those that for lack of funds are not usually represented in court.

How the Court Reasoned

Speaking again for the court majority, Judge J. Skelly Wright found this argument compelling. The case was argued in July 1973, before Congress reversed the Court of Appeals' injunction. At that time, the environmental lawyers appeared to have won the case. But the court took a long time to reach a decision. When the opinion was announced on April 4, 1974, the environmental plaintiffs clearly had lost the legal fight. Nevertheless, the Court of Appeals found in their favor on the financial claim. Said Wright:

> When violation of a congressional enactment has caused little injury to any one individual, but great harm to important public interests when viewed from the perspective of the broad class intended to be protected by that statute, not to award counsel fees can seriously frustrate the purposes of Congress. . . . Where the law relies on private suits to effectuate congressional policy in favor of broad public interests, attorneys' fees are often necessary to ensure that private litigants will initiate such suits. . . . Substantial benefits to the general public should not depend upon the financial status of the individual

volunteering to serve as plaintiff or upon the charity of the public-minded lawyers.

What effect would a rule giving payment to the plaintiffs' lawyers have on the defendants? In some cases, requiring defendants to pay might mean that it would be cheaper to give in to the plaintiffs' demands without even going to trial, rather than risk the huge fees that lawyers might charge if the trial goes on for months. That would be unjust, because it would mean that a defendant who deserved to win might be afraid to risk going to trial. But that was not the situation here, Judge Wright pointed out. Alyeska would scarcely have given in to the demands of the plaintiffs because of a fear that it would have to pay their lawyers. Its investment at the time of suit exceeded $1 billion; a few thousand dollars or even hundreds of thousands of dollars in legal fees for the opposing party would not cause it to capitulate.

But what did the plaintiffs accomplish? After all, the width limitation in the Mineral Leasing Act was scarcely one of the greater public issues of the day. It was so obscure, in fact, that few people knew about it until research for the suit began. Judge Wright's answer was as follows:

> But the dispute in this case was more than a debate over interpretation of [the Mineral Leasing] Act. [Alyeska's] primary argument was that, whatever the width restrictions in the Act originally meant, a settled administrative practice to evade those restrictions took precedence. In the final analysis, this case involved the duty of the Executive Branch to observe the restrictions imposed by the Legislative . . . and the primary responsibility of the Congress under the Constitution to regulate the use of public lands.
>
> The proper functioning of our system of government under the Constitution is, of course, important to every American, and in this sense appellants' suit had great therapeutic value.

> ... But requiring the Congress to revise the Mineral Leasing Act rather than permitting continued evasion of its clear, though anachronistic, restrictions has had other more concrete and equally important benefits. As a result of this suit, Congress has amended the Mineral Leasing Act to remove the restrictions of the 1920 statute and permit construction of the trans-Alaska pipeline. . . . The statute imposes several important new requirements designed to protect the public interest. Rather than continue the prior practice of permitting free use of Government land, the new statute requires the issuing agency to receive the "fair market value" of the right-of-way and empowers the agency to assess against the right-of-way recipient all reasonable administrative costs of processing an application and monitoring the right of way. . . . The statute contains special provisions making the operator of the pipeline strictly liable for damages resulting from use of the right-of-way. . . . The same section of the new statute requires the operator to maintain a $100,000,000 liability fund to satisfy the claims. . . . Forcing Alyeska to go to Congress to amend the 1920 Act certainly was not a sterile exercise in legal technicalities devoid of public significance.

Judge Wright also concluded that although his court had refused to rule on the NEPA issues, this should not affect the answer to the fee question. For the lawsuit did have an important legal effect. The plaintiffs' lawsuit served as a "catalyst to ensure that the Department of the Interior drafted an impact statement. . . . It must be recalled that when [the environmentalists] commenced this suit in 1970, the Interior Department, though ready to issue the necessary rights-of-way, had not yet drafted an environmental impact statement for the pipeline. . . . Requiring the Department to draft an impact statement as mandated by law not only benefited the public's statutory right to have information about the environmental consequences of the pipeline. It also led to the refinement of environmentally protective stipulations placed as conditions on the rights-of-way." Moreover, Judge Wright pointed out, early on the environmentalists were prepared to rest their entire case on the Mineral Leasing Act issue, but Alyeska refused and forced them to raise all the NEPA issues.

Why Alyeska Should Pay

But even given all these considerations, who should actually pay the attorneys' fees? The suit was technically filed against the United States Government, in the person of the Secretary of the Interior. So should he, or the United States, pay the fees? The answer to this question was clearly no, because a federal law prohibits courts from assessing attorneys' fees against the United States. The only party left to pay these fees was Alyeska. But it was not sued by the environmentalists.

The court pointed out that although Alyeska had not, in fact, violated any law or even been charged with any violation, nevertheless it had intervened in the lawsuit to protect its interests. Because the company was a "major and real party at interest in this case, actively participating in the litigation along with the Government, we think it fair that it should bear part of the attorneys' fees," Judge Wright said. The court decided that Alyeska should be forced to bear half the cost. Since the government could not be forced to pay the other half, that meant, the court said, that the plaintiffs' attorneys were entitled to recover half of their legitimate fees. The court remanded the case to the district court to determine how much they should be permitted to recover in dollar terms.

The Dissent

This decision of the Court of Appeals was not unanimous. Three judges vigorously dissented. "We are at a loss to know," said Judge Wilkey for himself and two of his colleagues, "who those 'particular individuals' enjoying 'substantial benefits' might be. It is hard to visualize the average American in this winter of 1973-74, turning down his thermostat and with a careful eye on his auto fuel gauge, feeling that warm glow of gratitude to those public-spirited plaintiffs in the Alaska Pipeline case."

In the dissenters' view, the environmentalists performed a net disservice to the American public:

> While no one questions the sincere motives of those "public interest" plaintiffs, it is not enough for a plaintiff to have a sincere feeling of self-righteous correctness in bringing litigation. There is the matter of *good judgment in assaying just where the public interest lies.* Did the plaintiffs exercise good judgment here in bringing suit to block the Alaska Pipeline? In retrospect, we submit they did not.
>
> And in retrospect is precisely the way the award of attorneys' fees is always judged. By delaying the obtaining of oil from the North Slope of Alaska for several years, the plaintiffs conferred *no public benefit* on the United States of America. . . .
>
> [P]laintiffs' net achievement [was] the amendment of the 1920 Mineral Leasing Act to authorize a wider right-of-way, quite the opposite of the plaintiffs' objective to limit the right-of-way to 25 feet on each side. Against this public service must be weighed the public *dis*service in blocking access to the much needed oil at a critical time in our history, and the enormously higher cost we must all pay. . . . Plaintiffs' litigation has lasted over three and a half years, the delay is at least as long as the litigation, so construction costs have been upped *at least* $637 million—well over half a billion dollars, all of which will be paid for by the American consumer, when the oil finally arrives.

Not surprisingly, Alyeska agreed with the dissenters. There was one thing left for it to do: appeal to the Supreme Court of the United States.

CHECKS AND BALANCES: PUBLIC *vs.* PRIVATE INTERESTS

The environmental lawyers lost the pipeline case —though in Congress, not in the courts. By filing and preparing the lawsuit, they saw themselves serving an important public interest: vindication of the public's right to have the laws obeyed. The lawyers wanted to be paid not merely as reimbursement for their time but so that they and others could in the future have a means of financing other lawsuits that they believed to be in the public interest. Having accomplished what they set out to do, they asked the court to order the losing defendants to pay them. This the court did, establishing a precedent that, if upheld on appeal, would permit many more important suits to be brought to test the rights of the public.

Chapter 7

In the Supreme Court

Final But Not Infallible

Every year more than 4,000 cases are appealed to the Supreme Court. Of this number, the justices pick fewer than 200 to hear oral argument and to write full-blown opinions. Except for a tiny category of cases that by law they are required to hear, the justices choose those that interest them, that they think are important, and that raise critical issues. In the fall of 1974, on a petition by Alyeska's lawyers, the justices agreed to hear an appeal from the decision of the U.S. Court of Appeals.

The Supreme Court is supreme because it is the highest court in the land and, therefore, final. In the famous words of Justice Robert H. Jackson, "We are not final because we are infallible, but we are infallible only because we are final." That does not mean that whatever the Supreme Court announces is the law forever. Just as the Court of Appeals could be reversed by Congress, so Congress can reverse the propositions of law announced by the Supreme Court, except in those cases in which the Court is expounding the meaning of the Constitution. But even the Court's constitutional rulings can be changed in our system of checks and balances, for the people always remain supreme. Three times in our history so far, the Court's constitutional decisions have been reversed by constitutional amendment (the Eleventh, Fourteenth, and Sixteenth amendments).

The Alyeska case caused considerable excitement in legal circles. If the Supreme Court were to sustain it, then dozens of public-interest lawyers would be given an important incentive to bring similar cases in the future. A number of associations and organizations came forward to submit briefs as *amici curiae*, or "friends of the court," to urge it to affirm the Court of Appeals. These included the Association of the Bar of the City of New York, the Lawyers' Committee for Civil Rights Under Law, the NAACP Legal Defense and Educational Fund, Inc., and the Center for Law in the Public Interest.

Unlike other appellate courts, the Supreme Court does not sit in separate panels. When it heard oral argument in the Alyeska case on January 22, 1975, seven of the nine justices sat behind their high bench in their large marble-colonnaded room. (Justices Douglas and Powell did not participate in the case. Although no reasons for their absence were stated, Justice Douglas was seriously ill at the time and would shortly retire after more than 36 years on the Court.) Nearly four months later, on May 12, the Court handed down its decision. By a 5-2 vote, it reversed. Alyeska would not have to pay its opponents' attorneys.

The Supreme Court Reverses

The majority opinion was written by Justice Byron R. White. Rather than considering whether the plaintiffs' attorneys deserved the fee award, he concentrated instead on whether the federal courts have the legal power to make the award. He concluded that they do not.

Justice White conducted a searching historical examination of the judicial power to award attorneys' fees. As early as 1796, he noted, the Supreme Court had declared that unless Congress authorized them to do so, the federal courts could not on their own make such awards. Nevertheless, over time, there developed in some courts the habit of awarding attorneys' fees in certain cases, usually because these awards were allowable under state law. In 1853, reacting to the great disparity among the courts—some awarding high fees, some awarding no fees—Congress enacted legislation to standardize the costs allowable in federal litigation. It set forth a table, stating the maximum rates that the courts could award to attorneys. By today's standards, these were quite small, on the order of $10-20 per case. This law continued virtually unchanged through various codifications of the law from then to the present day.

This law did not mean, Justice White explained, that the courts could never award winning attorneys' more substantial fees, for there exceptions were always recognized. But these exceptions were narrow. If the losing party acts in bad faith or disobeys an order of court, he may be forced to recompense the attorneys of the litigants forced to bring him to justice. But none of these exceptions applied to the Alyeska case.

However, when Congress by specific legislation has told the courts they can make attorneys' fee awards, then of course the courts may act. Justice White cited some 30 separate Congressional enactments permitting attorney fee awards. These included such statutes as the Perishable Agricultural Commodities Act, the Truth in Lending Act, the Copyright Act, various civil rights, antitrust, and environmental laws, and certain provisions of the Federal Rules of Civil Procedure. But not the Mineral Leasing Act.

In many of these statutes, Justice White noted, "it is true

that . . . Congress has opted to rely heavily on private enforcement to implement public policy and to allow counsel fees so as to encourage private litigation. . . . We have noted that Title II of the Civil Rights Act of 1964 was intended 'not simply to penalize litigants who deliberately advance arguments they know to be untenable but, more broadly, to encourage individuals injured by racial discrimination to seek judicial relief under Title II.' " Congress sometimes encourages private enforcement of the laws through lawsuits in which fees are recoverable. But that does not mean that courts can make such awards in the absence of Congressional authorization. In sum, concluded Justice White:

> Congress itself presumably has the power and judgment to pick and choose among its statutes and to allow attorneys' fees under some, but not others. But it would be difficult, indeed, for the courts, without legislative guidance, to consider some statutes important and others unimportant and to allow attorneys' fees only in connection with the former. . . .
>
> We do not purport to assess the merits or demerits of the "American rule" with respect to the allowance of attorneys' fees. It has been criticized in recent years, and courts have been urged to find exceptions to it. . . . [But the rule] is deeply rooted in our history and in congressional policy; and it is not for us to invade the legislature's province by redistributing litigation costs in the manner suggested by [the environmental groups] and followed by the Court of Appeals.

Now at last, five years after the suit was filed, it was finally over. Congress retains the power to change the legal rule concerning the awarding of attorneys' fees in future cases, but it could not act to change the rights of Alyeska or the Wilderness Society and its sister organizations. The Alaska pipeline case had come to an end.

CHECKS AND BALANCES: COURTS *vs.* COURTS

The Court of Appeals had ruled that it had the "inherent" power to order Alyeska to pay the fees of the plaintiffs' attorneys. This was not a power that was conferred on the court by Congress; no law said that the court could act as it did. But courts also draw their powers from the Constitution, and the judges believed that the power they exercised had ancient legal roots. The Supreme Court disagreed. Reversing the lower court's ruling, the justices thus limited their own power to consider the propriety of such payments in future cases—for, they said, there is no such power.

The Supreme Court having spoken, is that the end of the line? Not at all. If Congress chooses—if enough people push it to do so—it can pass a new law giving courts the power to order losers to pay the winners' legal costs. Congress has not yet acted so broadly, but the possibility will always remain open in a country that honors a system of checks and balances.

Chapter 8

The Land and the Pipeline

The legal effort to prevent construction of the pipeline or to change its nature as a trans-Alaskan pipeline to a trans-Canadian one had failed. But that did not end the government's involvement.

It took more than one year to complete the construction road, cut the tunnels into which the pipe would be laid through half its course, collect supplies and materials, and finish the other preliminary work that had to precede the laying of the pipe. Alyeska started welding the pipe and putting it into the ground on March 27, 1975. It was not an easy job and much went wrong. Most dramatically, the welds connecting many of the pipes were found to be defective. This was a serious danger, because a defective weld could spring a leak, and through a leak oil under pressure could spill out onto the ground in large quantities, tearing up the permafrost.

Government inspectors were at the work sites as the pipe was laid. They had authority and instructions to check every weld and, by government regulation, Alyeska was to X-ray each weld to insure that it had been completed properly. But it turned out that the company was falsifying many X-rays—for example, by X-raying a perfect weld and claiming that the X-ray was of a different weld, one that had not been checked. So serious did the problem become that a House subcommittee held "oversight" hearings to uncover what was happening. A 1976 hearing discovered that "an Alyeska audit of the 1975 pipeline welding program revealed 3,955 'problem welds' ranging from cracks in welds, falsified X-rays of welds, to missing and stolen X-rays, as well as other problems. At least half of these problem welds are already buried under the tundra and rivers of Alaska."

The falsification of X-rays came to light when Peter Kelley, a radiographer with a company hired to do the X-rays, objected to an order to change the weld numbers on his photographic plates. He was fired and he filed a lawsuit. In later testimony to the House subcommittee in Washington, Kelley recalled how the falsification worked: "It was [by] putting a number on a piece of film to correspond with that particular weld. This was put on another weld that had already passed inspection and so, in effect, you were saying that this piece of film is weld X when you were really X-raying weld Y."

The defective welds that were uncovered had to be replaced, of course, as did the many other defective parts, like the beams holding the pipeline up above the ground that frequently collapsed. What began as an attempt to rush through construction to avoid delays instead caused delays, as work had to be stopped and redone. All the while, federal government inspectors and Congressional committees watched, probed, asked questions, gave orders.

By 1977 the pipeline was finished and oil began to flow. By then the cost of construction had risen from the earliest optimistic estimates of $900 million to more than $8 *billion*. How much of the increase was due to the delay and inflation and how much due to Alyeska's haste, inefficiency, and waste may never be known—one government report suggested that at least $1.5 billion was due to construction inefficiencies alone. During that same time, the price of oil jumped precipitously, so that the oil companies stand to reap tens of billions of dollars more in profits than they had originally expected—and perhaps hundreds of billions of dollars, depending on how the price of oil continues to rise and on how much oil will eventually be found at Prudhoe Bay.

Nor did the government's involvement end with the completion of the pipeline. Then the question arose of how much Alyeska could charge for use of its pipeline, and the Interstate Commerce Commission, which has jurisdiction over pipeline tariffs, and the courts found plenty to occupy their time.

In the end, was the delay engendered by the complexities of the system of checks and balances that permeate our government worthwhile? It is a difficult question to answer. Perhaps delay for its own sake is never worthwhile, but delay is normally a by-product of a process of government that serves other ends. In this case, the ends to be served were multifaceted, as we have seen, ranging from the land claims of the Native Alaskans to serious concerns about the environment. Though the environmentalists failed to achieve what at least some of them wanted—abandonment of the project—they did force, through our system of checks and balances, a more sensible, ecologically sound construction, with which the nation can live in order to get the oil that it needs.

Appendix 1
Route of the Trans-Alaskan Pipeline

Appendix 2
Pipeline Chronology

(from the discovery of oil to President's signature 1968-1973)

February 1968—Substantial oil and gas reserves were discovered on the Alaskan North Slope at Prudhoe Bay.

October 1968—Pipeline Technologists, Inc., a pipeline consulting firm engaged by Atlantic Richfield Company and Humble Oil Company, completed a study on the feasibility of a pipeline system from Prudhoe Bay to the southern coast of Alaska. Pipe Tech. concluded that a secured pipeline could be constructed, operated, and maintained.

October 1968—Atlantic Richfield, Humble, and British Petroleum Oil Companies formed the Trans Alaska Pipeline System (TAPS) for the purpose of developing plans for and constructing a pipeline.

December 31, 1968—Task force established by interested oil companies concluded that an all-land route through Canada and Alaska was feasible, could be constructed within a reasonable time, and could be operated successfully.

February 1969—TAPS announced its decision to apply for permits to construct an oil pipeline from the North Slope (Prudhoe Bay) to the southern coast of Alaska (Valdez).

April 19, 1969—Secretary of the Interior Hickel established the North Slope Task Force to set guidelines for the development of federal land from the Arctic North Slope of Alaska.

May 9, 1969—The Interior Department task force was converted by President Nixon into an inter-departmental task force and directed to consider ways to explore and develop the oil resources of Northern Alaska, without destruction and with a minimum of disturbance.

APPENDIX 2   85

June 2, 1969—Several oil companies established McKenzie Valley Pipeline Research Ltd. (MVPL) to continue investigations into pipeline facilities from the North Slope of Alaska to Edmonton, Canada. Subsequent studies again confirmed its feasibility. *See* December 31, 1968.

June 10, 1969—TAPS filed a formal application for a pipeline right-of-way from Prudhoe Bay to Valdez.

August-December 1969—Public hearings on the proposed pipeline were conducted in Alaska and Washington, D.C.

September 15, 1969—Inter-Departmental Task Force submitted preliminary report to the President.

September 1969—State of Alaska received $900 million as a result of the lease sale covering 450,000 acres on the North Slope.

September 1969—Environmental stipulations were promulgated by the Task Force and subsequently approved by committees of both Senate and House.

December 1969—TAPS submitted an amended application for a single right-of-way, 54 feet in width, and 2 separate applications for Special Land Use Permits (SLUPs); one application for a 46-foot SLUP for additional access and construction space, and one application for a 200-foot SLUP for the construction of a haul road. Five additional oil companies joined the original three in the submission of this application.

December 1969—Secretary of Interior signed modification of Alaskan land freeze order to permit construction of a highway between Livengood to the Yukon River. Bureau of Land Management (BLM) issued mobilization authority allowing five road construction contractors to develop construction camps and mobilize for the construction of the road north of the Yukon River.

January 1, 1970—National Environmental Policy Act of 1969 (NEPA) became effective.

January 1970—TAPS was replaced by Alyeska Pipeline Service Co., Inc. *See* October 1968.

March 5, 1970—Secretary of Interior Hickel informed the President that he was prepared to grant permits authorizing the oil companies to construct a haul road from the Yukon to the North Slope—an act tantamount to ultimate approval of the pipeline itself.

March 26, 1970—Plaintiffs—Wilderness Society, Friends of the Earth, and the Environmental Defense Fund, Inc.—filed suit to enjoin construction of the pipeline.

April 3, 1970—The United States District Court for the District of

Columbia denied the plaintiffs' request for a temporary restraining order.

April 23, 1970—Ruling that the Secretary of the Interior must consider the full scope of a project before making decisions whether to approve part of it, the District Court granted the plaintiffs a preliminary injunction. The Court ruled that the applications for a 54-foot right-of-way, for a 46-foot SLUP and for a 200-foot SLUP were really a single application for a pipeline right-of-way in excess of the width permitted under section 28 of the Mineral Leasing Act of 1920, 30 U.S.C. §185 (1970).

January 1971—The Department of Interior released its Draft Impact Statement to the public and to other federal agencies.

March 1971—Alyeska applied for rights-of-way for 26 communication sites.

June 1971—Alyeska and the State of Alaska entered into a contract whereby the latter agreed to build a public highway along the route of the proposed haulway.

June 28, 1971—State of Alaska applied to the Bureau of Land Management for a highway right-of-way.

August 18, 1971—Alyeska withdrew its application of December 1969 for the 200-foot SLUP.

January 13, 1972—Decision of *NRDC* v. *Morton*, 337 F. Supp. 165, invalidated the Department of Interior's construction of NEPA and required the Department to consider a range of alternatives it had heretofore ignored.

February 4, 1972—Alyeska filed an amendment to its December 1971 application for a SLUP for construction purposes, requesting the temporary use of minimum amounts of land as may be reasonably necessary for construction of a pipeline.

February 1972—Revised technical and environmental stipulations were issued.

March 20, 1972—The Interior Department released its final study on the pipeline—a six-volume Impact Statement and three-volume Economic & Security Analysis. Comments were invited within a 45-day time limitation.

May 4, 1972—The plaintiffs submitted over 1000 pages of comments to the Department of the Interior.

May 11, 1972—Secretary of the Interior Morton announced his decision to approve the trans-Alaska pipeline and within a week issued a "Statement of Reasons for Approval."

August 15, 1972—District Court dissolved the preliminary injunction, denied a permanent injunction, and dismissed the complaint in *Wilderness Soc'y* v. *Morton*.

February 9, 1973—The United States Court of Appeals reversed the District Court's dissolution of the injunction and enjoined construction.

April 1973—Supreme Court denied certiorari, declining to review the Court of Appeals' decision.

July 17, 1973—Senate passed the Federal Lands Right-of-Way Act of 1973 and the trans-Alaska Pipeline Authorization Act (Gravel-Stevens amendment).

August 2, 1973—House of Representatives passed bill H.R. 9130 that contained pipeline authorization provisions similar to the trans-Alaska Pipeline Authorization Act.

November 16, 1973—President Nixon signed the House-Senate conference bill into law.*

* Peter H. Dominick and David E. Brody, "The Alaska Pipeline Case," *American University Law Review*, vol. 23, no. 2, 1973, pp. 387-89.

Appendix 3

Text of Public Law 93-153

[The Alaska Pipeline Act]

As enacted, the Alaska Pipeline Act appears in volume 87 of the *Statutes at Large*, p.576. It is officially cited as Pub.L. 93-153, meaning that it was the one-hundred-fifty-third law enacted by the Ninety-Third Congress. The provisions dealing with rights-of-way over federal lands appear as Section 185 of Title 30 of the *United States Code,* which deals with mineral lands and mining.

The text of Pub.L. 93-153 is set forth below and is reproduced from the version appearing in the *Statutes at Large.*

Public Law 93-153
93rd Congress, S. 1081
November 16, 1973

AN ACT

To amend section 28 of the Mineral Leasing Act of 1920, and to authorize a trans-Alaska oil pipeline, and for other purposes.

Be it enacted by the Senate and House of Representatives of the United States of America in Congress assembled,

TITLE I

SECTION 101. Section 28 of the Mineral Leasing Act of 1920 (41 Stat. 449), as amended (30 U.S.C. 185), is further amended to read as follows:

"Grant of Authority

"SEC. 28. (a) Rights-of-way through any Federal lands may be granted by the Secretary of the Interior or appropriate agency head for pipeline purposes for the transportation of oil, natural gas, synthetic liquid or gaseous fuels, or any refined product produced therefrom to any applicant possessing the qualifications provided in section 1 of this Act, as amended, in accordance with the provisions of this section.

"Definitions

"(b) (1) For the purposes of this section 'Federal lands' means all lands owned by the United States except lands in the National Park System, lands held in trust for an Indian or Indian tribe, and lands on the Outer Continental Shelf. A right-of-way through a Federal reservation shall not be granted if the Secretary or agency head determines that it would be inconsistent with the purposes of the reservation.

"(2) 'Secretary' means the Secretary of the Interior.

"(3) 'Agency head' means the head of any Federal department or independent Federal office or agency, other than the Secretary of the Interior, which has jurisdiction over Federal lands.

"Inter-Agency Coordination

"(c) (1) Where the surface of all of the Federal lands involved in a proposed right-of-way or permit is under the jurisdiction of one Federal agency, the agency head, rather than the Secretary, is authorized to grant or renew the right-of-way or permit for the purposes set forth in this section.

"(2) Where the surface of the Federal lands involved is administered by the Secretary or by two or more Federal agencies, the Secretary is authorized, after consultation with the agencies involved, to grant or renew rights-of-way or permits through the Federal lands involved. The Secretary may enter into interagency agreements with all other Federal agencies having jurisdiction over Federal lands for the purpose of avoiding duplication, assigning responsibility, expediting review of rights-of-way or permit applications, issuing joint regulations, and assuring a decision based upon a comprehensive review of all factors involved in any right-of-way or permit application. Each agency head shall administer and enforce the provisions of this section, appropriate regulations, and the terms and conditions of rights-of-way or permits insofar as they involve Federal lands under the agency head's jurisdiction.

"Width Limitations

"(d) The width of a right-of-way shall not exceed fifty feet plus the ground occupied by the pipeline (that is, the pipe and its related facilities) unless the Secretary or agency head finds, and records the reasons for his finding, that in his judgment a wider right-of-way is necessary for operation and maintenance after construction, or to protect the environment or public safety. Related facilities include but are not limited to valves, pump stations, supporting structures, bridges, monitoring and communication devices, surge and storage tanks, terminals, roads, airstrips and campsites, and they need not necessarily be connected or contiguous to the pipe and may be the subjects of separate rights-of-way.

"Temporary Permits

"(e) A right-of-way may be supplemented by such temporary permits for the use of Federal lands in the vicinity of the pipeline as the Secretary or agency head finds are necessary in connection with construction, operation, maintenance, or termination of the pipeline, or to protect the natural environment or public safety.

"Regulatory Authority

"(f) Rights-of-way or permits granted or renewed pursuant to this section shall be subject to regulations promulgated in accord with the provisions of this section and shall be subject to such terms and conditions as the Secretary or agency head may prescribe regarding extent, duration, survey, location, construction, operation, maintenance, use, and termination.

"Pipeline Safety

"(g) The Secretary or agency head shall impose requirements for the operation of the pipeline and related facilities in a manner that will protect the safety of workers and protect the public from sudden ruptures and slow degradation of the pipeline.

"Environmental Protection

"(h)(1) Nothing in this section shall be construed to amend, repeal, modify, or change in any way the requirements of section 102(2)(C) or any other provision of the National Environmental Policy Act of 1969 (Public Law 91-190.83 Stat. 852).

"(2) The Secretary or agency head, prior to granting a right-of-way or permit pursuant to this section for a new project which may have a significant impact on the environment, shall require the applicant to submit a plan of construction, operation, and rehabilitation for such right-of-way or permit which shall comply with this section. The Secretary or agency head shall issue regulations or impose stipulations which shall include, but shall not be limited to: (A) requirements for restoration, revegetation, and curtailment of erosion of the surface of the land; (B) requirements to insure that activities in connection with the right-of-way or permit will not violate applicable air and water quality standards nor related facility siting standards established by or pursuant to law; (C) requirements designed to control or prevent (i) damage to the environment (including damage to fish and wildlife habitat), (ii) damage to public or private property, and (iii) hazards to public health and safety; and (D) requirements to protect the interests of individuals living in the general area of the right-of-way or permit who rely on the fish, wildlife, and biotic resources of the area for subsistence purposes. Such regulations shall be applicable to every right-of-way or permit granted pursuant to this section, and may be made applicable by the Secretary or agency head to existing rights-of-way or permits, or rights-of-way or permits to be renewed pursuant to this section.

"Disclosure

"(i) If the applicant is a partnership, corporation, association, or other business entity, the Secretary or agency head shall require the applicant to disclose the identity of the participants in the entity. Such disclosure shall include where applicable (1) the name and address of each partner, (2) the name and address of each shareholder owning 3 per centum or more of the shares, together with the number and percentage of any class of voting shares of the entity which such shareholder is authorized to vote, and (3) the name and address of each affiliate of the entity together with, in the case of an affiliate controlled by the entity, the number of shares and the percentage of any class of voting stock of that affiliate owned, directly or indirectly, by that entity, and, in the case of an affiliate which controls that entity, the number of shares and the percentage of any class of voting stock of that entity owned, directly or indirectly, by the affiliate.

"Technical and Financial Capability

"(j) The Secretary or agency head shall grant or renew a right-of-way or permit under this section only when he is satisfied that the applicant has the technical and financial capability to construct, operate, maintain, and terminate the project for which the right-of-way or permit is requested in accordance with the requirements of this section.

"Public Hearings

"(k) The Secretary or agency head by regulation shall establish procedures, including public hearings where appropriate, to give Federal, State, and local government agencies and the public adequate notice and an opportunity to comment upon right-of-way applications filed after the date of enactment of this subsection.

"Reimbursement of Costs

"(l) The applicant for a right-of-way or permit shall reimburse the United States for administrative and other costs incurred in processing the application, and the holder of a right-of-way or permit shall reimburse the United States for the costs incurred in monitoring the construction, operation, maintenance, and termination of any pipeline and related facilities on such right-of-way or permit area and shall pay annually in advance the fair market rental value of the right-of-way or permit, as determined by the Secretary or agency head.

"Bonding

"(m) Where he deems it appropriate the Secretary or agency head may require a holder of a right-of-way or permit to furnish a bond, or other security, satisfactory to the Secretary or agency head to secure all or any of the obligations imposed by the terms and conditions of the right-of-way or permit or by any rule or regulation of the Secretary or agency head.

"Duration of Grant

"(n) Each right-of-way or permit granted or renewed pursuant to this section shall be limited to a reasonable term in light of all circumstances concerning the project, but in no event more than thirty years. In determining the duration of a right-of-way the Secretary or agency head shall, among other things, take into consideration the cost of the facility, its useful life, and any public purpose it serves. The Secretary or agency head shall renew any right-of-way, in accordance with the provisions of this section, so long as the project is in commercial operation and is operated and maintained in accordance with all of the provisions of this section.

"Suspension or Termination of Right-of-Way

"(o) (1) Abandonment or a right-of-way or noncompliance with any provision of this section may be grounds for suspension or termination of the right-of-way if (A) after due notice to the holder of the right-of-way, (B) a reasonable opportunity to comply with this section, and (C) an appropriate administrative proceeding pursuant to title 5, United States Code, section 554, the Secretary or agency head determines that any such ground exists and that suspension or termination is justified. No administrative proceeding shall be required where the right-of-way by its terms provides that it terminates on the occurrence of a fixed or agreed upon condition, event, or time.

"(2) If the Secretary or agency head determines that an immediate temporary suspension of activities within a right-of-way or permit area is necessary to protect public health or safety or the environment, he may abate such activities prior to an administrative proceeding.

"(3) Deliberate failure of the holder to use the right-of-way for the purpose for which it was granted or renewed for any continuous two-year period shall constitute a rebuttable presumption of abandonment of the right-of-way: *Provided*, That where the failure to use the right-of-way is due to circumstances not within the holder's control the Secretary or agency head is not required to commence proceedings to suspend or terminate the right-of-way.

"Joint Use of Rights-of-Way

"(p) In order to minimize adverse environmental impacts and the proliferation of separate rights-of-way across Federal lands, the utilization of rights-of-way in common shall be required to the extent practical, and each right-of-way or permit shall reserve to the Secretary or agency head the right to grant additional rights-of-way or permits for compatible uses on or adjacent to rights-of-way or permit area granted pursuant to this section.

"Statutes

"(q) No rights-of-way for the purposes provided for in this section shall be granted or renewed across Federal lands except under and subject to the provisions, limitations, and conditions of this section. Any application for a right-of-way filed under any other law prior to the effective date of this provision may, at the applicant's option, be considered as an application under this section. The Secretary or agency head may require the applicant to submit any additional information he deems necessary to comply with the requirements of this section.

"Common Carriers

"(r)(1) Pipelines and related facilities authorized under this section shall be constructed, operated, and maintained as common carriers.

"(2)(A) The owners or operators of pipelines subject to this section shall accept, convey, transport, or purchase without discrimination all oil or gas delivered to the pipeline without regard to whether such oil or gas was produced on Federal or non-Federal lands.

"(B) In the case of oil or gas produced from Federal lands or from the resources on the Federal lands in the vicinity of the pipeline, the Secretary may, after a full hearing with due notice thereof to the interested parties and a proper finding of facts, determine the proportionate amounts to be accepted, conveyed, transported or purchased.

"(3)(A) The common carrier provisions of this section shall not apply to any natural gas pipeline operated by any person subject to regulation under the Natural Gas Act or by any public utility subject to regulation by a State or municipal regulatory agency having jurisdiction to regulate the rates and charges for the sale of natural gas to consumers within the State or municipality.

"(B) Where natural gas not subject to State regulatory or conservation laws governing its purchase by pipelines is offered for sale, each such pipeline shall purchase, without discrimination, any such natural gas produced in the vicinity of the pipeline.

"(4) The Government shall in express terms reserve and shall provide in every lease of oil lands under this Act that the lessee, assignee, or beneficiary, if owner or operator of a controlling interest in any pipeline or of any company operating the pipeline which may be operated accessible to the oil derived from lands under such lease, shall at reasonable rates and without discrimination accept and convey the oil of the Government or of any citizens or company not the owner of any pipeline operating a lease or purchasing gas or oil under the provisions of this Act.

"(5) Whenever the Secretary has reason to believe that any owner or operator subject to this section is not operating any oil or gas pipeline in complete accord with its obligations as a common carrier hereunder, he may request the Attorney General to prosecute an appropriate proceeding before the Interstate Commerce Commission or Federal Power Commission or any appropriate State agency or the United States district court for the district in which the pipeline or any part thereof is located, to enforce such obligation or to impose any penalty provided therefor, or the Secretary may, by proceeding as provided in this section, suspend or terminate the said grant of right-of-way for noncompliance with the provisions of this section.

"(6) The Secretary or agency head shall require, prior to granting or renewing a right-of-way, that the applicant submit and disclose all plans, contracts, agreements, or other information or material which he deems necessary to determine whether a right-of-way shall be granted or renewed and the terms and conditions which should be included in the right-of-way. Such information may include, but is not limited to: (A) conditions for, and agreements among owners or operators, regarding the addition of pumping facilities, looping, or otherwise increasing the pipeline or terminal's throughout capacity in response to actual or anticipated increases in demand; (B) conditions for adding or abandoning intake, offtake, or storage points or facilities; and (C) minimum shipment or purchase tenders.

"Right-of-Way Corridors

"(s) In order to minimize adverse environmental impacts and to prevent the proliferation of separate rights-of-way across Federal lands, the Secretary shall, in consultation with other Federal and State agencies, review the need for a national system of transportation and utility corridors across Federal lands and submit a report of his findings and recommendations to the Congress and the President by July 1, 1975.

"Existing Rights-of-Way

"(t) The Secretary or agency head may ratify and confirm any right-of-way or permit for an oil or gas pipeline or related facility that was granted under any provision of law before the effective date of this subsection, if it is modified by mutual agreement to comply to the extent practical with the provisions of this section. Any action taken by the Secretary or agency head pursuant to this subsection shall not be considered a major Federal action requiring a detailed statement pursuant to section 102(2)(C) of the National Environmental Policy Act of 1970 (Public Law 90–190; 42 U.S.C. 4321).

"Limitations on Export

"(u) Any domestically produced crude oil transported by pipeline over rights-of-way granted pursuant to section 28 of the Mineral Leasing Act of 1920, except such crude oil which is either exchanged in similar quantity for convenience or increased efficiency of transportation with persons or the government of an adjacent foreign state, or which is temporarily exported for convenience or increased efficiency of transportation across parts of an adjacent foreign state and reenters the United States, shall be subject to all of the limitations and licensing requirements of the Export Administration Act of 1969 (Act of December 30, 1969; 83 Stat. 841) and, in addition, before any crude oil subject to this section may be exported under the limitations and licensing requirements and penalty and enforcement provisions of the Export Administration Act of 1969 the President must make and publish an express finding that such exports will not diminish the total quantity or quality of petroleum available to the United States, and are in the national interest and are in accord with the provisions of the Export Administration Act of 1969: *Provided*, That the President shall submit reports to the Congress containing findings made under this section, and after the date of receipt of such report Congress shall have a period of sixty calendar days, thirty days of which Congress must have been in session, to consider whether exports under the terms of this section are in the national interest. If the Congress within this time period passes a concurrent resolution of disapproval stating disagreement with the President's finding concerning the national interest, further exports made pursuant to the aforementioned Presidential findings shall cease.

"State Standards

"(v) The Secretary or agency head shall take into consideration and to the extent practical comply with State standards for right-of-way construction, operation, and maintenance.

"Reports

"(w)(1) The Secretary and other appropriate agency heads shall report to the House and Senate Committees on Interior and Insular Affairs annually on the administration of this section and on the safety and environmental requirements imposed pursuant thereto.

"(2) The Secretary or agency head shall notify the House and Senate Committees on Interior and Insular Affairs promptly upon receipt of an application for a right-of-way for a pipeline twenty-four inches or more in diameter, and no right-of-way for such a pipeline shall be granted until sixty days (not counting days on which the House of Representatives or the Senate has adjourned for more than three days) after a notice of intention to grant the right-of-way, together with the Secretary's or agency head's detailed findings as to terms and conditions he proposes to impose, has been submitted to such committees, unless each committee by resolution waives the waiting period.

"(3) Periodically, but at least once a year, the Secretary of the Department of Transportation shall cause the examination of all pipelines and associated facilities on Federal lands and shall cause the prompt reporting of any potential leaks or safety problems.

"(4) The Secretary of the Department of Transportation shall report annually to the President, the Congress, the Secretary of the Interior, and the Interstate Commerce Commission any potential dangers of or actual explosions, or potential or actual spillage on Federal lands and shall include in such report a statement of corrective action taken to prevent such explosion or spillage.

"Liability

"(x)(1) The Secretary or agency head shall promulgate regulations and may impose stipulations specifying the extent to which holders of rights-of-way and permits under this Act shall be liable to the United States for damage or injury incurred by the United States in connection with the right-of-way or permit. Where the right-of-way or permit involves lands which are under the exclusive jurisdiction of the Federal Government, the Secretary or agency head shall promulgate regulations specifying the extent to which holders shall be liable to third parties for injuries incurred in connection with the right-of-way or permit.

"(2) The Secretary or agency head may, by regulation or stipulation, impose a standard of strict liability to govern activities taking place on a right-of-way or permit area which the Secretary or agency head determines, in his discretion, to present a foreseeable hazard or risk of danger to the United States.

"(3) Regulations and stipulations pursuant to this subsection shall not impose strict liability for damage or injury resulting from (A) an act of war, or (B) negligence of the United States.

"(4) Any regulation or stipulation imposing liability without fault shall include a maximum limitation on damages commensurate with the foreseeable risks or hazards presented. Any liability for damage or injury in excess of this amount shall be determined by ordinary rules of negligence.

"(5) The regulations and stipulations shall also specify the extent to which such holders shall indemnify or hold harmless the United States for liability, damage, or claims arising in connection with the right-of-way or permit.

"(6) Any regulation or stipulation promulgated or imposed pursuant to this section shall provide that all owners of any interest in, and all affiliates or subsidiaries of any holder of, a right-of-way or permit shall be liable to the United States in the event that a claim for damage or injury cannot be collected from the holder.

"(7) In any case where liability without fault is imposed pursuant to this subsection and the damages involved were caused by the negligence of a third party, the rules of subrogation shall apply in accordance with the law of the jurisdiction where the damage occurred.

"Antitrust Laws

"(y) The grant of a right-of-way or permit pursuant to this section shall grant no immunity from the operation of the Federal antitrust laws."

TITLE II

SHORT TITLE

SEC. 201. This title may be cited as the "Trans-Alaska Pipeline Authorization Act".

CONGRESSIONAL FINDINGS

SEC. 202. The Congress finds and declares that:

(a) The early development and delivery of oil and gas from Alaska's North Slope to domestic markets is in the national interest because of growing domestic shortages and increasing dependence upon insecure foreign sources.

(b) The Department of the Interior and other Federal agencies have, over a long period of time, conducted extensive studies of the technical aspects and of the environmental, social, and economic impacts of the proposed trans-Alaska oil pipeline, including consideration of a trans-Canada pipeline.

(c) The earliest possible construction of a trans-Alaska oil pipeline from the North Slope of Alaska to Port Valdez in that State will make the extensive proven and potential reserves of low-sulfur oil available for domestic use and will best serve the national interest.

(d) A supplemental pipeline to connect the North Slope with a trans-Canada pipeline may be needed later and it should be studied now, but it should not be regarded as an alternative for a trans-Alaska pipeline that does not traverse a foreign country.

CONGRESSIONAL AUTHORIZATION

SEC. 203. (a) The purpose of this title is to insure that, because of the extensive governmental studies already made of this project and the national interest in early delivery of North Slope oil to domestic markets, the trans-Alaska oil pipeline be constructed promptly without further administrative or judicial delay or impediment. To accomplish this purpose it is the intent of the Congress to exercise its constitutional powers to the fullest extent in the authorizations and directions herein made and in limiting judicial review of the actions taken pursuant thereto.

(b) The Congress hereby authorizes and directs the Secretary of the Interior and other appropriate Federal officers and agencies to issue and take all necessary action to administer and enforce rights-of-way, permits, leases, and other authorizations that are necessary for or related to the construction, operation, and maintenance of the trans-Alaska oil pipeline system, including roads and airstrips, as that system is generally described in the Final Environmental Impact Statement issued by the Department of the Interior on March 20, 1972. The route of the pipeline may be modified by the Secretary to provide during construction greater environmental protection.

(c) Rights-of-way, permits, leases, and other authorizations issued pursuant to this title by the Secretary shall be subject to the provisions of section 28 of the Mineral Leasing Act of 1920, as amended by title I of this Act (except the provisions of subsections (h)(1), (k), (q), (w)(2), and (x)); all authorizations issued by the Secretary and other Federal officers and agencies pursuant to this title include the terms and conditions required, and may include the terms and conditions permitted, by the provisions of law that would otherwise be applicable if this title had not been enacted, and they may waive any procedural requirements of law or regulation which they deem desirable to waive in order to accomplish the purposes of this title. The direction contained in section 203(b) shall supersede the provisions of any law or regulation relating to an administrative determination as to whether the authorizations for construction of the trans-Alaska oil pipeline shall be issued.

(d) The actions taken pursuant to this title which relate to the construction and completion of the pipeline system, and to the applications filed in connection therewith necessary to the pipeline's operation at full capacity, as described in the Final Environmental Impact Statement of the Department of the Interior, shall be taken without further action under the National Environmental Policy Act of 1969; and the actions of the Federal officers concerning the issuance of the necessary rights-of-way, permits, leases, and other authorizations for construction and initial operation at full capacity of said pipeline system shall not be subject to judicial review under any law except that claims alleging the invalidity of this section may be brought within sixty days following its enactment, and claims alleging that an action will deny rights under the Constitution of the United States, or that the action is beyond the scope of authority conferred by this title, may be brought within sixty days following the date of such action. A claim shall be barred unless a complaint is filed within the time specified. Any such complaint shall be filed in a United States district court, and such court shall have exclusive jurisdiction to determine such proceeding in accordance with the procedures hereinafter provided, and no other court of the United States, of any State, territory, or possession of the United States, or of the District of Columbia, shall have jurisdiction of any such claim whether in a proceeding instituted prior to or on or after the date of the enactment of this Act. Any such proceeding shall be assigned for hearing at the earliest possible date, shall take precedence over all other matters pending on the docket of the district court at that time, and shall be expedited in every way by such court. Such court shall not have jurisdiction to grant any injunctive relief against the issuance of any right-of-way, permit, lease, or other authorization pursuant to this section except in conjunction with a final judgment entered in a case involving a claim filed pursuant to this section. Any review of an interlocutory or final judgment, decree, or order of such district court may be had only upon direct appeal to the Supreme Court of the United States.

(e) The Secretary of the Interior and the other Federal officers and agencies are authorized at any time when necessary to protect the public interest, pursuant to the authority of this section and in accordance with its provisions, to amend or modify any right-of-way, permit, lease, or other authorization issued under this title.

LIABILITY

SEC. 204. (a)(1) Except when the holder of the pipeline right-of-way granted pursuant to this title can prove that damages in connection with or resulting from activities along or in the vicinity of the proposed trans-Alaskan pipeline right-of-way were caused by an act of war or negligence of the United States, other government entity, or the damaged party, such holder shall be strictly liable to all damaged parties, public or private, without regard to fault for such damages, and without regard to ownership of any affected lands, structures, fish, wildlife, or biotic or other natural resources relied upon by Alaska Natives, Native organizations, or others for subsistence or economic purposes. Claims for such injury or damages may be determined by arbitration or judicial proceedings.

(2) Liability under paragraph (1) of this subsection shall be limited to $50,000,000 for any one incident, and the holders of the right-of-way or permit shall be liable for any claim allowed in proportion to their ownership interest in the right-of-way or permit. Liability of such holders for damages in excess of $50,000,000 shall be in accord with ordinary rules of negligence.

(3) In any case where liability without fault is imposed pursuant to this subsection and the damages involved were caused by the negligence of a third party, the rules of subrogation shall apply in accordance with the law of the jurisdiction where the damage occurred.

(4) Upon order of the Secretary, the holder of a right-of-way or permit shall provide emergency subsistence and other aid to an affected Alaska Native, Native organization, or other person pending expeditious filing of, and determination of, a claim under this subsection.

(5) Where the State of Alaska is the holder of a right-of-way or permit under this title, the State shall not be subject to the provisions of subsection 204(a), but the holder of the permit or right-of-way for the trans-Alaska pipeline shall be subject to that subsection with respect to facilities constructed or activities conducted under rights-of-way or permits issued to the State to the extent that such holder engages in the construction, operation, maintenance, and termination of facilities, or in other activities under rights-of-way or permits issued to the State.

(b) If any area within or without the right-of-way or permit area granted under this title is polluted by any activities conducted by or on behalf of the holder to whom such right-of-way or permit was granted, and such pollution damages or threatens to damage aquatic life, wildlife, or public or private property, the control and total removal of the pollutant shall be at the expense of such holder, including any administrative and other costs incurred by the Secretary or any other Federal officer or agency. Upon failure of such holder to adequately control and remove such pollutant, the Secretary, in cooperation with other Federal, State, or local agencies, or in cooperation with such holder, or both, shall have the right to accomplish the control and removal at the expense of such holder.

(c)(1) Notwithstanding the provisions of any other law, if oil that has been transported through the trans-Alaska pipeline is loaded on a vessel at the terminal facilities of the pipeline, the owner and operator of the vessel (jointly and severally) and the Trans-Alaska Pipeline Liability Fund established by this subsection, shall be strictly liable without regard to fault in accordance with the provisions of this subsection for all damages, including clean-up costs, sustained by any person or entity, public or private, including residents of Canada, as the result of discharges of oil from such vessel.

(2) Strict liability shall not be imposed under this subsection if the owner or operator of the vessel, or the Fund, can prove that the damages were caused by an act of war or by the negligence of the United States or other governmental agency. Strict liability shall not be imposed under this subsection with respect to the claim of a damaged party if the

owner or operator of the vessel, or the Fund, can prove that the damage was caused by the negligence of such party.

(3) Strict liability for all claims arising out of any one incident shall not exceed $100,000,000. The owner and operator of the vessel shall be jointly and severally liable for the first $14,000,000 of such claims that are allowed. Financial responsibility for $14,000,000 shall be demonstrated in accordance with the provisions of section 311(p) of the Federal Water Pollution Control Act, as amended (33 U.S.C. 1321(p)) before the oil is loaded. The Fund shall be liable for the balance of the claims that are allowed up to $100,000,000. If the total claims allowed exceed $100,000,000, they shall be reduced proportionately. The unpaid portion of any claim may be asserted and adjudicated under other applicable Federal or state law.

(4) The Trans-Alaska Pipeline Liability Fund is hereby established as a non-profit corporate entity that may sue and be sued in its own name. The Fund shall be administered by the holders of the trans-Alaska pipeline right-of-way under regulations prescribed by the Secretary. The Fund shall be subject to an annual audit by the Comptroller General, and a copy of the audit shall be submitted to the Congress.

(5) The operator of the pipeline shall collect from the owner of the oil at the time it is loaded on the vessel a fee of five cents per barrel. The collection shall cease when $100,000,000 has been accumulated in the Fund, and it shall be resumed when the accumulation in the Fund falls below $100,000,000.

(6) The collections under paragraph (5) shall be delivered to the Fund. Costs of administration shall be paid from the money paid to the Fund, and all sums not needed for administration and the satisfaction of claims shall be invested prudently in income-producing securities approved by the Secretary. Income from such securities shall be added to the principal of the Fund.

(7) The provisions of this subsection shall apply only to vessels engaged in transportation between the terminal facilities of the pipeline and ports under the jurisdiction of the United States. Strict liability under this subsection shall cease when the oil has first been brought ashore at a port under the jurisdiction of the United States.

(8) In any case where liability without regard to fault is imposed pursuant to this subsection and the damages involved were caused by the unseaworthiness of the vessel or by negligence, the owner and operator of the vessel, and the Fund, as the case may be, shall be subrogated under applicable State and Federal laws to the rights under said laws of any person entitled to recovery hereunder. If any subrogee brings an action based on unseaworthiness of the vessel or negligence of its owner

or operator, it may recover from any affiliate of the owner or operator, if the respective owner or operator fails to satisfy any claim by the subrogee allowed under this paragraph.

(9) This subsection shall not be interpreted to preempt the field of strict liability or to preclude any State from imposing additional requirements.

(10) If the Fund is unable to satisfy a claim asserted and finally determined under this subsection, the Fund may borrow the money needed to satisfy the claim from any commercial credit source, at the lowest available rate of interest, subject to approval of the Secretary.

(11) For purposes of this subsection only, the term "affiliate" includes—

> (A) Any person owned or effectively controlled by the vessel owner or operator; or
>
> (B) Any person that effectively controls or has the power effectively to control the vessel owner or operator by—
>
>> (i) stock interest, or
>>
>> (ii) representation on a board of directors or similar body, or
>>
>> (iii) contract or other agreement with other stockholders, or
>>
>> (iv) otherwise; or
>
> (C) Any person which is under common ownership or control with the vessel owner or operator.

(12) The term "person" means an individual, a corporation, a partnership, an association, a joint-stock company, a business trust, or an unincorporated organization.

ANTITRUST LAWS

SEC. 205. The grant of a right-of-way, permit, lease, or other authorization pursuant to this title shall grant no immunity from the operation of the Federal anti-trust laws.

ROADS AND AIRPORTS

SEC. 206. A right-of-way, permit, lease, or other authorization granted under section 203(b) for a road or airstrip as a related facility of the trans-Alaska pipeline may provide for the construction of a public road or airstrip.

TITLE III—NEGOTIATIONS WITH CANADA

SEC. 301. The President of the United States is authorized and requested to enter into negotiations with the Government of Canada to determine—

(a) the willingness of the Government of Canada to permit the construction of pipelines or other transportation systems across Canadian territory for the transport of natural gas and oil from Alaska's North Slope to markets in the United States, including the use of tankers by way of the Northwest Passage;

(b) the need for intergovernmental understandings, agreements, or treaties to protect the interests of the Governments of Canada and the United States and any party or parties involved with the construction, operation, and maintenance of pipelines or other transportation systems for the transport of such natural gas or oil;

(c) the terms and conditions under which pipelines or other transportation systems could be constructed across Canadian territory;

(d) the desirability of undertaking joint studies and investigations designed to insure protection of the environment, reduce legal and regulatory uncertainty, and insure that the respective energy requirements of the people of Canada and of the United States are adequately met;

(e) the quantity of such oil and natural gas from the North Slope of Alaska for which the Government of Canada would guarantee transit; and

(f) the feasibility, consistent with the needs of other sections of the United States, of acquiring additional energy from other sources that would make unnecessary the shipment of oil from the Alaska pipeline by tanker into the Puget Sound area.

The President shall report to the House and Senate Committees on Interior and Insular Affairs the actions taken, the progress achieved, the areas of disagreement, and the matters about which more information is needed, together with his recommendations for further action.

SEC. 302. (a) The Secretary of the Interior is authorized and directed to investigate the feasibility of one or more oil or gas pipelines from the North Slope of Alaska to connect with a pipeline through Canada that will deliver oil or gas to United States markets.

(b) All costs associated with making the investigations authorized by subsection (a) shall be charged to any future applicant who is granted a right-of-way for one of the routes studied. The Secretary shall submit to the House and Senate Committees on Interior and Insular Affairs periodic reports of his investigation, and the final report of the Secretary shall be submitted within two years from the date of this Act.

SEC. 303. Nothing in this title shall limit the authority of the Secretary of the Interior or any other Federal official to grant a gas or oil pipeline right-of-way or permit which he is otherwise authorized by law to grant.

TITLE IV—MISCELLANEOUS

VESSEL CONSTRUCTION STANDARDS

SEC. 401. Section 4417a of the Revised Statutes of the United States (46 U.S.C. 391a), as amended by the Ports and Waterways Safety Act of 1972 (86 Stat. 424, Public Law 92–340), is hereby amended as follows:

"(C) Rules and regulations published pursuant to subsection (7)(A) shall be effective not earlier than January 1, 1974, with respect to foreign vessels and United States-flag vessels operating in the foreign trade, unless the Secretary shall earlier establish rules and regulations consonant with international treaty, convention, or agreement, which generally address the regulation of similar topics for the protection of the marine environment. In absence of the promulgation of such rules and regulations consonant with international treaty, convention, or agreement, the Secretary shall establish an effective date not later than January 1, 1976, with respect to foreign vessels and United States-flag vessels operating in the foreign trade, for rules and regulations previously published pursuant to this subsection (7) which he then deems appropriate. Rules and regulations published pursuant to subsection (7)(A) shall be effective not later than June 30, 1974, with respect to United States-flag vessels engaged in the coastwise trade."

VESSEL TRAFFIC CONTROL

SEC. 402. The Secretary of the Department in which the Coast Guard is operating is hereby directed to establish a vessel traffic control system for Prince William Sound and Valdez, Alaska, pursuant to authority contained in title I of the Ports and Waterways Safety Act of 1972 (86 Stat. 424, Public Law 92–340).

CIVIL RIGHTS

SEC 403. The Secretary of the Interior shall take such affirmative action as he deems necessary to assure that no person shall, on the grounds of race, creed, color, national origin, or sex, be excluded from receiving, or participating in any activity conducted under, any permit, right-of-way, public land order, or other Federal authorization granted or issued under title II. The Secretary of the Interior shall promulgate such rules as he deems necessary to carry out the purposes of this subsection and may enforce this subsection, and any rules promulgated under this subsection, through agency and department provisions and rules which shall be similar to those established and in effect under title VI of the Civil Rights Act of 1964.

CONFIRMATION OF THE DIRECTOR OF THE ENERGY POLICY OFFICE

SEC. 404. The Director of the Energy Policy Office in the Executive Office of the President shall be appointed by the President, by and with the advise and consent of the Senate: *Provided*, That if any individual who is serving in this office on the date of enactment of this Act is nominated for such position, he may continue to act unless and until such nomination shall be disapproved by the Senate.

CONFIRMATION OF THE HEAD OF THE MINING ENFORCEMENT AND SAFETY ADMINISTRATION

SEC. 405. The head of the Mining Enforcement and Safety Administration established pursuant to Order Numbered 2953 of the Secretary of the Interior issued in accordance with the authority provided by section 2 of Reorganization Plan Numbered 3 of 1950 (64 Stat. 1262) shall be appointed by the President, by and with the advice and consent of the Senate: *Provided*, That if any individual who is serving in this office on the date of enactment of this Act is nominated for such position, he may continue to act unless and until such nomination shall be disapproved by the Senate.

EXEMPTION OF FIRST SALE OF CRUDE OIL AND NATURAL GAS OF CERTAIN LEASES FROM PRICE RESTRAINTS AND ALLOCATION PROGRAMS

SEC. 406. (a) The first sale of crude oil and natural gas liquids produced from any lease whose average daily production of such substances for the preceding calendar month does not exceed ten barrels per well shall not be subject to price restraints established pursuant to the Economic Stabilization Act of 1970, as amended, or to any allocation program for fuels or petroleum established pursuant to that Act or to any Federal law for the allocation of fuels or petroleum.

(b) To qualify for the exemption under this section, a lease must be operating at the maximum feasible rate of production and in accord with recognized conservation practices.

(c) The agency designated by the President or by law to implement any such fuels or petroleum allocation program is authorized to conduct

ADVANCE PAYMENTS TO ALASKA NATIVES

SEC. 407. (a) In view of the delay in construction of a pipeline to transport North Slope crude oil, the sum of $5,000,000 is authorized to be appropriated from the United States Treasury into the Alaska Native Fund every six months of each fiscal year beginning with the fiscal year ending June 30, 1976, as advance payments chargeable against the revenues to be paid under section 9 of the Alaska Native Claims Settlement Act, until such time as the delivery of North Slope crude oil to a pipeline is commenced.

(b) Section 9 of the Alaskan Native Claims Settlement Act is amended by striking the language in subsection (g) thereof and substituting the following language: "The payments required by this section shall continue only until a sum of $500,000,000 has been paid into the Alaska Native Fund less the total of advance payments paid into the Alaska Native Fund pursuant to section 407 of the Trans-Alaska Pipeline Authorization Act. Therefore, payments which would otherwise go into the Alaska Native Fund will be made to the United States Treasury as reimbursement for the advance payments authorized by section 407 of the Trans-Alaska Pipeline Authorization Act. The provisions of this section shall no longer apply, and the reservation required in patents under this section shall be of no further force and effect, after a total sum of $500,000,000 has been paid to the Alaska Native Fund and to the United States Treasury pursuant to this subsection."

FEDERAL TRADE COMMISSION AUTHORITY

SEC. 408. (a)(1) The Congress hereby finds that the investigative and law enforcement responsibilities of the Federal Trade Commission have been restricted and hampered because of inadequate legal authority to enforce subpoenas and to seek preliminary injunctive relief to avoid unfair competitive practices.

(2) The Congress further finds that as a direct result of this inadequate legal authority significant delays have occurred in a major investigation into the legality of the structure, conduct, and activities of the petroleum industry, as well as in other major investigations designed to protect the public interest.

(b) It is the purpose of this Act to grant the Federal Trade Commission the requisite authority to insure prompt enforcement of the laws the

Commission administers by granting statutory authority to directly enforce subpoenas issued by the Commission and to seek preliminary injunctive relief to avoid unfair competitive practices.

(c) Section 5 (1) of the Federal Trade Commission Act (15 U.S.C. 45(1)) is amended by striking subsection (1) and inserting in lieu thereof:

"(1) Any person, partnership, or corporation who violates an order of the Commission after it has become final, and while such order is in effect, shall forfeit and pay to the United States a civil penalty of not more than $10,000 for each violation, which shall accrue to the United States and may be recovered in a civil action brought by the Attorney General of the United States. Each separate violation of such an order shall be a separate offense, except that in the case of a violation through continuing failure to obey or neglect to obey a final order of the Commission, each day of continuance of such failure or neglect shall be deemed a separate offense. In such actions, the United States district courts are empowered to grant mandatory injunctions and such other and further equitable relief as they deem appropriate in the enforcement of such final orders of the Commission."

(d) Section 5 of the Federal Trade Commission Act (15 U.S.C. 45) is amended by adding at the end thereof the following new subsection:

"(m) Whenever in any civil proceeding involving this Act the Commission is authorized or required to appear in a court of the United States, or to be represented therein by the Attorney General of the United States, the Commission may elect to appear in its own name by any of its attorneys designated by it for such purpose, after formally notifying and consulting with and giving the Attorney General 10 days to take action proposed by the Commission."

(e) Section 6 of the Federal Trade Commission Act (15 U.S.C. 46), is amended by adding at the end thereof the following proviso: "*Provided*, That the exception of 'banks and common carriers subject to the Act to regulate commerce' from the Commission's powers defined in clauses (a) and (b) of this section, shall not be construed to limit the Commission's authority to gather and compile information, to investigate, or to require reports or answers from, any such corporation to the extent that such action is necessary to the investigation of any corporation, group of corporations, or industry which is not engaged or is engaged only incidentally in banking or in business as a common carrier subject to the Act to regulate commerce."

(f) Section 13 of the Federal Trade Commission Act (15 U.S.C. 53) is amended by redesignating "(b)" as "(c)" and inserting the following new subsection:

"(b) Whenever the Commission has reason to believe—

"(1) that any person, partnership, or corporation is violating, or is about to violate, any provision of law enforced by the Federal Trade Commission, and

"(2) that the enjoining thereof pending the issuance of a complaint by the Commission and until such complaint is dismissed by the Commission or set aside by the court on review, or until the order of the Commission made thereon has become final, would be in the interest of the public—

the Commission by any of its attorneys designated by it for such purpose may bring suit in a district court of the United States to enjoin any such act or practice. Upon a proper showing that, weighing the equities and considering the Commission's likelihood of ultimate success, such action would be in the public interest, and after notice to the defendant, a temporary restraining order or a preliminary injunction may be granted without bond: *Provided, however*, That if a complaint is not filed within such period (not exceeding 20 days) as may be specified by the court after issuance of the temporary restraining order or preliminary injunction, the order or injunction shall be dissolved by the court and be of no further force and effect: *Provided further*, That in proper cases the Commission may seek, and after proper proof, the court may issue, a permanent injunction. Any such suit shall be brought in the district in which such person, partnership, or corporation resides or transacts business."

(g) Section 16 of the Federal Trade Commission Act (15 U.S.C. 56) is amended to read as follows:

"SEC. 16. Whenever the Federal Trade Commission has reason to believe that any person, partnership, or corporation is liable to a penalty under section 14 or under subsection (l) of section 5 of this Act, it shall—

"(a) certify the facts to the Attorney General, whose duty it shall be to cause appropriate proceedings to be brought for the enforcement of the provisions of such section or subsection; or

"(b) after compliance with the requirements with section 5(m), itself cause such appropriate proceedings to be brought."

GENERAL ACCOUNTING OFFICE AUTHORITY

SEC. 409. (a) Section 3502 of title 44, United States Code, is amended by inserting in the first paragraph defining "Federal agency" after the words "the General Accounting Office" and before the words "nor the governments" the words "independent Federal regulatory agencies."

"(b) Chapter 35 of title 44, United States Code, is amended by adding after section 3511 the following new section:

"§ 3512. Information for independent regulatory agencies

"(a) The Comptroller General of the United States shall review the collection of information required by independent Federal regulatory agencies described in section 3502 of this chapter to assure that information required by such agencies is obtained with a minimum burden upon business enterprises, especially small business enterprises, and other persons required to furnish the information. Unnecessary duplication of efforts in obtaining information already filed with other Federal agencies or departments through the use of reports, questionnaires, and other methods shall be eliminated as rapidly as practicable. Information collected and tabulated by an independent regulatory agency shall, as far as is expedient, be tabulated in a manner to maximize the usefulness of the information to other Federal agencies and the public.

"(b) In carrying out the policy of this section, the Comptroller General shall review all existing information gathering practices of independent regulatory agencies as well as requests for additional information with a view toward—

"(1) avoiding duplication of effort by independent regulatory agencies, and

"(2) minimizing the compliance burden on business enterprises and other persons.

"(c) In complying with this section, an independent regulatory agency shall not conduct or sponsor the collection of information upon an identical item from ten or more persons, other than Federal employees, unless, in advance of adoption or revision of any plans or forms to be used in the collection—

"(1) the agency submitted to the Comptroller General the plans or forms, together with the copies of pertinent regulations and of other related materials as the Comptroller General has specified; and

"(2) the Comptroller General has advised that the information is not presently available to the independent agency from another source within the Federal Government and has determined that the proposed plans or forms are consistent with the provision of this section. The Comptroller General shall maintain facilities for carrying out the purposes of this section and shall render such advice to the requestive independent regulatory agency within forty-five days.

"(d) While the Comptroller General shall determine the availability from other Federal sources of the information sought and the appropriateness of the forms for the collection of such information, the independent regulatory agency shall make the final determination as to the necessity of the information in carrying out its statutory responsibilities and whether to collect such information. If no advice is received from the Comptroller General within forty-five days, the independent regulatory agency may immediately proceed to obtain such information.

"(e) Section 3508(a) of this chapter dealing with unlawful disclosure of information shall apply to the use of information by independent regulatory agencies.

"(f) The Comptroller General may promulgate rules and regulations necessary to carry out this chapter."

EQUITABLE ALLOCATION OF NORTH SLOPE CRUDE OIL

SEC. 410. The Congress declares that the crude oil on the North Slope of Alaska is an important part of the Nation's oil resources, and that the benefits of such crude oil should be equitably shared, directly or indirectly, by all regions of the country. The President shall use any authority he may have to insure an equitable allocation of available North Slope and other crude oil resources and petroleum products among all regions and all of the several States.

SEPARABILITY

SEC. 411. If any provision of this Act or the applicability thereof is held invalid the remainder of this Act shall not be affected thereby.

Approved November 16, 1973.

Glossary

AMERICAN RULE—the rule of law that requires each party to a lawsuit to pay his own lawyer's fees.
AMICI CURIAE—Latin for "friends of the court"; individuals or groups who file briefs in lawsuits in which they are not themselves involved.
ANSWER—the reply of a defendant to a lawsuit filed against him.
APPELLATE COURT—a court that hears appeals.
ARGUMENT—the oral discussion of the case that occurs in court by the lawyers before a judge.
BILL—the draft of a law being considered by a legislature.
BRIEF—a written document explaining a litigant's legal position to a judge.
CHAMBERS—a judge's private office in the courthouse.
COMPLAINT—the legal document with which a plaintiff begins a lawsuit.
CONFERENCE COMMITTEE—a joint committee of representatives and senators chosen to reconcile different versions of a bill passed by each house of Congress.
EIS—environmental impact statement.
FILING—the act of initiating a lawsuit in court.
FLOOR VOTE—a vote on a bill by the full membership of a house of Congress.
FTC—Federal Trade Commission.
INJUNCTION—a court order; usually an order not to do something harmful.
INTRODUCING A BILL—the act of starting a bill on its way through the legislative process.
ITEM VETO—a method of voting certain provisions in a bill passed by a legislature without vetoing the whole bill; the President does not have the power to veto in this manner.

GLOSSARY

LAND FREEZE—an order by the Secretary of the Interior prohibiting federal lands in Alaska from being used.

LEGISLATIVE HISTORY—the record of debates and reports over a bill that tells judges what the legislature intended the law to mean.

NEPA—National Environmental Protection Act.

OMB—Office of Management and Budget.

PRIVATE ATTORNEY GENERAL—a litigant who brings a lawsuit to vindicate a broad pubic interest.

PUBLIC INTEREST LAWYER—a lawyer who represents a group of people, usually for free or for a low fee, who cannot ordinarily afford to be represented in court.

REMAND—to send a case back to a lower court to follow the instructions of the appellate court.

REPORT A BILL—the act of approving a bill so that it can be voted on by the membership of a legislative body.

REVERSE—to upset or to overturn a decision of a lower court.

RIDER—a provision that is added to a bill but which usually has little or no relation to it.

RIGHT-OF-WAY—a legal right to use or to travel across someone else's land.

SEPARATION OF POWERS—the principle of government by which the legislative, executive, and judicial powers are exercised by different branches of government.

SLUP—special land use permit.

STAY—an order of a court preserving the status quo until a further ruling can be made.

TABLING MOTION—a motion in the legislature to defer or reverse a previous motion or to prevent it from being considered.

TAPS—Trans-Alaska Pipeline System.

VETO—an act of the President or a governor by which a bill that has been passed by Congress or a state legislature is prevented from becoming law.

Bibliography

Books

Berry, Mary Clay. *The Alaska Pipeline: The Politics of Oil and Native Land Claims*. Bloomington, Indiana: Indiana University Press, 1975.
   This book takes the story up to 1974, when the pipeline was under construction. As its title suggests, its principal concern is the impact of the oil discovery on the Natives.

Mead, Robert Douglas. *Journeys Down the Line: Building the Trans-Alaska Pipeline*. Garden City: Doubleday & Co., 1978.
   This book tells the whole story, beginning with the initial discovery and Alaskan history, and then the pipeline construction, its problems and impact.

Cases

Wilderness Society v. Hickel, 325 F.Supp. 422 (D.D.C. 1970).
Wilderness Society v. Morton, 479 F.2d 842 (D.C. Cir. 1973).
Wilderness Society v. Morton, 495 F.2d 1026 (D.C. Cir. 1974).
Alyeska Pipeline Service Co. v. Wilderness Society, 421 U.S. 240 (1975).

Congressional Hearings

Alyeska Oil Pipeline Oversight, Hearing Before the Subcommittee on Energy and Power of the Committee on Interstate and Foreign Commerce, U.S. House of Representatives, 94th Congress, 2d Session, June 21, 1976.

Index

Agnew, Spiro M., 56–7
Alaska
   Native claims to land, 17–25
   price of Natives' land, 25–6
   purchased from Russia, 18
   size of, 3, 4, 17
   statehood act, 22
Alaska Federation of Natives, 25
Alderson, George, 54
Alyeska Pipeline Service Company, 39, 44, 60, 67, 80–2
   ordered to pay lawyers' fees, 69–72
   Supreme Court reverses fee decision, 76–8
"American rule," 68
amici curiae, 76
"answer," 37
appeals courts, 13
   procedures in, 41–3
Ash, Roy L., 60

Bayh, Birch, 55
bill
   enactment of, 10
   making into law, 53–4
   veto of, 11
briefs, 42
Bureau of Indian Affairs, 23
Bureau of Land Management, 23, 47

Center for Law and Social Policy, 30–1, 41, 68
Chamber of Commerce, 61
Chugach National Forest, 21
"complaint," 37
conference committee, 54
Constitution, 8, 75–6
Council on Environmental Quality, 36
courts, power of to award attorneys' fees, 76–8
Cox, Archibald, 61
Cranston, Alan, 56

delegation of power, 11
Dellenback, John, 59
district courts, 12–13
Douglas, William O., 76

EIS, *see* environmental impact statement
Environmental Defense Fund, 29, 67
environmental impact statement, 34–5, 36, 37, 39, 40, 41, 43, 49
environmental issues, 29–30
executive branch, checks and balances in, 11–12

Federal Trade Commission, 57

Flannery, Dennis, 40, 43
fourth branch of government, 12
Friends of the Earth, 29, 54, 67

General Motors Company, 61
Goldberg, Arthur, 25
Gravel, Mike, 55, 61

Hart, George, 25, 37–8, 41, 42
Hickel, Walter J., 23, 30, 37, 39
House Interior Committee, 24
House of Representatives, 9, 10
House pipeline bill, 58–9

injunction, 41
Interstate Commerce Commission, 82

Jackson, Henry M., 54–5, 61
Jackson, Robert H., 75
Japan, sale of oil to, 5
Japanese steel, 5
judicial branch, checks and balances in, 12–15
jurisdiction of courts, 14

Kelley, Peter, 81

land claims, 17–25
  extinction of, 25
land freeze, 18, 23, 24
law, making of in Congress, 53–4
lawsuit, filing of, 37
legal fees, 67–8
legislative branch, checks and balances in, 9–11
legislative history, 45–6

majority rule, 7
Mineral Leasing Act, 31–4, 37, 38, 41, 43, 45, 46–8, 50, 53, 55, 59, 70, 71, 72, 73, 77

Mondale, Walter F., 55
Moorman, James, 30–1, 37–8, 40
Morton, Rogers C.B., 39, 40, 43
Mount McKinley National Park, 21

National Environmental Policy Act, 31, 34–7, 48–9, 50, 55, 57, 58, 71, 72
Native land claims, 18–27
Natives, settlement of claims of, 25–7
NEPA, see National Environmental Policy Act
Nixon, Richard M., 23, 27, 39, 52, 61
Northwest Ordinance, 19

Office of Management and Budget, 57, 60
oil, discovery of, 1–3
oil-lease auction prices, 3
oil shortage, 60
oral argument, 43
oversight hearings, 81

Pecora, William, 61
pipeline act (text), 88–111
  enacted, 61
  in House, 58–9
  in Senate, 57–8
  major provisions of (summary), 63–6
  President signs, 61
pipeline bill, 54–63
pipeline chronology, 84–7
pipeline construction, 40
pipeline, costs of, 81–2
pipeline, flaws in, 80–2
pipeline right-of-way, 44–8
pipeline route (map), 83

INDEX

Pittle, Herbert, 37–8
Powell, Lewis F., 76
private attorney general, 69
private power, as form of checks and balances, 15–16
proven reserves, 2
Prudhoe Bay, 2, 3, 30, 35, 40, 82
public interest law, 31, 69
public interest lawyers, 76

railroad rights-of-way, 31–2, 33
rider, 57
right-of-way on federal land, 31–4

Secretary of the Interior, 20, 23, 27, 35, 37, 38–9, 45, 47, 55, 59, 67
Senate
  composition of, 9–20
  pipeline bill in, 57–8
seniority of judges, 42n
separation of powers, 9–16
Seward, William H., 18
SLUPs, *see* special land use permits
special land use permits, 36, 38, 45, 47, 50

Stevens, Ted, 61
Supreme Court, 13–14, 75–6

tabling motion, 56
TAPS, *see* Trans-Alaska Pipeline System
Tlingit Indians, right of to sue U.S., 21
Tongass National Forest, 20–1
Trans-Alaska Pipeline System, 4–5, 17, 23, 24, 35–6, 39
treaty with Russia, 19

Udall, Stuart L., 23, 24
U.S. Geological Survey, 39

Valdez, 3
veto, 11

Watergate, 61
White, Byron R., 76–8
Wilderness Society, 29, 30, 67, 78
Wright, J. Skelly, 44–9, 69–72

Young, Donald E., 61

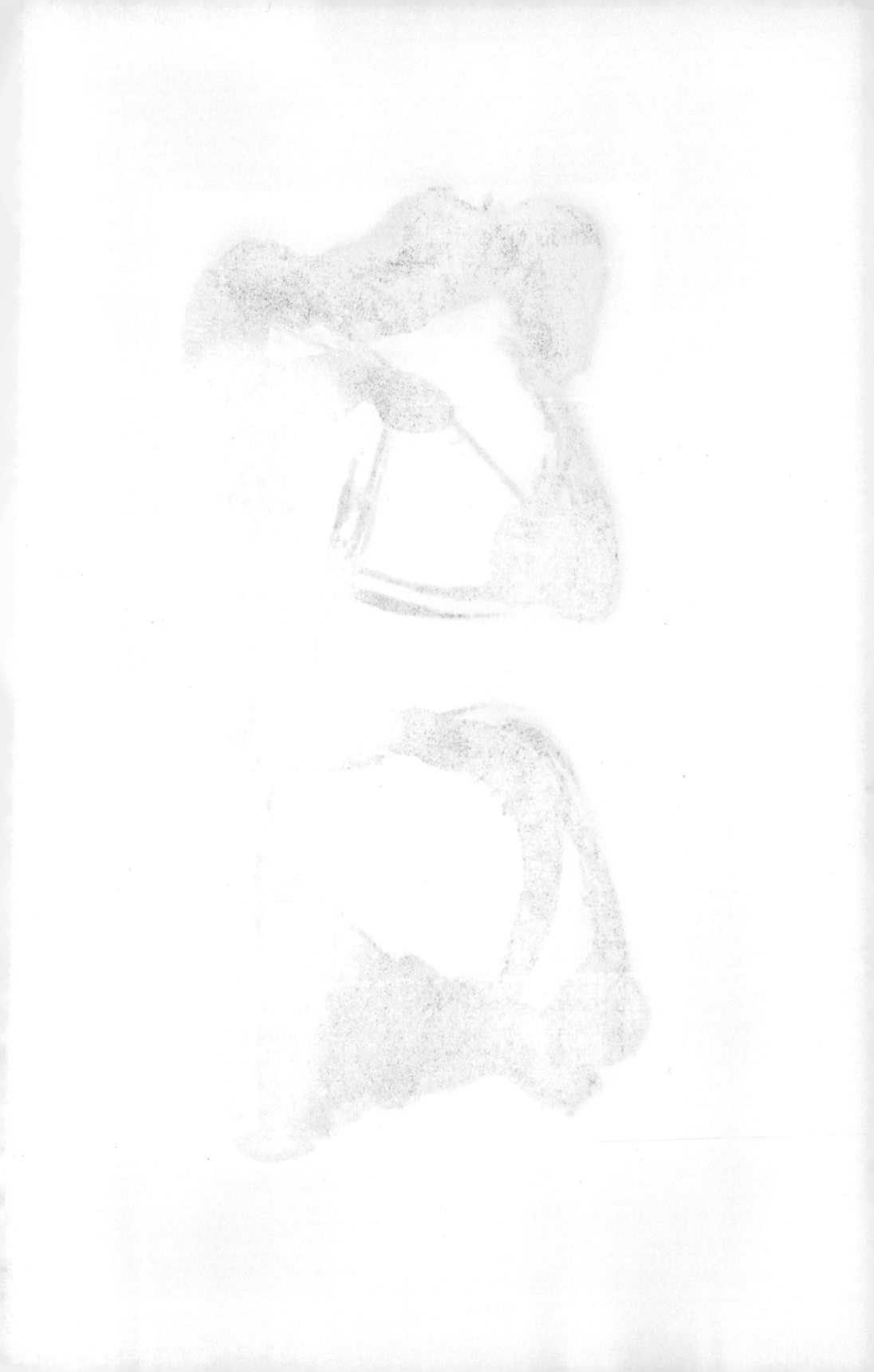

343.73 Lieberman, Jethro
L   K.
　　　　　Checks and balances

15369

ESEA
Title IV B
1981-82

DATE		
1/11/02		

**NORTH STAR HIGH
SCHOOL LIBRARY
BOSWELL CAMPUS**

© THE BAKER & TAYLOR CO

Risk, Safety, Expertise

A Pilot's Journey Into Risk and Resource Management

KD VanDrie
and
Brock Booher

Copyright © 2023 by KD VanDrie and Brock Booher
All rights reserved.
ISBN: 979-8-9883902-1-3

This book is dedicated to the hidden heroes of airline training and safety departments contributing to the world's safest mode of transportation and the Southwest Airlines Standards Department.

Table of Contents

Chapter One: Uncontained Engine Failure	1
Chapter Two: How Did We Get Here?	19
Chapter Three: The Need for Risk Management	27
Chapter Four: Master the Target	39
Chapter Five: Understand the Process	61
Chapter Six: Consider the Four Principles of Risk Management	77
Chapter Seven: Align Resources for Success	97
Chapter Eight: Recognize Risk Factors	123
Chapter Nine: Choose a Strategy	143
Chapter Ten: Cultivate Resilience	159
Chapter Eleven: Put It All Together	171
Conclusion	193
Acknowledgements	195
Appendix	205

Chapter One: Uncontained Engine Failure

April 17, 2018/1103 EDT/Boeing 737 N772SW/SWA Flight #1380 Climbing through FL320 enroute from KLGA (La Guardia) to KDAL (Dallas)

Bang! The aircraft shuddered and rolled to the left, continuing to vibrate and shake. The fire bell rang, sounding like some old-fashioned phone sitting on the office desk of a police precinct in the 1970s, as red lights illuminated on the glareshield. *Woosh!* All the air rushed from the cabin, like air rushing from an inflated balloon. For a moment, dust and vapor filled the flight deck. *Beep! Beep! Beep!* A nagging horn blared, warning the pilots of cabin pressurization loss. *Waaa! Waaa! Waaa!* The autopilot disconnect siren added to the cacophony of sounds like a crying baby in a noisy train station. Then to top it all off the voice of the aircraft warning system began repeating, "Bank angle! Bank angle! Bank angle!"

What would you do? A few moments before, it was a routine flight from New York City to Dallas. The conversation on the flight deck centered on checklists, procedural callouts, and food. Within a matter of seconds, the normal routine was replaced by a wave of abnormal sights, sounds, and sensations that overwhelmed the senses. Without quick action, the aircraft, along with its passengers and crew, would soon be hurtling at the earth uncontrollably. Only precise, immediate action could save the day.

The First Officer (the pilot flying) grabbed the yoke with one hand to return the aircraft to level flight. With the other hand, he pulled the quick-donning oxygen mask from its holder and placed it over his head. Life-saving oxygen filled his lungs keeping his brain functioning at full capacity and staving off deadly hypoxia. With his faculties intact, he focused on the most important task—flying the damaged aircraft.

The Captain donned her oxygen mask as well and worked to establish clear communication between the crew through the masks which reduced any normal flight deck conversation to strained exchanges. She assessed the engine instruments and silenced the bells and horns that only added to the stress of the dangerous situation.

The First Officer reduced the left engine to idle and the aircraft began descending.

The Air Traffic Controller, not knowing what had just happened in the aircraft less than a minute before, issued a clearance, "Southwest 1380 cleared direct VINSE V-I-N-S-E."

No response.

After a few seconds he repeated, "Ah you know what you… there ya go cleared direct VINSE V-I-N-S-E."

No response.

"Southwest 1380 New York?"

The Controller didn't know about the struggle happening on the flight deck and cabin of Southwest 1380. The Captain keyed the microphone, but at first only transmitted the sound of static.

"Southwest 1380 if you're trying to get me all I hear is static."

Two minutes after the explosion in the left engine the Captain transmitted over the radio. "Southwest 1380 has an engine fire descending."

Both the Captain and the First Officer knew they needed to make an emergency descent down into the thicker atmosphere below ten thousand feet before all of the oxygen for their passengers was depleted. Additionally, they knew they needed to land at the nearest suitable airport.

"Southwest 1380 ah you you're descending right now?" Asked the Controller.

"Yes sir we're single engine descending have a fire in number, one."

"Alright Southwest 1380 ah wh- okay where would you like to go to which airport?"

"Give us a vector for your closest."

"Uhmm okay."

The Controller suggested Harrisburg. The crew had a quick discussion and looked down at the map display and saw that Philadelphia (KPHL) was not very far and in front of them. "Philadelphia," the Captain stated over the radio.

After an initial vector the Controller issued the clearance. "Southwest 1380 cleared direct to the Philadelphia airport via direct." The First Officer turned the aircraft towards Philadelphia airport, still descending and still breathing the life-saving crew oxygen.

The explosion was caused when a fan blade in the left engine fractured at its root. The fan blade impacted the engine fan case, designed to contain just such a failure, and exploded into multiple fragments. Unfortunately, and uncharacteristically, some of the fan blade fragments traveled forward slicing into the inlet and fan cowl at the front of the engine. Portions of the inlet and fan cowl were ripped away from the aircraft. A large fragment slammed into the fuselage by the cabin window adjacent to seat 14A and shattered the dual-paned window on impact.

The passenger in seat 14A was pulled through the broken window with her seatbelt still buckled.

The A Flight Attendant was in the forward lavatory when she heard and felt the explosion. The C Flight Attendant was in the aisle abeam row five. The B Flight Attendant was standing in the aft galley preparing to begin service. Flight Attendants A and C rushed to their jumpseats with debris flying through the cabin as all the pressurized air was sucked out of the broken window at 14A. The B Flight Attendant, who only finished new-hire training six weeks earlier (and probably mildly hypoxic from the rapid decompression), didn't stop preparing to serve until a fellow employee riding on the aft jumpseat pointed out the oxygen masks had dropped. All of them buckled in and began breathing oxygen from the drop-down masks, as they had been trained to do.

The Captain made an announcement to the passengers. "Ladies and gentlemen this is your captain we're um, going into ah to Philadelphia. Ah... remain seated thank you." At the time she and her First Officer didn't know the extent of the damage or the state of the passengers in back. They were focused on flying the airplane and accomplishing the emergency checklists for the situation.

Twice more the warning system barked, "Bank angle!" The First Officer continued to fly the airplane and the Captain helped him adjust the rudder trim to achieve coordinated flight. They continued an emergency descent to eleven thousand feet with Philadelphia on the nose.

Following emergency procedures, the Flight Attendants retrieved the portable oxygen bottles from the front and aft stowage compartments and put them on. Now they could get up and check on passengers. Flight Attendant A arrived at row 14 first. The surreal scene must have been a shock to her system, but she didn't hesitate to take action. She began trying to pull the passenger in 14A back into the aircraft. The C Flight Attendant joined in the attempt. Somewhere during this time, the passengers from 14B and 14C moved to the aft galley, no doubt in trauma from the event but trying to give the flight attendants room to work.

Two men (from 8D and 13D) jumped up to help the flight attendants, without regard for their own safety. Together, they were able to pull the passenger from 14A back into the aircraft and laid her across the row of seats. The passenger from 8D, a paramedic, began CPR. A nurse from 11C jumped up and began assisting him. They both continued to administer CPR and first aid until after the aircraft landed.

Five minutes after the explosion, the aircraft was descending through seventeen thousand feet. The First Officer was still flying. ATC switched them to another center frequency.

"Center Southwest 1380 declaring an emergency going through seventeen thousand need your local altimeter," radioed the Captain.

"Ah, Southwest 1380 ah New York the ah Baltimore altimeter is ah two niner eight zero and you're descending to one one thousand?"

"Goin' down to one one thousand two nine eight zero." The Captain passed on the required information concerning souls on board and fuel remaining in time to the controller. She requested assistance from the fire trucks on the captain's side of the aircraft after landing.

Six minutes after the explosion, the Captain took control of the aircraft and the crew began to accomplish the required immediate action items, but before they could complete them they were interrupted by a frequency change to Philadelphia approach. They acknowledged and tuned the radio, but finished the immediate action items before checking in on the frequency. The approach controller cleared them down to six thousand feet and once again asked them about souls on board and remaining fuel in time.

"Okay one hundred and forty-nine souls on board. Five hours of fuel."

They continued descending as the approach controller vectored the aircraft for landing on runway 27L. The First Officer questioned the Captain, "Hey we're gonna need a few minutes right? to run a couple checklists? is that right?"

"Nope just keep goin'." She didn't want to delay the landing of the crippled aircraft.

Nine minutes after the explosion, the aircraft descended below ten thousand feet. The crew removed their oxygen masks and communication returned to normal on the flight deck. They continued working together to get the aircraft on the ground as soon as possible, but they still didn't know about the drama unfolding in the back of the aircraft. They asked for an extended final approach and began slowing.

The First Officer attempted to talk with the Flight Attendants, but initially got no reply. Then after a few seconds the Flight Attendants called the flight deck .

"We got a window open and somebody - is out the window," she told the First Officer. In spite of the extreme adverse circumstances in the cabin, the Flight Attendants remained calm and focused on their duties.

"Okay we're coming down is everyone else in their seats strapped in?" He asked.

"Yeah everyone still in their seats, we have people have been helpin' her get in I don't know what her condition is, but the window is completely out."

When the First Officer heard this, he immediately instructed the Captain, "Slow down to two hundred ten knots right now."

The Captain told the controller, "We're gonna need to slow down a bit."

"Southwest 1380, speed is your discretion. Maintain ah at any altitude above three thousand feet and you let me know when you want to turn base," answered Air Traffic Control.

The First Officer finished talking with the flight attendants and returned his focus to helping the captain land the crippled aircraft. He informed the captain, "Okay we have somebody that's flown outside the window."

Thirteen minutes after the explosion, the flight deck crew prepared for landing. Both members of the flight deck crew have worked together to descend the aircraft and prepare it for landing at the nearest suitable airfield. They have struggled to control the aircraft. They have struggled to communicate on the flight deck and with air traffic control. They are uncertain of the extent of the damage to their craft. Now, a few minutes before turning base and landing the aircraft, they learn that a passenger in their care is fighting for her life in row 14.

"Alright. Severe damage. Ah let's just ah. Let's just a let's do severe damage checklist and let's get it turned in," said the Captain.

She initially wanted a little more time to prepare for the emergency landing, but when she heard about the drama unfolding in the back of the aircraft, she decided not to delay.

The First Officer continued running the emergency checklist as directed. Concerned about the damage to the aircraft, the Captain announced, "Okay if we're going to do a flaps five landing (I believe)."

"Flaps five," answered the First Officer.

"Because I don't know the controllability of this thing," added the Captain. "Gimme flaps one."

The First Officer acknowledged and set the flap handle to the flaps one position. He continued to prepare the aircraft for landing by setting up the radios for the approach.

Worried about excess drag on the aircraft and the unpredictable flight characteristics of the damaged aircraft, the Captain did some mental math to determine her approach speed. She told the controller, "Southwest thirteen eight'd like to turn, start turning, inbound."

The controller cleared them for a turn towards the airport and advised that the airport was off their right and slightly behind them. Concerned about the buildings downtown, he cautioned them to maintain at or above the Minimum Vectoring Altitude.

The Captain turned toward the airport. "Okay could you have the, ah, medical meet us there on the runway as well we've got, ah, injured passengers."

"Injured passengers okay and are you is your airplane physically on fire?" queried the controller.

"No it's not on fire but part of it's missing. They said there's a hole and ahm, someone went out."

Incredulous, the controller asked, "Um, I'm sorry you said there was a hole and somebody went out?"

"Yes."

Keeping the crew focused on the task of landing the aircraft safely the controller directed, "Southwest 1380 it doesn't matter ah we'll work it out. There so the airport's just off to your right report it in sight please."

"In sight. Southwest 1380 airport's in sight."

The controller cleared them for the visual approach and switched them to tower frequency. As they lined up for the visual approach, Flight Attendant C in the aft galley announced that they were about to land. The good Samaritans administering CPR continued trying to save the life of the passenger from 14A. The company employee and one of the passengers from row 14 buckled into the aft jumpseat. Flight Attendant A, still focused on the passenger from 14A did not have time to make it back to the forward jumpseat and sat down in the aisle at row 5 with passengers holding on to her. Flight Attendants B and C sat on the aft galley floor along with one of the displaced passengers from row 14. When they sensed landing was imminent, they repeated the commands, "Heads down! Stay down!"

Fifteen minutes after the explosion, Southwest 1380 lined up for landing on runway 27L at Philadelphia. The Captain struggled to control the damaged aircraft and drifted below the instrument glideslope. The aircraft warning system announced, "Glide slope!" multiple times during the approach. To top it off, the winds were 280 at 19 knots with gusts up to 25 knots, not making the approach any easier.

The First Officer asked, "Flaps five are you sure? How about just fifteen? it's something we know."

The Captain asked for speeds commensurate with a flaps 15 setting, but decided to fly the aircraft at 180 knots and with flaps 5 selected to ensure controllability. The aircraft continued to descend faster than desired and the electronic warning voice became a refrain, "Glide slope! Glide slope! Glide slope!"

Above the sound of the warning voice, and only five hundred feet above touchdown, they completed the before landing checklist. The aircraft warning systems continued to bark about the glide slope as the aircraft barely continued to fly. One way, or another, the flight was about be over.

The Captain fought to maintain airspeed and glidepath and said a prayer under her breath. The First Officer dutifully called out trends and corrections. The flight attendants and passengers braced for the worst. The electronic warning voice continued to pester them as they crossed the runway threshold of runway 27L.

Seventeen minutes after the explosion at thirty-two thousand feet, the tires of Southwest 1380 touched down on the runway and the spoilers extended. The Captain deployed the remaining thrust reverser and slowed the aircraft to a taxi speed before exiting the runway near the waiting fire trucks and emergency response personnel.

Everyone breathed a collective sigh of relief, except for the passenger from 14A, and those administering CPR. They continued to fight for her life until the EMTs boarded the airplane and took over.

After clearing the runway and getting emergency personnel on board, the Captain and First Officer conducted a short debrief of the event.

They complimented each other on a job well done, and then the Captain added, "I know you didn't have time to go through all of it [checklists] but I could feel that it was just not in good condition is why—"

"And she [the aircraft] wasn't in good condition," added the First Officer.

"Is why I said give us a short one [short final approach]," offered the Captain. They continued to discuss their thought process surrounding the damage to the aircraft and their reaction to it.

"So that's just why I just wanted to know you don't have to defend my skipping of some of the checklists to get on the ground," said the Captain.

The First Officer responded with the common risk language he had been taught, "No. We were. We were in the Red."

"Yeah."

"We were in the Red."

"Yeah. we got put there real fast." Both the Captain and First Officer recognized how quickly their risk state changed when the fan blade separated and caused the damage to the aircraft. Safely on the ground, they took a moment to reflect and analyze their own performance.

The passenger from 14A became the first airborne fatality in the history of Southwest Airlines. It was also the first time a passenger window had been lost in the entire history of the B-737 fleet. (NTSB 2019)

However, it was NOT first time a fan blade had caused this much destruction in the engine of a Southwest airplane.

On August 27, 2016, Southwest 3472, enroute from New Orleans to Orlando, climbed through thirty-one thousand feet with 99 passengers on board. Bang! One of the fan blades separated and exploded into fragments. Some of the fragments traveled forward and sliced the engine cowl, causing it to separate. Debris from the separation impacted the fuselage above the left wing and left a 5x16 inch hole. The cabin depressurized. The aircraft shuddered and rolled to the left. All the same warning horns and sirens sounded on the flight deck. The crew initiated an emergency descent and landing into Pensacola, Florida, without injury to any of the 99 passengers or the crew. The final investigation of that accident had not been completed before the crew of SWA 1380 faced their fateful event. (NTSB 2018)

How did the crews of both Southwest flights manage uncontained engine failures successfully? What methodology did they apply to perform so well with such catastrophic failures? How were they trained and how did they prepare to deal with such an event? Or do we attribute their success to luck, or fate?

No doubt the experience of the crews was a factor. To achieve the rating of Air Transport Pilot required to fly for a major airline, the FAA requires a minimum of 1500 hours. The crews of both 3472 and 1380 were seasoned and experienced crews with thousands of flying hours between them. Experience is an able instructor, and certainly provides a solid foundation of knowledge, skill, and judgement to the aviator who accumulates flight hours.

However, experience alone is not a sure indicator of consistent performance, particularly in unusual situations. In addition to experience, deliberate training intended to develop resilience is needed. Unless a pilot has experienced all the possible emergency situations for a given aircraft, he or she will have knowledge gaps. Targeted training, built to develop specific skills and competencies, can fill the gaps left behind by experience alone.

In 1991 the Federal Aviation Administration released Advisory Circular 120-54 Advanced Qualification Program that provided "...a systematic methodology for developing the content of training programs for air carrier crewmembers and dispatchers." It replaced the previous requirements built on tasks and training time with data-informed training built to address specific needs and include Crew Resource Management. Airlines were encouraged to innovate using better methods and technology "...to achieve the highest possible standard of individual and crew performance." Under this program, air carriers, like Southwest, developed training and evaluation scenarios that require crews to work together in complex, time-sensitive scenarios. (US DOT 2004)

Using a systematic instructional design and development process based on the Volant Risk and Resource Management (RRM) model, Southwest Airlines developed and conducted training scenarios similar to the emergency situations faced by the crews of 3472 and 1380. Each of those pilots had received training and demonstrated their ability to handle a similar situation in the simulator under the scrutiny of training-center personnel *before* they faced it in the actual airplane.

Tailored training coupled with experience prepared the pilots to successfully deal with the life-threatening emergency.

But if we peel back another layer, what do we find? What philosophies or mindsets provided the underpinnings of their training? How did Southwest Airlines incorporate Crew Resource

Management into their tailored training? What tools and resources did the crew have at their disposal?

In 2011 Southwest Airlines partnered with Volant Systems to incorporate RRM into their operational philosophy. RRM provides framework and strategy to improve human performance and operational effectiveness for an individual, a team, or for an entire organization. Additionally, it provides an architecture that ties together human factors, psychology, operating documents design, curriculum design, standards of performance, an integrated data collection process, and a meta-data taxonomy to enhance data mining, analysis, and reporting. RRM was the toolbox used by training developers, administrators, and evaluators to build the custom-tailored training that enabled the crews of both flight 3472 and 1380 to succeed.

The tools provided by the Risk and Resource Management model gave both the training department and the crews themselves a common language and philosophy that increased performance in real-life situations. RRM gave evaluators the tools to find the root cause of deficiencies in performance and correct them in the training environment. RRM closed the loop on data collection so training developers could identify trends and correct them before they became an accident statistic. The robust philosophy and framework provided by RRM saved the lives of the passengers aboard flights 3472 and 1380, and contributed to the success of countless other flights which never made the news cycle.

Here is your opportunity to understand the philosophy, systematic approach, and tools to achieve success and safety in a high-risk environment. Risk is an inherent part of life, especially with more risky activities, like flying. Safety is the goal we seek and the state we hope to remain in, even when as we do things that could result in an unsafe outcome. Expertise is the combination of professional knowledge and skills in a given field. There are times when expertise alone can get you through a difficult situation, but in today's increasingly complex aviation environment success is more likely when you are able to use all available resources to reduce the risk.

This book is designed to help you manage risks, achieve safety, and expedite expertise using the Risk and Resource Management model.

Since 2007, there have been no fatal accidents attributed to pilot error for airlines that have approved Advanced Qualification Programs (AQP). (NTSB 2023)

Brock Booher

The first time I saw the Volant Risk and Resource Model, I thought, "What is all this psychobabble?" All the colors and blocks looked like some gimmick meant to get somebody in the headquarters promoted. We called it "CRM with colors." Then I set my cynicism aside, and, on a long flight, I took a hard look at the model. A funny thing happened. It started to make sense to me.

The first thing I noticed was how complete it was. It encompassed the emotional state of the pilot and the technical aspect of flying. It accounted for pilot workload and the process of managing the flight deck. It included policies, procedures, and techniques. It not only provided tools for assessing risk but also for managing it. It provided foundational principles to guide decision-making and concrete resources for executing decisions. There, on a three-by-five card, I found the framework needed for managing risk, improving operational performance, and achieving a safe outcome.

Not long after my "conversion," I found myself in an evaluator's role on the other side of the table, and my admiration for the model increased. The Volant RRM model gave me more precise language to discuss and debrief pilot performance. The nomenclature helped me to categorize parts of the process and properly identify the root causes of peak performance and errors. Furthermore, the model provided me tools for teaching other pilots to be successful risk managers. Using the RRM model and its language empowered me in ways I didn't expect.

The truth is that when you look at the RRM model, you may find nothing new there. Successful pilots have been using the tools and principles since the Wright brothers. Any pilot can manipulate the controls of an airplane, but professional pilots are risk managers.

The whole experience reminded me of my fifth-grade English teacher. She wore cat-eye glasses and walked around the room with a ruler scowling at students. Her specialty was diagramming sentences. I found the exercise to be pointless. I already spoke English. Why did I care? However, I learned to diagram sentences to avoid her wrath.

Years later, I found myself in South America and needed to learn Spanish. As I began to study a foreign language, the usefulness of diagramming sentences became evident. If you understand the parts of speech (verb, adverb, adjective, etc.), it is easier to learn a foreign language. All of my practice at breaking sentences apart and labeling their proper parts, and understanding their function made it easier to learn Spanish. I wanted to go back and hug my fifth-grade English teacher... well, maybe just send her a thank you note.

The Volant RRM model provides both the language and the structure for managing and analyzing risk. The graphic provides a visualization of the concepts, and the common language amplifies understanding and improves communication in difficult situations. Like diagramming sentences, RRM not only breaks down performance into various parts for proper evaluation, but also provides tools for improving future performance. It gives the user a language not only for identifying the parts, but also for implementing them efficiently and effectively in real time. In short, it is the language of successful risk management.

You may have picked up this book because you were curious. Maybe you picked up this book because someone insisted. I hope you are as skeptical as I was. Take the time to analyze it. Apply the principles you learn and recognize the places you are undoubtedly using the tools in your life already. You will find the language familiar and the nomenclature helpful for labeling risks, resources, and parts of processes that you already participate in.

Professional pilots are risk managers. RRM will elevate your risk management understanding and skills into the stratosphere.

"Simplicity is the ultimate sophistication."
-Leonardo Da Vinci

KD VanDrie

Risk and Resource Management is a framework and strategy for success. On the surface, it is quite simple.

- Three colors
- Four-steps
- Five blocks

Contained in that simplicity is the strategy for continuous improvement and success for working in dynamic, time-critical, high-risk environments; by yourself, when working with others; or in meeting the operational priorities of a large organization.

For application to personal success, we have learned that for Risk and Resource Management to be an effective tool, it needs to move beyond knowledge. It needs to impact what instructional designers call the 'affective domain.' Simply put, it needs to be integrated into both conscious and the intuitive processes, much like a musician learning music. For example, sometimes the information in a sheet of music goes straight from the written page to the actions of making the music without much conscious thought, but at other times there is a need to pay very close, intentional attention to each notation on the page; some actions are done at an intuitive level, and some need to be intentionally considered. This requires consistency in the way the music is written, a building block approach to learning, practice applying what has been learned, and a commitment to continuous improvement. Another parallel is that the level of mastery depends on personal goals.

Some folks are happy just playing by ear; others want to achieve greater precision or dig deeper into theory to exercise their own creativity.

We have also learned that the most effective introduction to RRM needs to be explained at a pace that it can be internalized into both conscious and intuitive thought processes and through application. This requires active learning, where the concepts are tried and applied to events on the path to success, followed by mindful consideration of what went well and what requires improvement. The RRM model is designed to aid in this process. But it only works when there is a commitment to continuous improvement.

Why use visual icons?

The use of visual icons in the application of RRM is essential. In addition to enhancing the explanation of the components, visualization helps to cement the RRM framework into the subconscious, which is what drives much of situational assessment, decision making, and communications. In addition, you will find the RRM terminology and graphics are effective tools for debriefing performance and identifying where improvements can be made.

In the simplest terms:
- The three colored **Green-Yellow-Red** "target" represents the likelihood of success *(colors directly relate to the impact of Risk Factors: task loading, additive conditions, and crew factors)*
- The five **Blocks** represent the Resources available to improve performance and trap/mitigate/eliminate errors *(includes consistency, job aids,*

ABCD

technology, other people, and personal preparation.)
- The four-step **ABCD** process is an acronym for a continuous loop to manage the Resources and to improve situation assessment, decision-making, communications, and continuous improvement. *(Integrates the foundational skills of Crew Resource Management (CRM) and the processes of Operational Risk Management (ORM))*
- As an added bonus, the arrow represents the Resilience needed to avoid or recover from the Red.

What can you expect to learn?
- How to use the three colors of the RRM target to recognize vulnerabilities and improve performance.
- How to develop and use the Resources needed to improve your own performance and work well with other people.
- How to use a very simple, continuous ABCD process to optimize
    - Situational Assessment
    - Decision Making
    - Communications
    - Continuous Improvement

Our challenge in writing this book was introducing the material, showing the practical application in an entertaining manner, and then providing a means to reflect on the lesson so that the information and strategies could be applied, internalized, and built upon. To accomplish this, each chapter is introduced with key points, followed by a fictionalized account to emphasize application, and finished with a discussion of the lessons learned.

We hope you will find the story engaging and helpful, but if you are more of a just-tell-me-the-facts type, feel free to read the bullets at the beginning of the chapter and the discussion at the end to learn the essence of the RRM approach.

To return to the music analogy, mastering RRM requires the same kind of commitment as mastering music. It cannot be done by simply reading about it. It must be practiced. Along the way as you make mistakes, you make corrections and to build new skills. And, as you integrate the concepts into your own thinking, you will discover new insights and RRM will become your own.

A Strategy for Learning RRM
1. Commit to professionalism
2. Observe yourself and others to recognize the impact of Green-Yellow-Red
3. Identify Risk Factors that lead to Yellow and Red
4. Internalize your priorities
5. Commit to running the ABCD loop
   - Consider when consistency could improve performance.
   - Consider when a job aid or checklist could improve performance.
   - Consider how use of technology improves or hinders success.
   - Use the Green-Yellow-Red observations to improve communication.
   - Recognize when there is a need to improve knowledge and skills.
6. Consider the internal drivers that impact perception and good decision making.

Chapter Two: How Did We Get Here?

> "The man who wishes to keep at the problem long enough to really learn anything positively must not take dangerous risks. Carelessness and overconfidence are usually more dangerous than deliberately accepted risks."
>
> Wilbur Wright

Key Concepts
- Risk management has been a part of aviation since the beginning.
- Aviation has not always been a safe mode of transportation.
- Aviation has become the safest form of transportation because of improvements in technology combined with effective risk management.
- Risk management is more than safety, it is the key to achieving success.
- Risk management philosophy, language, and methodology are incorporated in the concise and robust Risk and Resource Management (RRM) model.
- RRM can help you manage risk, achieve safety, and expedite your own journey toward expertise.

It was not a foregone conclusion that man would achieve powered flight when the Wright brothers began their trips to the windy beaches of North Carolina. On the contrary, most people thought it was an impossible feat and that God did not intend for man to fly. That fateful day in December, they proved it was not only possible for man to fly, but that the feat could be repeated safely over and over again. Their determination and persistence carried the day. The success of their first flight (and subsequent flights) can be attributed to good risk management.

In a letter to his father, Wilbur Wright once wrote, "The man who wishes to keep at the problem long enough to really learn anything positively must not take *dangerous risks*. Carelessness and overconfidence are usually more dangerous than *deliberately accepted risks*." (McCullough 2016) They understood, or at least partially understood that their endeavor was fraught with dangers and risks. "As time would show, caution and close attention to all advance preparations were to be the rule of the brothers." (McCullough 2016)

When Wilbur took the Wright Flyer to France to prove to the world that they had indeed achieved the feat of manned flight (many of the skeptics and critics of the day thought them frauds and pretenders), he would not be rushed in his preparations, in spite of mounting pressure from other "aviation experts" and the press. One observer of the press wrote, "Neither the impatience of waiting crowds, nor the sneers of rivals, nor the pressure of financial conditions not always easy, could induce him to hurry over any difficulty before he had done everything in his power to understand and overcome it." (McCullough 2016)

On Saturday, August 8, he opened the shed doors at the Hunaudières racetrack around three in the afternoon and rolled out the Wright Flyer, reconstructed after being shipped in crates from the United States to France, into the view of the eager crowd of dignitaries, press, and spectators. He continued his deliberate preparations, unfazed by the impatient onlookers, by preparing the catapult and surveying the field before positioning the aircraft for launch. Finally, around six thirty, he turned his cap backward and said, "Gentlemen, I'm going to fly."

Even after taking a seat and starting the engine, he was unsettled about some small detail and left his pilot's seat to check it. He would leave no detail to chance and spare no worthy preparation to ensure his success. After all, his life and reputation depended on the flight he was about to take. Then, after all, was in order, and he had mitigated every possible risk; he released the trigger and swept down the rail and into the air to hush the critics once and for all. (McCullough 2016)

Although the Wright brothers managed the risks of aviation successfully, not all the early aviators practiced good risk management. Consider the aviation daredevil Cal Rodgers.

On September 17, 1911, Cal Rodgers took off from the infield of a horse track in Sheepshead Bay, Brooklyn, in an attempt to fly from New York to California in thirty days or less. Dressed in a suit and tie with a cigar in his mouth, the handsome thirty-year-old football star with only sixty flying hours to his name took off in his cloth-covered biplane covered in advertising for his sponsor *Vin Fiz*, a popular grape soda. His plan was to follow the train tracks, or what pilots of the day called the "iron compass," to navigate his way to California. There were no airports, no fueling stations, and no air traffic control. His motivation was the $50,000 prize offered by William Randolph Hearst to the first person who could accomplish the feat.

Over the next forty-nine days, he experienced multiple crashes requiring so many repairs that by the time he got to California, the only original parts of the airplane were the vertical rudder, the oil pan, and a single wing strut. He suffered multiple injuries — a lacerated skull, broken leg, burns, cuts, and bruises. In spite of all of his difficulties and the fact that he didn't win the purse because he took too long, a crowd of twenty thousand people greeted him when he landed in Pasadena and paraded him through the streets wrapped in an American flag. Three days later, he flew to the Pacific shore, where his engine failed, and he crashed into the beach. He broke both legs, several ribs, and his collarbone. Finally, in April 1912, while chasing a flock of seagulls over Long Beach, one of the birds got stuck in his rudder. The aircraft spun out of control and crashed, killing Cal Rodgers in the process. (Groom 2015)

Cal Rodgers' story was not that unique in the early days of aviation. Aircraft crashes were commonplace as the new mode of transportation developed into an industry. Each accident pushed the aviation industry towards better manufacturing and better technology—aluminum construction, radial engines, and instrumentation for flying in the weather. Each accident or incident increased the "corporate knowledge" in the industry, improving the pilot's ability to manage the risks and produce a safer outcome.

Even though technology and pilot abilities improved over time, airliner accidents and fatalities continued to increase steadily with increasing flights until they reached a peak in 1972. (Ranter 2023) Accident investigations pointed less and less to mechanical failures and more and more toward pilot error. In order for aviation safety to improve, pilot skills had to improve, but not in managing the airplane. Pilots needed improved interpersonal communication skills, decision-making skills, and leadership skills. Pilots needed to be better risk managers.

The first attempt to improve the "soft skills" of pilots was called Cockpit Resource Management (CRM). United Airlines was one of the first major airlines to create and implement a CRM training curriculum for its pilot group. Then in July of 1989, Captain Al Haynes and his crew crashed a United Airlines DC-10 in Iowa, that by all accounts, should have resulted in the death of everyone on board. Instead, 184 passengers of the 296 on board survived. The flight deck crew also survived (and eventually returned to flying duties). In the aftermath, Captain Al Haynes said, "So if I hadn't used CRM, if we had not let everybody put their input in, it's a cinch we wouldn't have made it." (Andino 2014) With this resounding endorsement, CRM training became an industry staple.

In February of 1993, the FAA issued an Advisory Circular (AC 120-51) outlining "guidelines for developing, implementing, reinforcing, and assessing Crew Resource Management (CRM) training for flight crewmembers and other personnel essential to flight safety." The purpose of the training was to improve "situation awareness, communication skills, teamwork, task allocation, and decision making within a comprehensive framework of standard operating procedures." (US DOT 2004) Since the issue of the original Advisory Circular, the FAA has strengthened its stance on CRM and made it a mandatory part of training for professional pilots.

As aviation professionals began teaching and implementing the elements of CRM into their operations, they began to realize that even though it provided valuable training, it did not fully capture the complex risks involved in today's modern flight deck. How do you measure someone's situational awareness? With standard operating procedures in place, why do pilots continue to commit simple procedural errors? What does good decision-making look like? How do you manage catastrophic events outside the scope of control?

With these questions, several models for managing risk emerged. James T. Reason, from the University of Manchester, introduced the Swiss Cheese Model discussing the layers of protection for managing risk and preventing accidents. (Reason 2021) In 1994 psychologists at the University of Texas developed Threat and Error Management (TEM), an overarching safety philosophy built on the principles of the Swiss Cheese Model that assumes pilots will commit errors and encounter unforeseen risks during flight operations. (Merritt, Ph.D and Klinect, Ph.D. 2021)

During this same timeframe, the Volant Risk and Resource Management (RRM) model was developed on the philosophy of combining the risk management needs of the organization, the flight crews, and the individual pilot into a single model. The model utilizes fundamental principles of risk management as a foundation. RRM incorporates the soft skills of CRM, a layered approach of resources similar to the Swiss Cheese model, and the recognition of human error (and the need to trap those errors). Additionally, the RRM framework provides more robust process tools that include skills for managing the flight deck and the internal and external resources, to achieve a safe, and successful, outcome. RRM provides a systematic methodology for analyzing risk at the personal and operational levels both before and after an incident.

Risk and Resource Management is designed to manage risks, achieve safety, and expedite expertise from the organizational level down to the individual level.

Innovation requires courage and bold action, but progress seldom is made by the careless thrill seeker intent on garnering publicity without considering and mitigating the risks. The pioneers of aviation understood the risks and labored to manage them well enough that people with less courage or sense of adventure felt comfortable boarding an airplane and taking to the air. Improvements in technology have reduced the risks associated with mechanical deficiencies, but the burden of managing the risks of flight remains squarely on the shoulders of professional pilots. The risk-management strategies of the pilot have become an essential and integral part of aviation safety.

In February of 2009, *New York* magazine put Sully on the cover and stated: "The Last Aviator, Why they don't make pilots like Sully anymore." (Kolker 2019) While we applaud the piloting skills and decision-making of Captain Sullenberger, it is disingenuous to state that we have stopped training pilots of his caliber. In fact, the opposite is (and should be) true. Aviation is the safest form of travel in the world, not only because of the technological advances in aircraft design and manufacturing but also because we continue to train better. (IATA 2022)

In fact, during the accident investigation of the Miracle on the Hudson, they concluded: "US Airways CRM and TEM training, which was integrated into all aspects of US Airways training, including ground school and flight training, gave pilots the skills and tools needed to build a team quickly, open lines of communication, share common goals, and work together." Robert Sumwalt, the Director of the NTSB at the time, stated, "This speaks well for the crew, it speaks well for their training, and it speaks well for the benefits of

CRM. And this, this is exactly why the NTSB wants CRM in part 135 operations. That very issue is on our most wanted list." (NTSB 2009)

Today's student pilots will learn to fly with one hundred years of aviation wisdom at their beck and call. Simulation tools allow today's student pilots to train for a wide variety of emergency situations, including the one faced by Captain Sullenberger. The curriculum for even the private pilot includes the elements of risk management and decision-making. Modern aviation training can, and should, produce thousands of pilots as capable as Captain Sullenberger.

This book is our attempt to provide the pilot with the risk management tools that can help him or her manage the risks and use the resources available from the first flight as a student pilot to the last flight as an airline pilot and beyond. We hope that it will also appeal to risk managers outside of the aviation world.

In keeping with the long-standing tradition of learning about aviation from the stories of other aviators, we have organized the lessons in this book using a fictional story. You will follow the protagonist, Luke "Risky" Rogers, on his journey from teenage driver to airline pilot. In each chapter of Risky's journey, he will learn about a different aspect of the RRM model and decision-making in a fictional setting. By using this story-telling teaching technique, the concepts will be easier to understand and retain. We will break from the fictional narrative at the beginning of each chapter to summarize the key concepts, occasionally as needed throughout the text to emphasize or explain, and at the end of each chapter to summarize. We hope you enjoy following the protagonist as he learns about and employs the Risk and Resource Management model in each scene.

Chapter Three: The Need for Risk Management

"So we shall let the reader answer this question for himself: who is the happier man, he who has braved the storm of life and lived or he who has stayed securely on shore and merely existed?"
—Hunter S. Thompson

Key Concepts
- Safety is a state of being free from harm or loss.
- We can accomplish more through good risk management than by simply trying to "be safe."
- Safety is the product of good risk management. Safety is the goal, but not the method or means.
- Risk is the probability and magnitude of deviation from a desired result.
- Risk management is the methodology that optimizes performance and produces a safe outcome.
- We accept different levels of risk based on our goals, experience, value system, and perceptions.
- Risk-based thinking is something we do naturally.

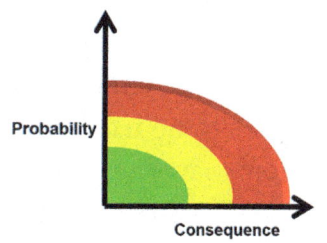

Luke slept through his alarm and only woke up when his father pounded on his door. "I'm awake," he shouted. His parents had divorced a few years ago, and he was staying in Arizona with his father over the summer. His mother had just moved to Cincinnati. He would be joining her at the end of the summer.

"I'm headed to work and won't be back until after dinner," said his father. "What are you going to do on your first day of summer break?"

Luke rolled over and fluffed up his pillow. "I was thinking about heading up the canyon with some friends. Can I borrow the truck?"

There was a long pause before his father answered. "Yeah, I guess so. Just make sure you take out the trash before you go."

"Will do Dad." He yawned and reached for his cell phone.

"Promise me you'll drive safe."

"I will. I will." Luke checked his social media feed.

"What time will you be home?"

"Midnight?"

"Okay, be safe."

"Yep." Luke heard his father's footsteps on the stairs as he was leaving. He fired off a group text to several of his buddies. *Bonfire in the canyon tonight with Lucky Luke! Who's in?* Soon the texts came pouring in, and the event was set for that evening.

Luke was happy to see the gas tank of the truck was almost full when he climbed in. That would save him some time and money. When the truck started, the radio began playing jazz music, his father's favorite genre. He shook his head and began backing out of the driveway as he fumbled with his phone to connect and play his favorite playlist. From the corner of his eye, he noticed a kid on a bicycle pedaling down the sidewalk, apparently having just gone behind the truck. "Stupid kid!" he muttered to himself. "Do you have some sort of death wish?" He turned up the music volume and backed into the street.

He drove down the street from his house and took a left turn onto the suburban street that would take him out of the neighborhood. His phone chimed, and he reached down and grabbed it. One of his friends texted – *Are you bringing firewood?* With one hand on the wheel, he texted back – *Yep, I'll get some.* When he put down his phone and looked up, he saw a woman walking a dog crossing the street in front of him. He slammed on the brakes and came to a screeching stop. His cell phone slid into the passenger side floorboard. The woman gave him a dirty look and continued walking with her dog across the street. He leaned over and grabbed his cell phone. "I guess that's why they call me Lucky Luke," he mumbled to himself.

He didn't see any cars as he approached the intersection for the main road and slowed down to be sure. When he was sure it was clear, he stepped on the gas and made a left turn onto the road. He stopped at the local supermarket and grabbed a couple of bundles of firewood for the bonfire, and picked up three of his friends before heading up the canyon road with the music blaring and the windows down.

"Here, hold my phone for me," he told his friend in the passenger seat. "I want to post a video before we lose the signal in the canyon." His friend held up the phone and gave him the thumbs up. With one hand on the wheel and the other hand moving with the music, Luke looked over at the camera and said, "Lucky Luke here. Headed up the canyon to the usual spot for a bonfire tonight with my best buds! Come and find the party!"

"Did it take?" he asked.

"Yep! Turned out great." He handed the phone back to Luke, who promptly posted it to social media.

The speed limit on the canyon road was forty-five miles an hour, with slower speeds in the curves. Luke barreled along the mountain road making the tires squeal in turns laughing with his friends who jostled from side to side. On one corner, he misjudged and crossed the double yellow line. An oncoming motorcyclist swerved to miss the hurtling truck and blared his horn. They all laughed it off and continued up the road with the engine revving.

The bonfire party was a big success. They were one of the first people into the park and staked out the best spot for the party. Soon the fire was roaring, and as the sun went down, other partiers arrived to enjoy the festivities. They played music and danced. Several people brought cold beer. They laughed and partied until around midnight, when they ran out of firewood, and all they had left to keep them warm in the cool mountain air was a few coals. Car by car, they left the party and headed down the mountain.

Luke yawned when he climbed into the truck. He left the window down so the cool mountain air would help keep him awake on the drive home. They had only gone a few miles, and all the passengers in the truck had passed out, sound asleep. His head bobbed occasionally, but he stuck his face into the wind to stay awake. More than once, the sound of his tires hitting the gravel on the side of the road jerked him awake. He fought off the fatigue and continued home. After dropping off his friends, he finally pulled into the driveway around two in the morning and stumbled into bed.

The next morning, he got out of bed a little before noon and was surprised to see his father working at the kitchen table when he sauntered in to find something for breakfast.

"Good morning," said his father. "Glad to see you made it home in one piece. I bought some doughnuts this morning, but they might be stale by now."

Luke rubbed his eyes. "Thanks, Dad." He grabbed a doughnut and took a bite. "They're still good," he said through a mouthful of doughnut. "What are you doing home today?"

His father stared at his computer through his glasses and continued typing. "Oh, I thought it might be good to catch up some with you this morning. I told them I was working from home today." He stopped and closed his laptop. "Come grab a seat."

Luke grabbed another doughnut and started for the kitchen table. He noticed several empty beer bottles lined up on the table as he sat down, and when he looked up at his father, he could tell this wasn't going to be a social chit-chat with Dad. He shoved another bite into his mouth and looked out the window.

"What time did you get home last night?" asked his father.

"A little after midnight."

"Can you be more precise?"

Luke shrugged. "I dunno. One AM?"

"According to the home security system, 2:37 AM. You told me you would be home by midnight."

"The bonfire lasted a little longer than expected."

His father clenched his jaw and took a deep breath. "Did you know that I got one of those dashcam driver-monitoring systems for the truck? It monitors everything when you drive it." He opened up his laptop and pulled up a video of the truck cameras.

Luke choked down the mouthful of doughnut and stared at the screen, feeling a knot form in his stomach.

"So, the best I can tell from the downloaded information you weren't a very safe driver last night."

"What do you mean? I was safe—no injuries and not a scratch on the truck. I made it home safe and sound."

"Okay, let's look at the footage." His father began scrolling through the footage. First, he showed the kid on the bicycle dodging the truck as it backed out of the driveway. Then, the truck screeching to a stop for the lady walking the dog. It was clear that he ran the stop sign and gunned the truck into the intersection from the video. The bright yellow jacket of the motorcyclist popped against the green mountain fir trees that lined the curve of the highway, where the truck swerved across the double line and into oncoming traffic. More than once, the footage showed the truck drifting off the edge of the road and into the gravel shoulder on the drive back down the canyon. Without saying anything, his father pulled up the video Luke had posted on social media. As if to punctuate the entire scene with an exclamation point, he slid the beer bottles in between them.

His father glared and narrowed his eyes. "You call that safe driving?"

Even through the lenses of his father's glasses, Luke could feel the angry glare. He looked away and stared out the window and mumbled. "What do you want? I'm not perfect, but I made it home safe. No one got hurt."

"You're lucky no one got hurt!"

"But no one did get hurt." Luke shrugged and grinned. "I guess that's why my nickname is Lucky Luke."

His father shook his head and frowned. "Luck isn't going to protect you. When you take risks like that, sooner or later your luck runs out." He closed the laptop. "Until you learn the difference between taking unnecessary risks and being safe, you're not driving my truck anymore."

"What am I supposed to do? Sit around the house all summer? Can't I just have a little fun?"

"Fun? You almost ran over a pedestrian. You posted to social media while driving. You crossed the double line and almost hit a motorcycle. You stayed out too late and were obviously too tired to drive." He pointed at the beer bottles. "You were drinking and driving." He shook his head. "You take too many risks. We should call you 'Risky' not 'Lucky.'"

"First of all, those beer bottles aren't mine. I'm not stupid enough to drink and drive. Besides, I'm not old enough to drink anyway." Luke went to the fridge for a glass of milk and to give himself a moment to think. "Maybe I do take some risks, but isn't that what makes life worth living? Life would be boring without taking a few risks." He took a drink and sat back down across from his father. "Haven't you been telling me to make the most of my life? Seize the day? How can I do that if I don't take a few risks and live on the edge a bit?"

"Living on the edge? It's okay to take a few calculated risks to have fun, and achieve something, but you were way past the edge several times last night." He shook his head. "Okay, 'Risky Rogers,' I think you need a couple of weeks without driving my truck to help you learn to be safe."

"No!" Luke put his face down on the table.

Perhaps you have been part of a similar conversation before. Have you ever told someone to be safe? What did you mean when you said that? What does it mean to be safe?

By definition, safe means to be free from hurt, injury, or danger. (Dictionary.com 2023) Was Risky safe? Did he injure anyone? Was there any damage to the truck? He achieved an outcome free from harm or loss. He did exactly what his father asked him to do. He returned home safely without a scratch on the vehicle. By definition, he was safe.

Perhaps his father should have set a different expectation before allowing Risky to drive the truck. Maybe he should have instructed him to properly manage the risks associated with driving, but that doesn't roll off the tongue so easily. It is, however, what Risky's father wanted him to do. Essentially the father assumed his son knew how to manage the risks of driving by following some simple rules—no texting and driving, obeying traffic signs, driving at or near the speed limit, avoiding distractions while driving, leaving the party before he was fatigued, and most importantly, not driving after consuming any alcohol.

Why did the father want Risky to follow those basic rules? Because he understood that by following those rules, he would be mitigating the risks associated with driving a vehicle, and by mitigating and managing the risks by default, would achieve a safe outcome. That's what his father meant when he told Risky—"Be safe."

On the other hand, what did Risky want? To maximize the fun! But whether it was due to inexperience, a youthful attitude toward invulnerability, or some other reason, he didn't see the risks.

Risk management is the process that allows us to achieve both results: maximize the desired outcome while minimizing any associated risks.

Perhaps we should change our language to say what we really mean when we tell a loved one or friend to be safe. Maybe we should say, "Watch out for the hazards and manage the associated risks." But that isn't as easy as telling someone, "Be safe!" It is, however, what we mean.

Safety is the desired outcome, the product we seek and hope to achieve. It is not a process. It is the end result. You are either safe (free from harm or loss), or you are not.

Risk management is the process of achieving our goals, including a safe outcome. It involves recognizing associated risks, mitigating and managing those risks, and achieving a safe outcome in spite of the possibility of experiencing harm or loss. It is the methodology we employ when we strive to be safe. In addition to achieving a safe outcome, good risk management also enables us to accept risks for the purpose of achieving a desired outcome, like driving a mountain road to get to a party with our friends. Taking risks is a necessary part of any worthwhile endeavor. Managing those risks is an essential part of success in any undertaking.

Some people have difficulty recognizing or at least quantifying the level of risk. Risk managers use charts or tables to visualize and quantify risk, but that's not practical in our daily life. One of the goals of this book is to help you create an intuitive sense of increased risk and the impact it can have on your performance and success.

Luke rode his bicycle to a friend's house over five miles away. When he rode up his friend was wiping down a motorcycle. "Hey Mark, when did you get the motorcycle?"

"Yesterday," Mark answered as he continued to work on the motorcycle. "That's why I didn't come to the bonfire. I was finishing up the rider's safety course."

Luke glanced down at his bike and then back at the motorcycle with its shiny gas tank, powerful engine, and fat racing-style tires. "How fast does it go?"

"Fast enough." He looked at Luke's bicycle and grinned. "Definitely faster than your bike."

"Aw man! That hurts! Can I take it for a spin?"

Mark gave him a sideways look. "Do you have a motorcycle endorsement?"

"No but I've ridden dirt bikes before."

Mark shook his head. "My insurance won't cover you without an endorsement."

Luke nodded in understanding, still staring at the bike and imagining himself screaming down some winding road with the wind blowing through his hair.

Mark went back to cleaning and asked. "Why did you ride your bike? Trying to get some exercise?"

"Nah, my dad grounded me from using the truck. He doesn't want me to have any fun this summer."

"You should take the motorcycle course and get yourself something a little faster than you can pedal."

Luke's eyes lit up.

That evening after dinner, Luke volunteered to wash the dishes and clean up. His father immediately picked up on the change. "Thanks son, but cleaning up won't shorten your grounding."

He kept cleaning. "Actually, I was thinking about something else."

His father raised an eyebrow. "Oh, let's hear it?"

"Well, remember how you have been trying to teach me to be more independent and self-reliant?"

His father nodded. "Uh huh."

"Well, if you want me to be self-reliant, I need to get my own vehicle."

"That's a great idea, but cars are expensive. Last time I checked you don't have enough money."

Luke nodded. "I don't have enough money for a car, but I do have enough money for a motorcycle."

His father started laughing. "You get grounded from my truck for unsafe driving and you want to get a motorcycle? Sounds like the nickname 'Risky' really does fit you."

Luke blushed and tried not to get upset. "Well, Risky Rogers does have a nice ring to it." He rinsed off one of the pots from dinner. "I have enough money saved to take the rider's course and still get a cheap motorcycle. That way I wouldn't have to rely on you for transportation."

His father grabbed a towel and started drying the dishes. "Tell you what. You get a job first, and then we can talk about it again."

Not wanting to give up so easily, Luke persisted. "You always tell me I should learn from my mistakes. How can I learn to be a better driver if you don't let me drive?"

"Good point, but how can you I let you learn without putting you, and others, in danger?"

"I'm not dangerous." He shoved another pot into the soapy water. "I just want to have an *actual* life."

His father leaned against the counter as he dried off one of the pans from dinner. "Do you know what I wanted to be when I grew up?"

"No." Luke wondered where this conversation was going. The thought that his father had not achieved his childhood dream was new to him.

His father got a wistful look on his face. "I always wanted to be a pilot, specifically a fighter pilot. But I didn't have 20/20 vision. So, the military turned me down."

Luke stopped washing and looked at his father. "I never knew that. Why didn't you try another route?"

"Actually, I did. I took a few flying lessons in college, but I ran out of money. Then I met your mother." He shrugged. "Life happened while I was making other plans, and before I knew it, I had to support a family." He smiled at his son. "I don't regret the family part, and I've achieved success in my career, but I always wondered how my life would have been if I had been able to pursue that dream."

Luke grinned. "And now you're keeping your only son from pursuing his dreams by grounding him from driving. Just think of the opportunities I'm missing."

His father laughed and playfully punched Luke in the shoulder. "You are NOT getting a motorcycle, Risky Rogers. But I have an idea. Why don't you take a couple of flying lessons while you're grounded?"

> I'M NOT READY TO TRUST YOU WITH TRUCK KEYS WHILE YOU'RE GROUNDED

> HOW ABOUT SOME FLYING LESSONS?

Luke stopped washing and gave his father a puzzled look. "Seriously? You won't let me drive the truck, but you'll let me fly an airplane?"

His father nodded. "I'll let you fly an airplane with an instructor. I became a better, safer driver after taking a few flying lessons. You don't have a lot of room for taking unnecessary risks in an airplane. You have to be methodical and calculate every move to be a safe pilot." He grinned. "Besides, you want to be 'ungrounded.'"

Luke rolled his eyes and said, "Dad jokes."

"Seriously though," his father continued. "I think you could learn some things and would probably enjoy it. If you're smart, you'll apply what you learn to other areas of your life. Then you can live on the edge without hurting yourself, or anyone else."

Luke went back to washing the dishes in the sink, but his imagination had already taken to the air. "Are you going to tell Mom about this?"

His father reached up and tousled Luke's hair. "Well Risky Rogers, I'll tell her that if she doesn't let you take flying lessons, I'm going to buy you a motorcycle."

Chapter Four: Master the Target

"How many people operate at 100 percent all the time? By definition, half of your time you are performing below your average. And if you've been around flying long enough, I'm sure you've walked away from flights where you said, 'I should not have flown, I should not have taken that flight.' It's really useful to be lucky, but it's hard to control."
—*Immanuel Barshi*

Key Concepts
- The target provides a visualization of potential risk and its impact on human performance. It is color-coded into Green, Yellow, and Red areas, where the rings further from the center represent increasing levels of risk.
- The target can describe the state of an individual, a crew, or an entire operation.
- Recognizing the current risk state is the first step of returning the risk state to the Green.

- **Green**—Represents a high likelihood of a positive outcome. This is a combination of good situational awareness, management strategies, and Resources in place to improve performance and capture errors. Communication is effective. Problems are anticipated and managed. Errors are minimized or trapped. Operational priorities are followed.
- **Yellow**—Represents increased risk due to higher task loading, additive conditions, and/or crew factors. Situation assessment becomes more difficult. Situational awareness could be decreasing. Errors may go unnoticed. Communication may become strained. Operating in the Yellow may require adjusting the plan (based on time available), balancing priorities, and using available Resources.
- **Red**—Represents a high potential for a serious error or operational failure. The time available and/or Resources are not in place to capture errors. Clear thinking and decision-making become much more challenging. Communication must be more direct to prevent misunderstandings. Operating in the Red can result in tunnel vision leading to severely diminished situational awareness. Recovery is necessary, which often requires the flexibility to change the immediate goal.
- The key skill is to recognize both the level of risk and the impact the risk has on performance.
- The target is not a visual representation of ability. Even proficient and skilled professionals will inevitably be in the Yellow or Red when faced with difficult conditions.

Risky got out of the truck and followed his father along the sidewalk to the flight school. After a few steps, his attention shifted, and he stopped to watch the airplanes overhead. Several airplanes circled the airfield in Chandler, Arizona. He heard the twin engines of an aircraft on the runway come to life and propel it down the runway for takeoff. A helicopter flew by and landed on the asphalt in front of the control tower. He couldn't believe his father was actually going to let him fly an airplane.

His father came back and stood next to him. "Exciting, isn't it?" he asked.

Risky continued to watch, feeling the excitement build in his gut like the first time he rode a roller coaster. "Yeah it looks like fun," he answered, trying to hide his excitement.

When they walked into the flight school, a young woman with black hair pulled back in a ponytail stood to greet them with a big smile. "Hello, I'm Vicky. Are you Mister Rogers?" she asked.

Risky's father extended his hand and smiled back. "Yes, I am, but without the cardigan."

She gave him a puzzled look.

"You know... Mister Roger's Neighborhood?"

"My dad is trying to be funny," interrupted Risky. He rolled his eyes. "Dad jokes."

She looked at Risky and back at his father. "This must be your son that you mentioned over the phone. I can certainly see the resemblance."

"I must admit that he gets his dashing good looks from me." He reached up and flicked one of his ears. "He certainly didn't get those ears from his mother."

Risky shook his head. "Thank goodness I got my mother's sense of humor. Can we just get to the flight?"

The instructor smirked and stepped in. "I think I can take it from here Mister Rogers." She ushered Risky towards a hallway. "Let's go to the first briefing room on the right." She looked back at the father. "Come back to pick him up in about an hour and half."

Risky plopped himself down in the chair and looked around the room. It was decorated with cockpit posters and safety notices. "So, do we get to do anything fun today?" He asked before the instructor could close the door.

She smiled and stood at the whiteboard. "First of all, let me introduce myself again. My name is Victoria Young, but everyone calls me Vicky. I got interested in becoming a pilot when I was a flight attendant and I've been flying about two years. I've been a Certified Flight Instructor for about six months." She wrote her name on the board. "Tell me about yourself."

Risky leaned back in the chair and balanced on the back two legs. "I'm Luke Rogers, but my friends call me Lucky Luke." He smirked and added, "Or lately Risky Rogers."

Vicky continued smiling and wrote Luke Rogers on the board. "Your father mentioned a little about your new nickname and the events that led to this lesson today. I understand you like to live on the edge a bit."

"Life isn't any fun without a few risks."

"I agree. That's why you're here today — learn to manage a few calculated risks and have some fun." She drew a bullseye on the board with a green center outlined with a yellow circle and surrounded by a red circle. "Do you like roller coasters?"

"Love 'em! My buddies and I rode one five times in a row once. It was dope."

"Okay, tell me what you remember about the first time."

"It was awesome and we screamed a lot."

"Do you remember any details from the first ride?"

Risky paused. "I remember we were in the last car and got whipped around a lot in the turns."

"Now tell me what you remember about the fifth and last time you rode it."

"Well, on the last ride I was sitting next to my buddy, Chuck, and we waited for the front seat of the front car. When the coaster got to the top, you know, the place where it hangs for a moment before you start dropping like a rock, Chuck and I high-fived each other. Then when we got to the loop, I looked down at the ground and saw a bunch of people's stuff that must have fallen out of the coaster and started laughing. Then when we finally started coasting to a stop,

Chuck was quiet and looked a little pale. He had like this one bead of sweat trickling down the side of his face, and as soon as the harness released, he went running to the nearest trash can and threw up." He laughed. "We all started laughing and saying, 'What up Chuck?' It was hilarious."

Vicky smiled and chuckled. "I'm sure it was. Notice how you remember a lot more details from the last ride than the first ride? Why do you think that is?"

"I guess because I knew what to expect after a few rides."

"That's right. At first, your perception of risk caused your senses to shut down a bit because you didn't know what to expect. Your expectations didn't align with what was happening and that pushed you into the Red. After a couple of rides, you had good situational awareness, because of your previous experience." She pointed to the target on the whiteboard. "On your first ride your situational awareness put you somewhere in the Red or Yellow and by the last ride you were more in the center in the Green. But your safety on the roller coaster really didn't depend on your situational awareness. As long as you stayed strapped in and all the safety features functioned properly, you were going to be safe.

Today when we go flying it's like a roller coaster we control. We, along with the laws of aerodynamics, determine if we go up or down. You might feel uncomfortable at times, but it's as safe as the roller coaster."

"Can we do a loop?"

Vicky shook her head. "Not in this airplane, but if you like that type of flying, you can take an aerobatics course once you get your license. Besides, I don't think you're ready for aerobatics, unless you want to end up like your buddy Chuck."

Risky scowled. "I never get sick."

"Good. Today, since it's your first time flying, your situational awareness will most likely be somewhere in the Red or Yellow. If you were in the airplane by yourself, your level of risk would also be in the Red or Yellow and most likely wouldn't produce a safe outcome. However, I'm going to be in the airplane with you to make sure we manage the risks and land safely." She pointed at the target. "From time to time during the flight today I will ask you where you are in the target. Just tell me Green, Yellow, or Red, depending on how you feel and how much you think you are understanding. In fact, if I asked you right now, where do you think you are in that target?"

Risky gave her a thumbs up. "I'm in the Green for sure."

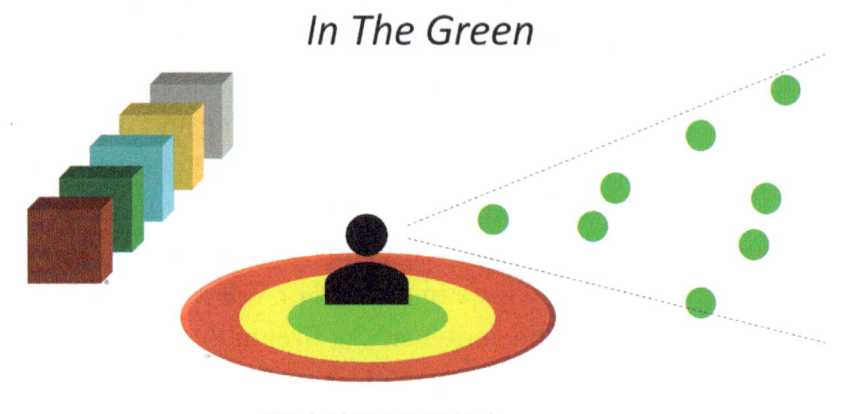

In The Green

- Situational Awareness is Good
- Resources are in Place to Protect Goals

Vicky smiled. "Good. Now let's go over today's flight …"

For some reason, Risky thought he would feel safer in the airplane than he actually did. The slim aluminum doors didn't feel like they would provide him with much protection, and the seat wasn't very comfortable. He buckled the seatbelt but then had to get help from Vicky to figure out the shoulder strap. The headset pinched the ears he inherited from his father, and he cursed the genetic inheritance under his breath. Even though the weather was mild and sunny, it started getting warm the moment Vicky closed the door. It smelled like musty carpet and vinyl seats.

He watched her prepare the aircraft for flight, flipping switches and checking things, but he had no idea what she was doing. He sat there with his hands in his lap, trying to keep up with her pace, but eventually gave up and stared out the window until his headset suddenly came to life.

"Can you hear me?" asked Vicky.

"Yeah, I can hear you," he answered, but he sounded muted.

Vicky reached over and adjusted the microphone close to his mouth. "Try talking again."

"I can hear you," he repeated. This time he could hear his own voice in the headset.

"Where do you think you are in that target we talked about?"

Everything felt foreign and strange to Risky, but he shrugged and said, "I'm in the Yellow."

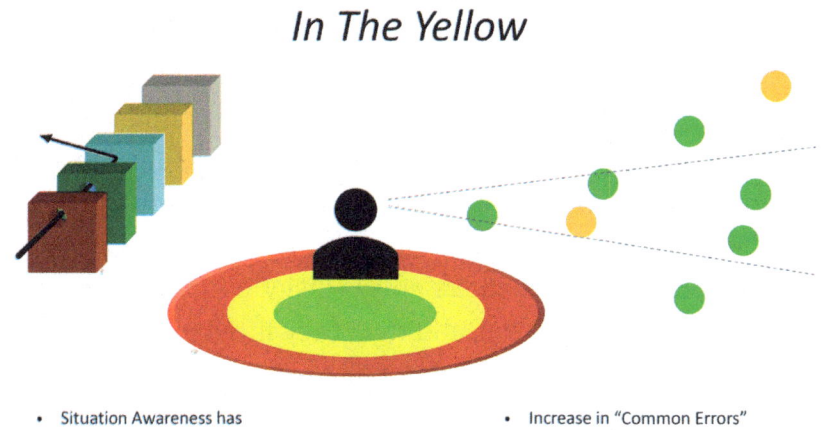

In The Yellow

- Situation Awareness has Narrowed
- Resources are beginning to fail
- Increase in "Common Errors"
- Impacts Communication Style
- Need to Reprioritize

"Good call! I'm glad you recognize where you are. I'll try to explain what I'm doing as we go along. Just like in the roller coaster, it gets easier as you get accustomed to the new environment. Let me get the ATIS, the automated weather report, and we'll be on our way."

Vicky turned a knob, and an automated voice came over the headset. "Chandler Airport information Sierra, winds 210@5 …" Risky tried to make sense of the combination of words and numbers, but it might as well have been a foreign language. He looked over at the runway and watched another airplane take off.

"Don't worry if you don't understand all that. It gets easier to understand when you know what to expect in the information." She turned and smiled, then continued, "Okay, we're going to start the engine now. It's going to get noisy." She reached over and pulled a knob back twice. She yelled through the open window, "Clear prop!" Then she reached over and turned the key in the ignition. The propellor turned a few times, and then the whole aircraft shuddered as it came to life. The smell of exhaust lingered as a blast of wind entered the cockpit.

"Okay are you ready to go fly?" she asked as she closed the window.

The headset pinched his ears. The vibration from the propellor rattled his bones. The lingering exhaust smell made his stomach queasy. He felt lost. Risky smiled but gave her a thumbs up.

Risky tried to keep up with her actions and radio calls, but it was overwhelming. After a few minutes, he just enjoyed watching the other airplanes take off and land. He got excited when they lined up on the runway, but when she pushed up the power, it felt like the whole airplane might shake apart. Vicky was trying to explain something about their speed, and then they lifted off.

The light craft felt like a kite as it climbed away from the ground, and a sudden sense of awe overcame him as the nearby houses and streets began to fall away beneath him. He was flying!

"How are you doing?" asked Vicky.

Risky continued to look out the window. "This is totally lit, but I feel like such a newb."

Vicky laughed. "Well newb, let's learn some flying skills. Hold the controls with me."

"Seriously?"

"Yes, seriously. Hold the controls loosely and follow my movements. Put your feet on the rudder pedals as well. I'll explain more about the aerodynamics when we get back to the briefing room but for now just get a feel for how the airplane responds to your inputs."

Risky put his hands and feet on the controls.

"First, it's always good to know where you need to be looking. So, let's start by establishing a sight picture for level flight at a cruise power setting. See where the horizon is in the windscreen? With this power setting this is what level flight looks like. You're in level flight as long as you have that sight picture. You can confirm that by glancing down here at the altimeter. But mainly, you want to keep your eyes outside for now."

Risky looked at how the horizon cut across the windscreen.

"Here's how you turn the aircraft. Use aileron and rudder together for a coordinated entry into the turn, and establish the turn. Then neutralize the controls and add a little back pressure. See how the sight picture changes?"

Risky could feel the movements and watched the aircraft turn. He looked out the side window at the ground.

"Reverse the process when you want to roll out of the turn. Use the horizon to keep the aircraft level." She rolled the wings level with the horizon.

"Okay, are you ready to fly?" Risky nodded. "You have the aircraft," she announced as she released the controls. "Turn the aircraft to the right," she directed. Risky turned the yoke, and the nose of the aircraft searched for stability. "Don't forget to add a little rudder in the direction of the turn as you roll the aircraft into and out of the turn."

"How do I add rudder?"

"With the foot pedals. Pull back a little bit. We're descending."

Risky pulled back on the yoke. "Too much," said Vicky. "Now we're climbing. Use the horizon to help you stay level. Remember the sight picture you used before."

Soon he felt like he was getting the hang of it. "Are you sure we can't do a roll?" he asked again.

She shook her head. "That would definitely put us both in the Red since this aircraft wasn't designed for aerobatic flight. Too much risk."

Risky smiled. "You're no fun."

"It seems like you are feeling pretty good about things. Would you say you're in the Green?"

"Yeah, I don't feel like such a newb anymore."

"Okay, we can't do a roll or loop, but we can do some power-on stalls. I have the aircraft. Put your hands in your lap and your feet flat on the floor."

Risky did as instructed and watched her add power and raise the nose of the aircraft. Vicky narrated. "You can see, and feel, the aircraft slowing down as we approach the stall. When the speed is too slow, and the wings don't have enough airflow to create lift... the aircraft will stall." The nose of the aircraft fell abruptly, and Risky felt like he was back on the rollercoaster with his stomach in his mouth. "When the nose drops, the air begins to flow over the wings again to create lift and we're back to flying. With these training aircraft, you can almost let go of the controls, and they'll recover themselves."

When she recovered the aircraft back to level flight, Risky was still trying to figure out what had happened.

"Now you do it. I'll talk you through it. You have the aircraft." He grabbed the controls and followed her instructions as best as he could, but when the aircraft wings stalled and the nose dropped, it also rolled, and he felt like he was falling sideways out of the sky.

Vicky took the controls. "I have the aircraft." She righted the wings and smoothly returned to level flight. "Still in the Green?"

"Let me try it again," he insisted. He took control of the aircraft and tried to mimic her actions, but once again, the aircraft tilted to one side, and she took control. Before he even realized it, he felt queasy, and a cold sweat broke out on his forehead.

It was quiet for a moment on the headset, and he stared straight ahead at the spinning propellor, trying to keep his bearings. He noticed the aircraft was in a gentle turn and descending.

Vicky's voice broke the silence on the headset. "That's probably enough for today. Let's head back to the pattern and get you back on the ground." She leveled the wings and continued an easy descent. "Hold the controls with me. It will make you feel better."

Risky nodded and put his hands on the yoke.

"Put your feet on the rudder pedals also," instructed Vicky. "Do you have the aircraft?"

Risky nodded, not wanting to speak.

"We always want to verbalize when we transfer aircraft control. Do you have the aircraft?"

"Yeah. Yeah I got it." The sweat from his palms made the yoke feel slippery, and he gripped it tighter.

"Still in the Green?" asked Vicky.

"No, definitely in the Red right now."

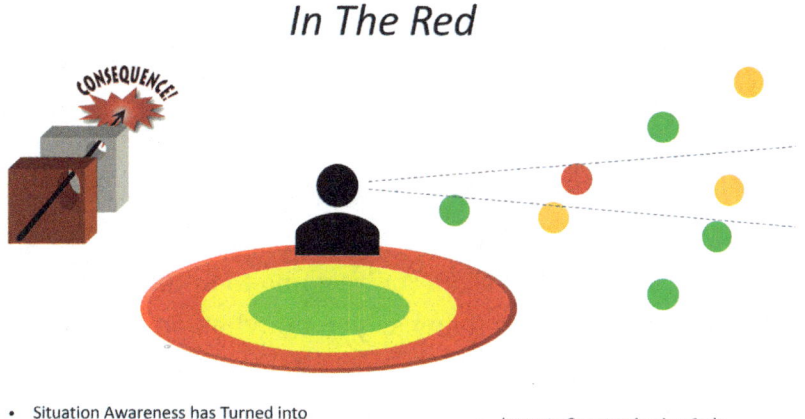

In The Red

- Situation Awareness has Turned into Tunnel Vision
- Difficult to Self-Diagnose
- Impacts Communication Style
- Requires a Recovery

"I'm glad you realize that. It's important to recognize, when we can, that we are not performing to our normal abilities. That allows us to get the help we need from other resources." She reached up and tuned the radio. The same automated voice gave the current airfield information. "Okay, raise the nose a little bit and add some power. We are approaching the pattern altitude."

Risky wrestled with the controls as they reentered the traffic pattern. Feeling the craft respond to his inputs did help him feel better, but he was glad when Vicky took control and landed the aircraft. When they taxied clear and opened a window, the queasiness began to subside. He could see his father standing at the fence when they parked. As soon as the propellor stopped, he unbuckled and got out of the airplane, back on solid ground. He held on to the wing strut and tried to look casual as his stomach returned to normal.

"Feeling better?" asked Vicky as she tied down the airplane.

"Much better, yeah."

"You get over it with time. I threw up the first time I went flying in a small plane."

"You did? And you kept flying?"

"Sure. I wasn't going to let a little temporary airsickness keep me from flying. I knew that as my situational awareness improved, the queasiness would go away." She grabbed the keys from the ignition and closed the door. "The most important takeaway for you today is to be honest about where you are in that target. Next time we fly, you'll be able to absorb more of the experience, just like the roller coaster ride."

As they walked back into the building, Risky headed toward his father, seated in the lobby. "Hang on there," said Vicky. "We still need to debrief today's lesson. You're going to find that you learn as much in the debrief after flying as you do when you are actually in the aircraft."

Risky shrugged at his father and followed Vicky back into the room. As they sat down, Vicky asked, "So, did you ever get into the Yellow or Red today?"

Risky laughed, "A better question would be, did I ever get out of the Yellow or Red?"

Vicky smiled. "I love your candor. It's going to serve you well. As you get used to the environment and know what to look for, your perceptions will improve, and your reactions will be more appropriate. But you did well today for your first flight. Let's talk about the things we learned today."

Vicky reviewed the maneuvers they performed and explained the aerodynamic control surfaces they manipulated. Then glancing up at the posters on the wall, she continued, "Flying not only involves manipulating the controls but also understanding human factors. You got to experience some of this today as you moved from Green to Yellow to Red and back to Green. Did you notice any of that attention narrowing we talked about?"

"Yes indeed." Risky replied.

"Well, as we continue our training, or when you're off doing your own thing, try to recognize it. We already talked about how the perception of danger or risk can cause it, but there are other factors also. You did a good job recognizing your Green-Yellow-Red state today during the lesson. See if you notice it any other time. You can see it in yourself and even in other people when you get the hang of it. You're going to find it not only impacts perceptions; it can affect the ability to think through problems and even communicate with other people. "We'll talk about it more next time." She glanced at her watch and stood to signal the end of the debrief. "Let's go talk to your father about scheduling your next flight."

Two days later, Risky's father dropped him off for another flight lesson. This time Risky had prepared. He had downloaded some material to study and learned about basic aircraft controls. He watched a few videos online about flying. He even downloaded a free flying game for his gaming console. At first, he stared at the virtual instruments while he was flying, but then he remembered Vicky's instruction about sight picture. He practiced flying straight and level and then incorporated turns. Soon he could manage the basic maneuvers. Confident in his new skills, he tried a few aileron rolls and even a loop. It took a few hours, but he was determined to demonstrate his skills and not get airsick this time. Mostly, he really wanted to try an aileron roll.

When he got to the briefing room, Vicky was writing on the whiteboard. She had already drawn the same target on the board and was putting up a list of maneuvers.

"I'm going to stay in the Green today," stated Risky as soon as he walked in.

"I'm not sure that's even possible," replied Vicky. She looked at him and grinned. "Not to mention you're wearing a red t-shirt."

"This is the shirt I wore that day on the roller coaster. It's lucky." Risky frowned. What do you mean you don't think it's possible?"

"Even professional pilots with years of experience get pushed into the Yellow and Red. It isn't always about staying out of the Yellow or Red. It's about recognizing when you are out of the Green so you can use a resource to get you back there." She sat down. "That's why it's called Risk and Resource Management. You have to recognize how the changing risks affect you and manage them with resources."

"What's a resource?" he asked.

"Right, we were going to talk about that. Resources are controls that are in place to reduce your risks, like the traffic laws for driving. You remember how we used a checklist before we took off? Well, that checklist is a resource to prevent us from missing an important step. Resources help us improve performance and manage or reduce risk." She pointed back at the posters. "See how when the block has a hole in it a mistake can get through, but when the block is solid the mistake bounces off? That is just a visualization of how using Resources can catch an error before it causes an undesired outcome."

"Oh, like that irritating light in my dad's car that goes off every time you exceed the speed limit."

"Right. So you don't get a speeding ticket."

"Yeah, but it is still irritating."

She rolled her eyes. "We'll talk about that more later. Let's talk about flying now."

Risky nodded. "I studied the things you told me to, and I watched some videos online. I don't want to look like such a newb today."

"Great! I'm glad you came prepared. Do you play any sports?"

"I play soccer."

"What are some of the basic skills you need to be a good soccer player?"

"Let's see... dribbling, passing, shooting, trapping, and learning not to touch the ball with your hands, unless you're the goalie."

"When you first started playing, how did you develop those skills?"

"Our coach made us do drills."

"You mean you couldn't just read about playing soccer?"

"Like that would work," scoffed Risky.

"Well, it's the same with flying." She pointed to the list on the board. The first two Resources you need to develop are knowledge and skills. You studied the materials I assigned to gain knowledge. In the airplane today, we'll focus on skills—manipulating the controls. Knowledge and skill are two basic Resources to help you stay in the Green and get back into the Green. Let's talk about the flight controls and how to manipulate them correctly."

Vicky continued the briefing by discussing the flight controls and how to fly the airplane through a variety of basic maneuvers. Risky listened, but the whole time he was thinking about how he had learned all of this through watching the videos and practicing his flying skills on the video game. He was determined to stay in the Green all day today, and secretly he was thinking about doing an aileron roll.

This time Risky learned about the preflight and actually understood some of the things Vicky explained to him. He was able to buckle into the seat and get his headset on without any help. He even understood some of the preflight procedure. The information from the ATIS made a little more sense, and he was able to start the engine with her coaching. Overall, he felt like he was getting the hang of it.

When the tower cleared them for takeoff, she said, "Put one hand on the throttle and the other hand on the yoke. On the ground, steer with the gentle inputs from the rudder pedals. Rotate at 65 knots on the airspeed indicator."

"You're going to let me do the takeoff?"

"This is a flying lesson, isn't it?"

"Yeah."

"Then you need to fly, just like you needed to practice those soccer skills."

"Sweet!" He did as she instructed, and in a few moments, they were airborne. The sight picture on takeoff and climb looked similar to the video game. He practiced coordinated turns, holding straight and level flight, and even practiced a few stalls without getting nauseous. He felt like he was able to keep up much better today. He even felt confident at the controls on this flight, like he could actually become a pilot if he wanted.

"You're doing much better today. Are you ready to go back to the pattern and try some landings?" asked Vicky.

"Sure." He turned the aircraft and pointed it back in the general direction of the city.

"Let me get the latest ATIS," said Vicky, and she changed the frequency on the radio. The automated voice began broadcasting the latest weather conditions at the airfield.

Risky had a sudden impulse to do an aileron roll and show Vicky how much he had learned. He had mastered it in the video game. How hard could it be? He looked at the ground. It looked like he had enough altitude. He could see Vicky focused on getting the ATIS. He rolled the yoke and extended the ailerons to the stops and the aircraft began to fall like a rock as the wings rolled.

"I have the aircraft," shouted Vicky over the headset. She snapped the controls out of his hands about the time the aircraft reached ninety degrees of bank. She reversed the controls and then gently recovered from the dive that resulted from the attempt. Once they were back in level flight, she looked directly at him. "What was that all about?"

He shrugged. "I wanted to try an aileron roll. I've done them on this video game I got and they looked fun."

"They looked fun?" She shook her head. "Yeah, they're fun all right, until your engine quits because it can't get fuel, or you exceed the limitations of the aircraft, or get disoriented and crash into the ground. Yeah, just loads of fun."

She turned the aircraft towards the pattern entry point. "You're done flying for today. Keep your hands in your lap until we get on the ground."

"You're not going to tell my dad are you?"

She let out a sigh. "We're not even going to discuss that right now. Just sit there. We'll discuss it in the debrief."

Risky nodded and stared out the window as she flew them back to the airport and landed.

Vicky began the debrief. "So, did you reach your goal of staying in the Green all day today?"

Risky was a little surprised by the question after the way the flight had ended. "I know that you had to help me a lot, but I feel like I stayed in the Green. I felt comfortable in the airplane today."

"And what about your attempt at an aileron roll?"

"I really thought I could do it. I'm sorry."

"Okay, thank you for the apology, but do you think you were in the Green when you attempted the aileron roll?"

Risky frowned. "I felt really good about everything today. I guess I got carried away."

"Even though you felt good and considered yourself in the Green, that was an excellent example of how inexperience and lack of knowledge caused you to underestimate the risk. Any time you exceed the performance limitations of the aircraft, the expectations of the other crew member, or break an FAA rule, you have definitely pushed yourself, and everyone in the aircraft, into the Red." She shook her head. "And you nearly accomplished all of those. You might feel comfortable, but you have definitely accepted enormous unnecessary risk." With that, she stopped talking and stared at him with a blank face. "A lucky t-shirt won't save you."

Risky looked at the floor. "I'm sorry. Please don't tell my dad. He'll ground me from driving even longer."

Vicky paused for a moment and then pulled out a pen and ripped a piece of paper from her notepad, and began writing. "Okay Risky," she said, emphasizing his nickname like it was unpleasant in her mouth. "I'm writing down the four principles of risk management. If you lose this piece of paper, you can find them in the Pilot's Handbook of Aeronautical Knowledge, and it certainly wouldn't hurt you to read the whole book."

She verbalized the concepts as she wrote.
- "Accept no unnecessary risk.
- Anticipate and manage risk by planning.
- Accept risk when benefits outweigh the cost.
- Make risk decisions at the right level.

If you can memorize these before the next lesson, I will let you keep flying with me, and I won't tell your dad." She handed him the piece of paper.

Risky looked up. "Thank you! I'll do it. I promise."

Vicky cut him off with her hand. "BUT. If you ever try a stunt like that again, you will have to find a new instructor and I will explain to your dad that you certainly deserve the nickname 'Risky' and don't need to be anywhere near the controls of an airplane or a motor vehicle. Am I clear?"

"Yes, crystal clear." Risky let out a sigh of relief. "Thank you."

Vicky stood and opened the door. "Get out of here before I change my mind, and don't come to the next lesson without memorizing those four principles."

> "IT'S COOL! I DID THIS ALL TIME IN STARFOX!"

JUST BECAUSE THE PILOT-IN-COMMAND LOOKS *LIKE* THEY'RE IN THE GREEN —

IT DOESN'T MEAN THEY ARE!

Learning to recognize our risk state is the first step to managing risk. This is true for the individual pilot flying solo, a flight crew working together on a crew aircraft, and for an entire flight operation. How do you know when you have exceeded an acceptable level of risk? How do you know when your situational assessment has narrowed, or you have lost situational awareness? How can you recognize deteriorating conditions or capabilities in yourself or in others?

The target represents our risk state. It is a tangible expression of our current level of risk. Even expert pilots will find themselves susceptible to common human deficiencies that allow us to drift into the Yellow and Red.

Often, we don't recognize the increase in risk and/or decrease in capability until we have committed an error we normally do not commit or find ourselves in a high-risk situation we would normally have avoided. Sometimes we sense that something isn't right, but can't put a finger on it. When we are working with other people, we may find communication becomes strained or misunderstandings increase. At the individual level, it can manifest itself as an emotion or gut feeling that's difficult to describe.

Although it may be difficult to describe at times, we can recognize the symptoms—making small mistakes, having more difficulty communicating, losing your sense of humor, channelized attention, inattention, delayed reaction or responses, difficulty managing distractions, taking shortcuts instead of following regular policies and procedures. Because it's easier to see in others than in ourselves, we should learn to recognize when others are entering the Yellow or the Red because it will influence how we respond to their input and needs. For example, Vicky's reaction to Risky's attempted aileron roll clearly indicated she was in the Red. That made it obvious to Risky that the time for joking was over.

Perhaps the most important feature of the target is that it gives us a common language to address the increasing risk and decreasing performance. When we verbalize, "I'm in the Red," to someone else who understands the target, it immediately communicates the current risk state and should trigger a response—assess or reassess the situation, monitor performance, attempt to provide more time, or offer assistance. The common language is easier to understand and reduces reaction time, while increasing the application of Resources to move the individual, the aircraft, or the operation back into the Green as soon as possible.

It's also important to remember that risk in one area of your life can impact performance in another. For example, a stressful interaction at home can impact performance on the job. Learning to recognize when stress or risk is impacting your personal performance is critical to consistent success.

Yellow and Red can also be contagious. It's easy to be drawn into the Yellow or Red if someone you care about, follow, or respect is already there. It's better to step back and maintain a Green perspective so can provide constructive help. Keep in mind advice is sometimes hard to accept when people are currently in the Yellow or Red.

Think about a stressful time in your life. What did it feel like? What were the emotions you experienced? How did you perform? What Resources did you use to reduce the impact of the stress? How did others treat you during the experience? How did you treat others? What was the final outcome?

Imagine going through the same experience again, armed with a language to communicate your emotional/awareness state. Imagine how having Resources to help you cope with the situation would have changed it. What if you could reach out to people you trusted with a simple phrase to alert them or call them into action on your behalf? Would the experience be the same? Would the final outcome be the same? Even if nothing bad happened, could you have excelled?

Once Risk is recognized, it can be verbalized. The target provides simple language to communicate potential risk. It is one of the fundamental tools of RRM that can reduce risk, achieve safety, and expedite expertise.

Chapter Five: Understand the Process

ABCD

"Excellence is a continuous process and not an accident."
—A. P. J. Abdul Kalam

Key Concepts
- Effective risk decision-making requires a continuous process that integrates four fundamental leadership skills: situational assessment, decision-making, communication and a commitment to continuous improvement.
- **ABCD** is a fast and continuous process that maintains situational awareness, balances priorities, communicates intentions, promotes action, and facilitates continuous improvement.
- **Assess**—Assess the Green-Yellow-Red status. Maintain situational awareness. Continuously evaluate what is happening now to identify, integrate, and apply the critical elements of information and determine how it affects the future outcome.
- **Balance**—Balance the amount of time available, operational priorities, and available Resources. Make decisions to maintain redundancy and distribute workload.
- **Communicate**—Communicate risk and intentions. Effectively communicate in the appropriate style (Green, Yellow,

or Red) to gather additional information and create a shared mental model is established.
- **Do and Debrief**—Do execute the plan in timely manner and Debrief the results. Perform basic and complex tasks to the best of your ability, then continuously work toward improving performance and reducing risk by improving the application of Resources and management skills. Commit to continuous improvement by conducting self-debriefs and learning from others.
- Over time this process becomes intuitive, but understanding the elements of the process helps us analyze our performance and improve it.

Risky drove to the airport with his work uniform on. He would have to go straight to work after his flying lesson today, but Vicky was true to her word. He showed up for the next lesson with the material memorized, and she didn't tell his father about the attempted aileron roll.

After a few lessons, he struck a deal with his father. As long as he worked at least 20 hours a week and contributed half of his pay to the lessons, his father would cover the rest of the cost until he got his private pilot certificate. Not only that, but he ungrounded him early so he could drive to work at the sandwich shop.

Risky felt like the summer was shaping up rather nicely. He wanted to get as much flying done as he could before he had to go back to live with his mother in the fall, maybe even finish his private pilot license. His mother hadn't reacted well to the news of the flying lessons, and he was worried she would stop them when he went back to live with her. If that was going to happen, he needed to do well on his landings today.

When he walked into the briefing room, Vicky was already writing on the whiteboard. "Do you know your ABCs?" she asked.

"Doesn't everyone?" he replied with a chuckle. He took a seat and saw she had put up the letters A, B, C, and D.

She turned and sat across from him. "Well, today I'm going to teach you the ABCs of flying. I'm going to help you develop your process for managing the tasks and risks of a flight."

"Okay, that sounds kind of complicated. I was hoping to just get the landings down."

"It's not difficult. Easy as ABC." She scooted her chair closer to the whiteboard. "In fact, it ties in nicely to the traffic pattern and your landings. For example, you are in the Casa Grande pattern on downwind for runway 23." She drew a long rectangle representing the runway. "The winds are 200 at 10 knots." She drew an arrow representing the wind direction. "You make a mental **Assessment** of what the winds will do to your pattern." She put check mark by the A in the circle.

"Then you **Balance** that information with any procedures or policies, like crosswind limits. Those winds are clearly within our limits." She put a check mark by the B.

"Then you **Communicate** your position to other aircraft in the pattern with a radio call. What is the radio call as you turn base?"

"Um... N6156S turning base," answered Risky.

"Don't forget to start with 'Casa Grande traffic' so that everyone knows where you are, and you should include the runway. Try again."

Risky paused and then stated, "Casa Grande traffic, N6156S turning base for runway 23."

She put a checkmark by the C. "Good. Now the most important part of the process, **Do**. You simply execute your intentions. In this case, it means turning base for runway 23 in Casa Grande while adjusting for the winds, watching for any traffic, and communicating with everyone else in the pattern. ABC*D*."

Risky felt a bit overwhelmed, but he nodded.

"I see a bit of confusion in your face," said Vicky.

Risky let out a sigh. "How am I going to remember all this stuff?"

"Did you think about driving to the airport today? Do you remember anything about the drive?"

Risky reflected for a moment. "About the only thing that stands out is some lady texting at the light when it turned green. I had to honk my horn to get her to move."

"You mean you don't remember turning the steering wheel to make the turns or stepping on the brake at the stop lights?"

"Well… I know I did those things, but they don't stand out in my memory. I just did them without thinking about them."

"So, driving has become almost subconscious?"

Risky shrugged. "I guess so."

"The same will happen with manipulating the controls of the aircraft. Think about what you do behind the wheel of a car." She pointed at the A on the board. "You're constantly assessing the path of the vehicle." She drew an arrow between the A and the D. "And you turn the wheel to make it go where you want it to go."

Risky frowned. "What about the B and the C?"

"This isn't a linear process. Sometimes you make intuitive decisions based on your past experiences. Do you need to balance and communicate every time you turn the wheel of the car? For the simple process of keeping the car on the road, you simply assess and do. But what if you are driving on a narrow mountain road at night during a rainstorm? What would be different?"

"I would probably turn on my windshield wipers."

"Would you go the same speed?"

"No, I would slow down."

"Why?"

"Because I don't want to slide off the road."

She put a checkmark beside the A on the board. "You assessed that the road conditions were different. You balanced the priority of driving fast or staying on the road and decided that staying on the road was more important. There isn't a need to communicate if you are driving by yourself, but if you tap on the brakes to slow down, you are communicating your intentions to the cars behind you. Then you slowed down and drove slower." She put a cap on the marker and put it down. "ABC*D*."

"Don't get too hung up on the mechanics of the process. It will feel natural, just like driving, as you practice. In fact, once you create the habit pattern, the only time you consciously run through the ABC*D* process is if you sense the situation may be going into the Yellow or Red, or maybe before you begin a new phase of flight."

She picked back up the marker. "But whether you are doing it from habit or intentionally, the process and language are useful both in the airplane and in the debrief." She circled the *D*. "In fact, you may have noticed that the D is italicized. That's because it stands for 'Do' and 'Debrief.' This model helps us breakdown a complex process into simpler pieces so that we can better understand how to improve it."

"Kind of like the team meeting with the coach after a soccer match?"

"Exactly. You spend some time after the game discussing the details and how to improve or reinforcing the things you did well."

Risky nodded. "I guess your debrief the other day was like the time the coach threatened to bench me if I didn't start passing the ball a bit more."

Vicky smiled. "Yeah, kind of like that. Now, let's talk about the traffic pattern in Casa Grande..."

They spent the remainder of the briefing discussing traffic pattern operations. She talked through each phase step-by-step emphasizing the continuous process of flying an airplane. When they walked out of the briefing room to the airplane, Risky felt a little overwhelmed by all the information, but when he started the walkaround, everything seemed to fall into a familiar rhythm under Vicky's watchful eye.

Risky ran a finger along the propellor blade. "I wanted to thank you again for not telling my dad about the aileron roll. I promise it won't happen again."

"I must admit, that pushed me into the Red," answered Vicky.

Risky checked the engine oil. "Yeah, I could tell during the debrief."

"Well, I apologize for being in the Red during the debrief, but it's a good lesson on how communication changes when we're under stress." She stopped and folded her arms. "As a flight attendant I've seen how communication has to change when someone moves from the Green to the Yellow, or Red."

Risky continued the walkaround. "Yeah? Like what?"

"Well, one time we lost pressurization and all the oxygen masks dropped. I stopped my service and immediately sat down and started using oxygen, but my coworker kept filling drinks." She shook her head and laughed. "I had to practically yell at him to get him to sit down. Granted he was probably hypoxic."

"Hypoxic?"

"It's when you don't have enough oxygen getting to your brain and you're not able to think clearly."

Risky smirked. "That's what happened to me right before I tried the aileron roll."

Vicky shook her head and smiled. "When we're in the Green, like right now, we communicate using body language, nuance, and humor, but when we move into the Yellow or Red, it interferes with our perception and can lead to misunderstanding. When someone is in the Red, we have to be more direct, maybe even forceful to get them out of the Red."

Risky checked the rudder. "Kind of like taking the aircraft and telling me not to touch the controls?"

Vicky smiled. "Exactly. But did you trust me when I took the controls?"

Risky nodded and moved along the fuselage. "Yeah, of course."

"Why?"

He shrugged. "Because I knew you were a professional."

"So, you trusted me when I had to be direct. When you follow policies and procedures it builds trust with the other crew members and they're more likely to listen to you and cooperate when they get into the Red."

Risky grinned. "To be honest, I was also afraid of you, at least a little bit."

Vicky gave him a blank stare. "A healthy respect for authority is good." Then she broke into a laugh. "C'mon. Let's go fly."

Risky took off without any intervention from Vicky and felt the familiar rush of watching the ground fall away beneath him. It was a typical Arizona summer day, and the temperature was on the rise, bouncing the aircraft around in the building thermal convection.

"Chandler Tower, N6156S departing the pattern to the southwest," he said over the radio as he turned towards the practice area and continued his climb. As he rolled out of the turn, he felt the power come back, and the propellor slowed to idle. He looked down and saw that Vicky had pulled the power to idle.

"You just lost your engine," said Vicky. "What are you going to do?"

Risky felt a sense of panic, and even though he opened his mouth, no words came out. He let the nose fall and started a glide.

"Okay, remember the ABCDs," said Vicky. "First assess. The engine quit. So, we need to maintain control of the aircraft and give ourselves as much time as possible to handle the situation. Establish a glide speed that gives the best range, or our L/Dmax. For this aircraft that's 65 knots. Trim the aircraft to hold 65 knots with the power off."

Risky held the nose up and trimmed it to establish the glide.

"See. You already went from A to D without even thinking about the letters. Now we reassess and start looking for a forced landing site. What do you see that might work?"

Risky looked off the nose and saw a golf course. "How about that golf course?"

"That would work. We could line up on the fairway and set it down." Risky made a slight turn to line up on the fairway.

"If there's any time, we can go back and assess. Why did the engine quit?

Check the fuel selector. Check the ignition. If you are flying with another pilot, you would use the "C" and communicate to talk about the problem and balance the workload. One of you can fly, and the other can continue to analyze the situation and communicate with ATC. We can talk about this more in our debrief."

Risky looked at the horizon, and even though he knew it was an artificial situation, he felt his grip tighten on the yoke.

"After assessing and analyzing the problem, we determine the motor isn't going to restart, and we continue with Do and focus on the emergency landing." She pushed the throttle in half way and initiated a climb. "Go ahead and add power to resume the climb."

Risky pushed the throttle to the stop and resumed the climb.

"You see the ABCD process is really just a continuous, nonlinear process. The parts only become obvious when we are faced with potential risk or an unusual situation. It just takes experience and practice."

Once Vicky saw him relax a bit, she continued, "One of the good things about the ABCD is that it can reduce that 'panic' feeling by providing a defined, and eventually instinctive process for handling something unexpected. We can talk more about that in the debrief."

A few minutes later, they approached the pattern at Casa Grande from the North. Vicky pointed at the moving map display. "Okay, we are about fifteen miles away from the airfield. We have assessed that they are using runway 23 from the AWOS. How will we enter the pattern?"

Risky looked down at the display. He could see that if they continued on this heading, they would fly over the middle of the runway. He frowned because he had a hard time visualizing the pattern entry. "Should I turn so that we can line up for the runway?"

"Okay, what is the direction of the traffic pattern?"

"Left?"

"Correct." She held her pen up to the display and aligned it with the runway in use. "So if you turn left after takeoff..." She moved her pen to demonstrate. "This is what it will look like." She put her pen over their position. "We are coming from this direction. What if we crossed over midfield and then turned left to join the traffic pattern?"

Risky could visualize the pattern now and understood. "Yeah, that would work."

"Great! We accomplished the A. Now let's move to the B and C." She tuned the radio to the pattern frequency. "What are we going to say over the radio?"

"Uh...Who they are...who we are...and what we want. N6156S entering the pattern from the North?"

"That's close, but remember to announce, 'Casa Grande Traffic' and tell them who you are; where you are; and your intentions." She pointed to the display. "We are about ten miles north of the airfield."

"Casa Grande traffic, N6156S, ten miles north of the field... um, entering the pattern?"

"Entering the pattern for a midfield downwind runway 23," she added. "Key the mike and make the call."

Risky hesitated and then keyed the microphone. "Casa Grande traffic, N6156S, ten miles north of the field, entering midfield for runway 23."

"Okay, not bad. Now we listen up on the radio for traffic and build our situational awareness as we do what we told everyone we would do. ABCD. Easy peasy."

She coached him through the pattern entry, and they entered the downwind.

He struggled to control the aircraft as they changed airspeeds, altitudes, and configurations, but he enjoyed being close to the ground. They lined up for landing and extended the flaps.

Vicky began talking him through the corrections. "Okay now we focus almost entirely on the A and the D, just like driving, but with an extra dimension. You can see we are getting a little high. Think of it this way on approach, use power to control descent rate and pitch to control airspeed. We drift a little to the left and you make a small correction with the ailerons. We are getting a little fast. Make an adjustment with the pitch. It is a constant process of assessing and doing, and the quicker you can assess the change, the quicker you can adjust your flight path. Aimpoint. Airspeed."

Risky pulled back too much on the yoke for the first landing, and the aircraft rose like a balloon away from the runway. When he adjusted to land, Vicky intervened.

"Go around," she directed.

He pushed up the power, and she coached him through the procedure. "Okay, when you get in that situation, you have to make a quick assessment and balance your priorities. You ballooned. You wanted to land, but you don't want to land so hard that you break something. This is a case where you use a personal policy to create a mindset of 'if I balloon, I will go around.' That way, after you've made the assessment, your decision will be better AND faster. In other words, you can balance your priorities quickly and take the required actions. Constant ABCD. Eventually, you'll be able to do all of this without any coaching or help from me."

For the next forty-five minutes, Risky struggled to control the aircraft in the traffic pattern, make the radio calls, and accomplish some good landings. Every time he felt like he could accomplish one of the tasks, he would struggle with another. It felt like he was holding on to the tail of the airplane, and it was pulling him around the pattern. One landing would be good, and the next one would be a disaster. He wondered if he would ever be able to do it all together. When they departed the pattern in Casa Grande and headed back to Chandler, Risky wondered if he was cut out to be a pilot.

"Nice job!" said Vicky. "Let's go back and do one more landing in Chandler and call it a day."

Risky nodded but didn't say anything. "You okay?" asked Vicky.

"Well, I thought I would do better today. I really wanted to get my landings down so I can get my Private Pilot Certificate before I have to leave at the end of the summer."

"You're learning a complex skill. It takes practice. I thought you did quite well. Just focus on this last pattern and then we can talk about it all in the debrief."

Risky nodded and renewed his focus on the task at hand. He listened to the weather information and used the techniques Vicky had shown him to assess the pattern. Then he selected the tower frequency and tried to build his situational awareness through the radio calls. With her help, he made the pattern entry radio call. He found himself constantly assessing his path and the pattern, balancing the workload, communicating over the radio, and making the necessary adjustments. When he lined up on final, he shifted all of his focus to flying the final approach and made a nice landing without any help from Vicky.

"As simple as ABC*D*," she said as they cleared the runway.

When they got to the briefing room, Vicky circled the D on the whiteboard. "This letter separates the professionals from the amateurs. Professionals are constantly striving to improve their performance and learn from their mistakes. How do you think it went today?"

Risky shook his head. "I felt like such a newb. It felt like I was holding on by the tail of the airplane."

"Okay, what do you need to improve?"

"Everything."

Vicky smiled. "So, basically you are saying that you stunk, and in order for you to get better, you need to stink less?"

Risky laughed. "Yeah, I guess so." "Is that a helpful debrief?"

He shook his head. "Not really."

"Why not?"

He shrugged. "I don't know what to work on. I don't know what I need to do to improve."

"Exactly! In order for the debrief to be effective, we have to be specific. We have to focus on the things you can learn and improve before you go fly again. The easiest way to do this is to break our flight down into smaller phases of flight. What did you think about the takeoff, climb, and navigation to the practice area?"

"Actually I think that went well," he replied. "I'm even getting familiar enough with the route to the practice area to have a moment to feel sorry for all the folks stuck in traffic down there."

She gave him a complimentary chuckle. "Okay the repetition is helping you stay in the Green on the departure. What happened when I pulled the power back for our simulated engine failure."

He grimaced. "Yellow for sure with maybe a sprinkling of Red."

"That's normal when an aircraft malfunction startles us. That's why we train and practice. Our goal in training is to create an instinctive reaction to that feeling. You sense something is different, ensure your priorities remain intact, possibly communicate to get more information, or as in this case, we needed to go straight to the "Do" to maintain control of the aircraft and establish the best glide speed. Once we established the glide and you picked out your landing spot, did you feel yourself sliding back toward the Green?"

"Not really. I kinda froze for a moment."

"That's not unusual the first time, but keep in mind, we practice simulated emergency operations for two reasons. One is to ensure you have the knowledge and skill to perform the correct actions, but the other is to develop resilience in unexpected events."

"Resilience?"

She nodded. "When you can intuitively recognize your Green-Yellow-Red state and automatically respond with the ABCD, beginning with situation assessment, instead of letting your brain shut down, you'll be resilient in stressful situations."

"I could use a little resilience when I'm trying to get a date."

Vicky smiled. "Well loverboy, these principles apply to more than just flying." She stood to write on the whiteboard. "Let's talk about pattern operations."

For the next few minutes, she discussed all the policies and procedures for normal pattern operations. She gave him some homework assignments to study and encouraged him to listen to the traffic pattern radio to practice his radio communication. Then she talked to him about chair flying the pattern before his next lesson. When he finished, he had specific items to review and practice before the next flight.

He hopped in the truck and started the drive to work, still thinking about today's lesson. When he pulled into the parking lot, he barely remembered the drive. Just like Vicky said, the process of driving had become almost subconscious for him.

"As simple as ABC*D*," he mumbled to himself and wondered if flying would ever be that easy for him.

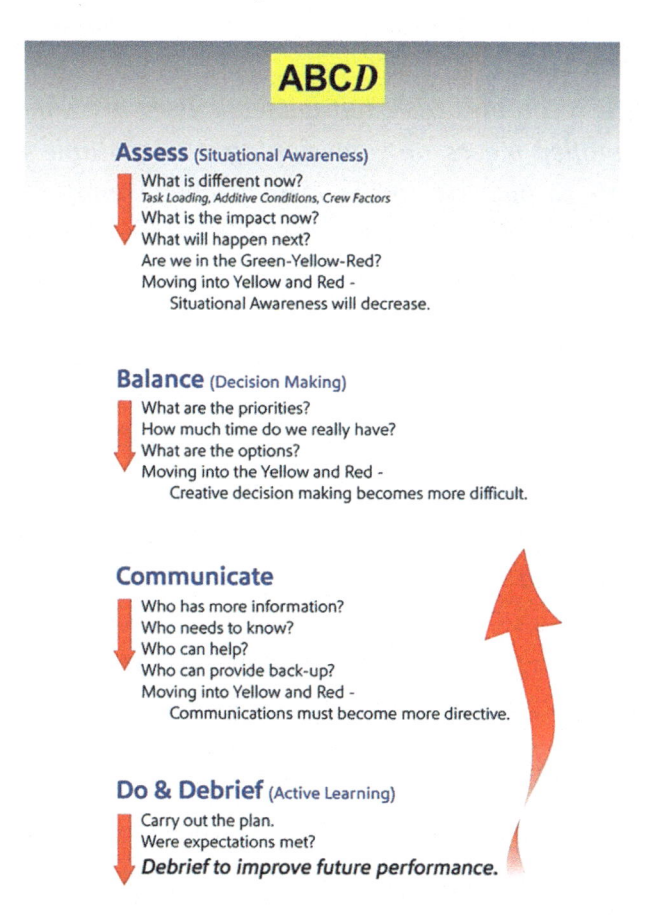

ABC*D*

Assess (Situational Awareness)
What is different now?
Task Loading, Additive Conditions, Crew Factors
What is the impact now?
What will happen next?
Are we in the Green-Yellow-Red?
Moving into Yellow and Red -
   Situational Awareness will decrease.

Balance (Decision Making)
What are the priorities?
How much time do we really have?
What are the options?
Moving into the Yellow and Red -
   Creative decision making becomes more difficult.

Communicate
Who has more information?
Who needs to know?
Who can help?
Who can provide back-up?
Moving into Yellow and Red -
   Communications must become more directive.

Do & Debrief (Active Learning)
Carry out the plan.
Were expectations met?
Debrief to improve future performance.

Life is a journey, not a destination. The same is true of flying (and managing risk during a complex procedure); it is a process, not an event. What is the process we use to accomplish complex and risky tasks in order to achieve a safe outcome or improve performance?

In life, we develop our risk management process through trial and error without really thinking about the components and pieces of the process. It's almost a natural or subconscious act that we perform in rapid succession to achieve our goal. However, we didn't start by knowing the process. We learned it.

Do you remember learning to use a spoon? Probably not, but your parents most likely remember the first time you attempted the process. They taught you to perform that simple process and many other more complicated processes by breaking them down into simple, repeatable steps.

Flying is a complex task, but we learn it by breaking down the task into smaller pieces and developing a repeatable process for combining those pieces into the larger, more complex whole. The pioneers of aviation had to learn by trial and error. We have the advantage of years of experience broken down into small bite-size pieces. Aviation can, at times, be a high-risk, time-critical, complex operation. This requires intentional attention to the risk management process.

The ABCD process described in this chapter was not invented in the classroom. It is the result of observing successful pilots as they managed complex, time-critical tasks over several years. It was developed and refined as part of an instructional development strategy designed to train airline pilots. Data was collected on the human factors strategies used by successful crewmembers as well as the errors they made. This data helped define a simple process that integrated proactive risk management with crew resource management.

It may seem academic at first; however, practicing this until it becomes intuitive pays dividends. This fast, continuous, and nonlinear process maintains situational awareness, improves decision-making, and greatly improves communications. Most importantly, debriefing performance improves not only future performance but also improves personal resilience when you find yourself in the Yellow or Red.

When dutifully practiced, this process and the underlying skills lead to more complex attitudes and skills such as adaptability, flexibility, intentional attention (monitoring skills), teamwork, leadership, workload management, and resilience.

The components could have been labeled differently (indeed, others have), but in the end, the process is still the same — constantly observing, assessing, and reassessing; deciding what actions are the most urgent and important and applying available Resources; communicating with others; taking necessary actions; striving for continuous improvement.

Of interest, an Air Force fighter pilot, Colonel John Boyd, developed a process known as the OODA loop (which stands for Observe, Orient, Decide, Act) to describe how fighter pilots attain a competitive advantage. His observation was that the faster a pilot could complete the OODA loop, the better their advantage. The OODA loop model is still in use in many businesses and law enforcement. The RRM process is similar but combines the steps a bit differently and emphasizes the need for communication and debriefs.

As you continue your training, you will find that there is a much deeper level to each step of the ABCD process. Because the Green-Yellow-Red target and ABCD process are based on general Human Factors, these concepts and tools are not limited to airplanes or even just limited to safety. They can be applied to any situation or task, which means they can become an intuitive part of everyday life.

You will develop a process for situation assessment, balancing your Resources and workload to maintain your priorities and communicating your perceptions of risk and intentions. Keep it simple at first. The goal is for it to become a mostly subconscious process working in the background until you need to intentionally work through the steps when faced with higher risks. The RRM target and the ABCD process employed in the RRM model give you a starting point if you are new, and if you have years of experience, it can help you refine and improve your process. Using these tools will help you manage risks, achieve safety, and expedite expertise.

Chapter Six: Consider the Four Principles of Risk Management

"The essence of risk management lies in maximizing the areas where we have some control over the outcome while minimizing the areas where we have absolutely no control over the outcome."

—Peter L. Bernstein

Key Concepts
- Accept no unnecessary risk.
- Anticipate and manage risk by planning.
- Accept risk when benefits outweigh the cost.
- Make risk decisions at the right level.
- Risk and Resource Management is an integration of classic Crew Resource Management and Operational Risk Management.
- Risk management allows the pursuit of potential high-risk endeavors by creating controls and processes to decrease or mitigate the risk.

Risky woke up before his alarm went off and grabbed his phone to check the weather. It was going to be a clear day in the Phoenix area, but the winds were forecast to pick up before lunch. He wondered if the winds would keep him from completing his first solo flight today. He hoped not because he only had a few days before he had to go back to live with his mother.

A text came through from his father – *Hey son! I left early for work but I'm going to be near the airport on business today and wanted to watch you solo. What time is your flight?*

He shook his head and smiled. He knew his father didn't have any business in the area. His father had left early for work so he could be there to watch him solo today. He texted back – *My briefing starts at 0800. Should be airborne by 0900.*

His father texted back. *I should be there right before you get airborne.*

His stomach did a flip as he thought about his father watching as he flew solo for the first time. He was nervous enough already and having him there would only make it worse. *I'm in the Yellow and I haven't even left the house.* Then he laughed at himself, amused at thinking about the target spontaneously.

"I guess that's progress," he said to himself. He started to text his father back to ask him not to be there, but he knew it wouldn't do any good. He would sneak in to watch anyway. Nothing he could say would keep him away. Instead he texted—*Okay pops I'll look for you. Take some pictures for me.* He pulled on his lucky red t-shirt and headed out the door.

Risky sat in the briefing room, fidgeting with his phone, when Vicky walked in with two bottles of water. "I see you're wearing your lucky t-shirt," she said with a grin as she put a bottle of water in front of him. "Make sure you stay hydrated. It helps with the butterflies in your stomach as well."

He put down his phone and took a sip from the bottle. "Do you think I'll be able to solo today? I mean … the crosswinds might be out of limits by the time we get airborne."

She put down her water bottle and started writing on the whiteboard with her back to him. "Well, if you want to solo, you have to be able to make that decision. You'll be the Pilot in Command. What do you think?"

Risky wasn't really thirsty, but he took another drink of water to help himself think. "Well, the forecast winds during our scheduled time are right at crosswind limits for solo students. My father is driving up to watch me, and that makes me even more nervous. I'm not sure I want to risk looking like an idiot trying to land in strong crosswinds with him watching."

Vicky put down the marker and sat down. "Funny you should mention risk, since you'll be responsible for managing the risks as the PIC today." She smiled and pointed to the whiteboard. "Remember these Risky Rogers?"

He looked up at the whiteboard. She had written four bullets— the four principles of risk management. He knew about them, but only because she had insisted that he learn them. He blushed and nodded. "How can I forget?"

She smiled. "Yeah, I figured. How do they apply today?" she asked.

He shrugged. "I'm not sure. Every time I read these, they seem so... abstract."

"Well, let's see if we can apply the abstract and make it a little more concrete." She pointed at the board. "I like to start with number three – Accept risks when the benefits outweigh the cost. If we can't get past that one, none of the others matter anyway. Flying is risky, as you know. Flying solo for the first time is even more risky. What are the benefits of you flying solo today?"

"Well, I need solo time to get my Private Pilot certificate."

"Okay, you need solo time to achieve your goal. That's worth some risk. What else?"

He stared at the board, trying to think of an answer. "Because it would be fun?"

"There's nothing wrong with a little calculated risk taking in the name of fun, and flying an airplane by yourself is definitely fun."

He leaned back on the back legs of his chair. "Well, I want to solo before I have to go back to live with my mom. And my dad is coming to watch me today."

"Ooh! Parental pressure, or peer pressure, definitely can be a distraction, but it's also a good reason to fly today. If we can." She picked up a marker and put a checkmark next to the principle. "Now let's look at number one – Accept no unnecessary risk. What does that mean?"

"Well, we don't have to fly today."

"No, we don't, but we have already determined that there are some benefits with flying today. What would be an unnecessary risk?"

"If I took off in the airplane without your approval. He blushed and gave a sheepish grin. "Or tried to do an aileron roll in the pattern. Something like that?"

She chuckled. "Yeah, something like that, or if we ignored the crosswind limits simply because we wanted to please your father." She put another check on the board. "Yes. Definitely unnecessary! How do we accomplish the second one – Mitigate risk by planning?"

"Isn't that why we do a preflight briefing before we fly?"

"Yes, but how do we specifically mitigate risk for this flight today? What are the conditions that are pushing us toward the Yellow today?"

He chuckled. "You know what's weird? I actually thought about being in the Yellow this morning when my dad texted me to tell me he was coming to watch. Weird right?"

"That's not weird. That's progress. What else might push you into the Yellow today?"

"The winds. I don't want to look incompetent landing in crosswinds with my dad watching."

"Okay, you've actually mentioned several things in that one sentence. The winds are a hazard. It's your first solo. And your dad is watching. We call those additive conditions." She put three blocks on top of each other on the whiteboard. "When we look at risk, it's important to look at the whole picture. Mishaps are rarely caused by a single hazard, but more often when multiple conditions stack up."

"Let's talk about mitigating them one at a time. Do you think I would sign you off to solo if I didn't think you were ready?"

Risky shook his head. "No, you would definitely make me prepare more."

She crossed out one of the blocks. "We've adequately prepared for your first solo. What have you done to push aside your concern about your dad watching?"

"I realized he is going to come watch no matter what I do." He shrugged. "I guess I just accepted it."

She crossed out another block. "You've pushed aside your concern for your dad's reaction. What about the winds?"

Risky frowned. "The forecast calls for some increasing crosswinds."

"You're right. The winds are a hazard, and the risks associated with strong crosswinds are things like running off the side of the runway or having to divert to another field if they go out of limits. How can we plan for those risks and prepare to manage them?"

"We can get a good weather briefing."

"That's a good resource to start with, but what do we do with the information?"

"Talk about crosswind landing procedures?"

"Another good resource. What's your plan if the winds go out of limits while you're in the pattern? Where will you go?"

The room seemed to be getting warmer, and it felt like his forehead was about to burst into perspiration. "I didn't think I was allowed to go anywhere else on my first solo."

"You're not supposed to, under normal conditions, but we're planning for contingencies. We're mitigating risk by planning." She grabbed her iPad and opened a chart. "You remember going over to Mesa Gateway? If the winds are as forecast—300@10—that's a direct crosswind here for runway 04/22." She pointed to the diagram for the nearby airport. "But that's a headwind for runway 30/12 at Mesa Gateway. Why can't we use that airfield as an option for planning?"

"I never thought of that because I didn't think I was allowed to go there."

Vicky smiled and put another check on the board. "That leads us to the last principle – Make risk decisions at the right level. You're right. Our school policy doesn't allow you to leave Chandler Airpark's airspace on the first solo, under normal circumstances. That means that we have taken that risk decision away from you and made it at a higher level. What is the crosswind limit for the C-172 we will be flying today?"

"15 knots."

"Okay, does the school have a stricter crosswind limit for solo students?"

The question stumped him, and he felt even more nervous than when the briefing started. "I don't know."

"The school policy dictates that the maximum crosswind limit for solo students is 10 knots. In other words, you don't get to make that risk decision. The decision has been made at a higher level. All you have to do is follow the policy." She put a checkmark next to the principle. "Now that we understand how to apply these principles in this situation let's go back and mitigate more risk by planning out this flight."

She made him talk through the crosswind landing procedure and techniques for maintaining aircraft control with crosswinds. They pulled up the information for Mesa Gateway and briefed the steps for diverting there in the event of an emergency or if the crosswinds exceeded the limit. They went through the flight step-by-step, discussing the hazards, risks, and Resources available, and rehearsed several emergency procedures.

At the end of the briefing, she stood and began to erase the whiteboard. "You will be the PIC when I get out of the aircraft, but remember, I'll be on the radio if you need to use me as a resource."

His father was sitting in the lobby when he walked up to the desk to check out the airplane. He smiled and gave him a thumbs up but didn't say anything. Risky smiled back and gave him a thumbs up as well, trying to look confident, but his stomach did a somersault. For years he had complained about not having enough freedom and independence. Now he was about to fly solo, and all he felt was nervous.

He grabbed the keys and clipboard for the Cessna 172 and walked to the aircraft. The sky was clear, and like a typical August morning in the Valley of the Sun, it was starting to heat up. He could see the windsock fluttering. He was going to have to deal with the crosswind, but that didn't bother him as much as knowing his father was going to be watching.

He focused on the tasks at hand and completed the preflight as Vicky walked up and climbed into the airplane. Working to control his nerves, he walked in front of the airplane and turned to face it. "No chocks. No chains. No taxi obstacles," he said to himself. "Let's go fly."

He climbed into the left seat of the aircraft, buckled up, and began running the checklist. When he listened to the ATIS, the winds were 300 degrees at 8 knots—8 knots of crosswind, just within limits for a solo. With the checklist complete, he was ready to start the engine. He glanced at Vicky, but she just smiled at him and sat there like a passenger.

"Clear prop!" he shouted. The motor sputtered to life when he turned the ignition, and the propwash poured into the hot cockpit and filled it with the smell of exhaust. He glanced back at the FBO and saw his father taking pictures.

He keyed the microphone. "Chandler tower, Cessna N6156S, taxi from the FBO for pattern work, with information Sierra."

"N6156S, taxi to runway 22R."

"Taxi to runway 22R." He pushed up the power and began taxiing out. Vicky sat in the right seat, observing his actions with her hands in her lap like she was a passenger.

After completing his runup, the tower cleared them for takeoff. He aligned the nose of the aircraft with the runway and pushed in the throttle. He felt the winds push the craft and adjusted the controls appropriately for a crosswind takeoff. Within a few seconds, they were airborne and climbing up to pattern altitude.

Without any help, he flew around the pattern and lined up on final approach with all of the checklist items complete. Tower cleared them for the option. Feeling good about the pattern and confident in his abilities for the moment, he smiled to himself and focused on the landing aimpoint.

As he maneuvered the aircraft through about one hundred feet above the ground, Vicky finally spoke. "Go around."

He glanced at her at first, trying to figure out what he had missed, but then he smoothly applied power and executed the go-around procedure without a problem. When he got to pattern altitude, he looked at her and asked, "What was wrong with the approach? Why did you send me around?"

She smiled. "Nothing was wrong with approach. I just wanted to make sure you could do a go around without my help. Nice job!"

He shook his head and prepared for the next landing. The approach wasn't as good as the last one, but he corrected and accomplished a good touch-and-go with crosswind controls. Without any help, he completed three more patterns, his confidence growing with each one.

Vicky seemed pleased but then surprised him. "Tell the tower you want to depart for Mesa Gateway. Let's go do one landing over there."

He gave her a funny look but keyed the microphone and got the clearance. Just as they had briefed, he switched frequencies and contacted the tower. With some coaching from Vicky, he entered the pattern and accomplished a touch-and-go at Mesa Gateway. The runway looked huge compared to the ones at Chandler, and he also noticed that the winds were almost a direct headwind. After one pattern, they headed back to Chandler.

"Tell the tower this one will be a full-stop landing," directed Vicky.

He landed the aircraft, taxied it back to the FBO, and shut it down. He could see his father lingering under an awning by the FBO.

"How do you feel?" asked Vicky.

He nodded. "I think I'm ready." Then he grinned and added, "And I promise not to do any aileron rolls."

She shook her head and smiled. "If you do, you better turn south and go to Mexico for political asylum." She unplugged her headset and stepped out of the aircraft. She secured the seatbelt for the right seat and reached into her pocket. She pulled out a pair of plastic wings and handed them to him. "You're the PIC now. Bring these wings back to me."

With that, she closed and secured the door before walking into the FBO. Risky tucked the wings into his flight bag. He noticed that the cockpit got very quiet for a moment. This was it. He was about to fly solo. He contained his excitement and focused on his tasks, and completed the checklist.

"Clear prop!" Just like he had practiced, he started the engine and taxied out for takeoff. The first pattern went smoothly. It felt strange being the only one at the controls. Nobody was there to save him. No one was there to fix a bad pattern or deal with an emergency. No one else was there to decipher a difficult radio call or monitor the fuel. He only had himself to blame if he made a mistake, but he also got all the credit if he handled it well.

The first pattern didn't go as well as he had hoped. He struggled to keep the aircraft lined up with the runway. The wind gusts seemed to push the aircraft off the centerline no matter how much he wrestled with the controls. He decided to go around and try again, but when he got on downwind, he heard Vicky's voice over the radio.

"N6156S the wind gusts here at Chandler are exceeding the limits for solo students. What would you like to do?"

At first, he thought this was some sort of test. "What are the current winds?"

"Winds are 300 10 gust 15," answered the tower controller.

He didn't have to look at the chart to know she was right. For a moment, he felt panic begin to creep into his chest, but then he took a deep breath. *Assess. Am I in the Green, Yellow, or Red?* He checked his fuel and confirmed he had enough gas to fly around the pattern for at least a couple of hours. He could see Mesa Gateway's runways off to the East. He realized that he was prepared to deal with this and relaxed. *Green is good.*

He keyed the microphone with confidence. "Chandler tower, I'm going to fly around the pattern a couple more times to see if the winds calm down. If they're still out of limits, I'd like clearance to Mesa Gateway."

"N6156S approved as requested. Cleared to fly the pattern. Maintain pattern altitude and let us know when you want to depart."

"N6156S, roger." He turned base for the runway but maintained pattern altitude. He looked down at the airfield and aligned with the runway, and adjusted his throttle and trim. For the first time, he noticed details—the crab of the aircraft into the wind, the traffic on the nearby roads, the shopping center nearby. He checked his alignment with the runway and adjusted his crab into the wind. When he turned downwind again, he felt surprisingly calm about the entire situation and smiled.

As he turned crosswind after the second pattern, he keyed the microphone. "Chandler tower, say winds."

"Winds are still 300 @10 gust 15."

"N6156S request departure from downwind to Mesa Gateway."

"N6156S, approved as requested. Contact Mesa Gateway tower as you depart. Your instructor wanted me to relay that she will meet you on the ramp at Mesa Gateway. She wants you to do a full stop landing over there and give her some time to drive over and meet you."

"Okay... um roger."

Just as he had briefed and practiced, Risky contacted the tower at Mesa Gateway and entered the pattern. His confidence soared, and he didn't really want to make a full-stop landing. He was having too much fun. He checked the fuel and decided to do one more pattern since he knew it would take twenty minutes for Vicky and his father to arrive anyway. He did a touch-and-go on the first pattern and then made a full stop on the second pattern. When he taxied into the ramp, he saw her standing by the fence with his father.

The propellor came to a stop, but the gyros continued to hum as he completed the checklist and opened the door. He was grinning from ear to ear as Vicky and his father approached the airplane.

Vicky extended her hand. "Congratulations! Nice job!"

Instead of shaking her hand, he reached into her flight bag, pulled out the plastic wings, and offered them to her. "You wanted these back, right?"

She laughed. "Just keep them. You earned them today." They shook hands.

His father interrupted. "Let me get a few pictures of you both next to the airplane."

They posed for a couple of pictures together, and then he posed by himself as well. Then his father asked, "Can I take you both to lunch to celebrate?"

"Well, let me debrief him and then I'll take the airplane back to Chandler. The two of you can go celebrate without me. Give me five minutes." His father nodded and headed back to the fence.

"So, how do you think you did?" she asked as he put his flight bag into the aircraft.

He grinned. "I didn't do any aileron rolls."

She chuckled. "That's a good thing because I can't see you living on the lam in Mexico."

Risky thought back over the events of the flight. "I think it went pretty well. I was nervous at first, but I settled down."

"Why do you think it went so well?"

"Honestly, it went well because you made sure I was prepared."

"Did you follow the principles we talked about in the briefing?"

He thought about their discussion. "Yeah, I guess I did, but I really didn't think about them while I was flying, except I did think about the ABCD and being in the Green."

"Well, there you go. You certainly did. Think about it." She held up a hand and began counting off each principle. "You accepted the risk because the benefits outweighed the costs. It was important for you to solo today for multiple reasons, and you did it. You didn't accept any unnecessary risks—no crazy stunts, unacceptable patterns, or making up your own rules. More than anything, we mitigated risk by planning. We briefed the crosswind procedures. We discussed options if the winds went out of limits. We even practiced our contingency plan together. And of course, we made risk decisions at the right level. We didn't ignore the crosswind policy and used our Resources to accomplish everything within our policies and procedures."

He nodded. "Yeah, I guess we did." He realized she hadn't noticed the extra pattern.

"You see. All that abstract stuff we talk about does apply."

"Did you notice that I did an extra pattern here?" asked Risky.

She gave him a funny look. "No, I didn't notice. Tell me what prompted that decision?"

He shrugged. "I was having fun and didn't want to land yet. I had plenty of gas and the weather was good. I figured it wouldn't hurt anything."

"Well, you were the pilot in command for the flight. It sounds like you assessed the situation and acted like a pilot in command. Technically, you should have made the first one a full stop, but it was your decision." She started her preflight walkaround. "Make sure you annotate the landing in your logbook. Now, go celebrate with your father!"

He grabbed his flight bag and headed for the fence, feeling like he was walking on air.

His father snapped another picture with his cell phone as he got close. "Nice job! You did it."

"Thanks! Did you get to see any of my landings or get any pictures of me flying."

"No, I didn't have a good angle in Chandler at first, and by the time I moved, you were diverting to here. I'm proud of you for doing the right thing." He pointed at the commercial aircraft parked at the passenger terminal down the ramp. "If you keep making good decisions like you did today, Risky Rogers, you can take me up in one of those in a few years."

Four principles of Risk Management improve the odds of reaching your goals:
- **Accept no unnecessary risk.**
- **Anticipate and manage risk by planning.**
- **Accept risk when benefits outweigh the cost.**
- **Make risk decisions at the right level.**

These principles came from the distillation of real-world experiences. They weren't handed down in tablets of stone from some mountaintop. They are written in the blood of aviators and etched in the mangled metal of once airworthy aircraft.

"Principles are concentrated truth, packaged for application to a wide variety of circumstances." (Richard G. Scott) *These four principles for managing risk certainly ring true and can be applied to a wide variety of situations, but sometimes it's difficult to move them from the abstract world of philosophical discussion into the real world of application.*

It's easy to repeat the principles in the classroom and the briefing room, but if we don't understand how they actually apply to our behavior, then they are no better than the fuel in the fuel truck when we are about to run out of gas in the air. Abstract concepts and principles have little value if we can't apply them.

How do we learn to understand and apply these principles? We follow Vicky's example. We discuss specifically how to apply them in the classroom and briefing room. We use the Volant RRM Model to apply them during the flight. We debrief their application, again using the RRM Model to improve our future performance by making them more automatic in our thought processes in concrete terms after we fly. We move the principles from the abstract world of philosophy to the real world of beating hearts and aluminum airplanes.

In short, the Volant RRM Model is designed to help integrate the four principles of Risk Management into an intuitive thought process when faced with time-critical or high-risk decisions.

- **A**SSESS *the situation*
  - **Are we in the Green, Yellow, or Red?**
    - *1) Are there any unnecessary risks?*
- **B**ALANCE *the use of time and Resources?*
  - **Are we able to stay in or return to the Green?**
    - *2) Can we anticipate and manage risk by planning?*
  - **Can we return to the Green?**
    - *3) Did we make risk decisions at the right level, complying with personal policies or following established policies and procedures?*
- **C**OMMUNICATE *risks and intentions*
  - **Can we gather more information or improve coordination and cooperation in the right manner considering the Green-Yellow-Red of the situation?**
- **D**O *what must be done*
  - **Can we continue in the Green or do we need to continue in the Yellow or Red?**
    - *4) Did we accept risks because we thought the benefits outweighed the costs? How did it work out?*
- **D**EBRIEF *to improve future performance*
  - *Most likely, you will find some room for self-improvement and shift your understanding of these concepts from the abstract to the concrete.*

You can see the four principles of risk management are embedded in the RRM Model. The ABCD provides a process, and the Green-Yellow-Red provides a language to help quantify the impact of the risk. These principles can be applied in a wide variety of situations and help us achieve our goals and manage risks.

The explanation above is provided to illustrate how the parts begin to fit together, but it is more academic than needed for real-time application. The next time you fly, or do another activity for which you

want to improve your performance, take a moment for self-examination by asking the following questions:
- What was the Green-Yellow-Red status?
  - Was risk of not achieving my goal ever in the in the Yellow or Red?
  - Or was my perception ever in the Yellow or Red?
- If so, how could I have improved performance?
  - Better anticipation of the risk?
  - Better use of time?
  - Better management of available Resources?
  - Better communication with others?
- What will I do in the future?

Risky got out of bed early so he could catch his father in the kitchen before he left for work. He ambled into the kitchen as if it was normal for him to be awake at this hour and grabbed a bowl from the cupboard. "Hey, Pops, can I borrow the truck this evening?" He grabbed the milk from the refrigerator. "Since I'm leaving next week, it's my last chance to go hang out with my friends." He sat down at the table next to his father, who was reading emails.

His father gave him a sideways glance and smirked. "You're up early. Must be important." He closed his laptop and looked at Risky. "Where are you going?"

Risky poured a bowl of cereal, trying not to look at his father. "We were thinking about heading up the canyon this afternoon to get out of the heat."

"Hmmm… I remember how that went last time. Can I trust you to be safe?" asked his father.

Risky smiled as he poured some milk over his cereal. "You can trust me to use good risk management in order to produce a safe outcome." He shoved a bite into his mouth.

His father chuckled. "Wow! Sounds like you've been rehearsing that line."

Risky answered through a mouth full of cereal. "Well, you were right. I have learned a lot from flying about managing risks and keeping safe."

His father shook his head and smiled. "Apparently it hasn't taught you any table manners." He pushed back from the table and took a long look at Risky. "Yes. Yes, you have learned a lot. I'm proud of you. Where will you be going and when will you be home?"

"You mean you'll let me go?"

"Where will you be going and when will you be home?"

Risky's eyes lit up. "I wanted to go up the canyon this afternoon to get out of the heat."

"Okay, what are the hazards and risks to this outing?"

Risky gave him a funny look. "Have you been talking to Vicky?"

"Let's just say, I checked up on my investment in you."

"Okay, well first of all, the fire danger is high, so we won't build a fire. Then we have all the standard additive conditions associated with driving — traffic, distractions (like cell phones), road conditions, fatigue, pedestrians, and so forth. I guess the risks are that I might crash the truck and get injured or killed." He held up a finger before his father could interject. "BUT! I can manage the risks by not texting or calling while driving, not staying out too late, slowing down on winding roads or in poor road conditions, and keeping a constant lookout for pedestrians and other drivers on the road. I can keep myself, and the vehicle, in the GREEN."

"In the GREEN?"

"Yeah, it's the risk target Vicky taught me. GREEN is the center where risks are recognized and are being properly managed. YELLOW is the next ring where risk increases so you may need to change your plans a bit, and RED is the outer ring where risk has increased to the point where you may need to adjust your goals to end up with the best outcome. I promise to keep it in the GREEN."

His father shook his head and smiled. "Okay! Okay! You convinced me. What time will be home?"

"Midnight?"

"Too much risk for me."

"Eleven?"

"Deal."

Still grinning, Risky carried his bowl to the sink. "Y'know, it's not too late for you to sign up for flight lessons yourself. You might learn something about being safe."

After his father left for work, Risky fired off a group text to several of his buddies. *I'm heading up the canyon this afternoon to get out of the heat. Who's in?* Soon the texts came pouring in, and the event was set.

Risky groaned when he saw the gas tank of the truck was almost empty when he climbed in. He took a moment and thought about where to get gas along his route and mapped it out on his phone. When he started up the truck, the radio began playing jazz music. He left the truck in park and connected his phone, and started his favorite playlist. He looked back over his shoulder and noticed some kids coming down the street and waited until they passed before pulling out of the driveway.

He took a left turn at the end of his street and heard his phone chime. At first, he reached for it, but then he decided to wait until he got to the gas station to check it. At the next intersection ahead, he saw a couple crossing the street and slowed down. They waved to him as they cleared the street, and he continued on.

Even though he felt like he needed to hurry, he came to a complete stop at the intersection out of his neighborhood, and checked for traffic before making the left turn. At the gas station, he checked his messages while the pump was running. None of the messages were urgent. The group was excited to get together and coordinated rides and assignments. He answered a couple of questions while he was stopped.

He made a couple of stops to pick up his buddies and they headed out of the valley to escape the heat. The music was loud, and the conversation was louder. Risky felt odd, like the distractions inside the vehicle made it more difficult for him to concentrate on driving.

Then it dawned on him. *I'm actually drifting into the YELLOW. ABCD.* He reached over and turned the music down a bit, and made sure both hands were on the wheel.

His buddy, Mark, in the front seat, held up his phone and started taking a video. "Hey, Luke, say something to all my followers."

"All two of them?" Risky smiled but didn't take his eyes off the road or hands off the wheel. "It's been a great summer here in Arizona and I wish I didn't have to go back to Ohio."

As the truck slowed around a sharp curve, Mark stopped recording. "Looks like those flying lessons really did make you a better driver."

The winding canyon road was fun to drive, but Risky made sure to stay below the speed limit and manage the turns without drifting into the oncoming lane. They arrived at the arranged site without incident and with plenty of time to enjoy the sunset in the cooler mountain air as the rest of their friends arrived. They danced to their music and talked about their plans for the fall. It was a huge success.

Knowing that it would take at least an hour to get home, Risky began saying goodbyes and gathering up the buddies riding in his truck around nine-thirty. A few of them protested, but he was firm in his commitment to get home on time. They left the party with more than an hour to get home before his curfew. Not once did he struggle to stay awake on the way home. He dropped off his friends and pulled into the driveway at 10:50 pm, ahead of schedule.

His father was watching TV when Risky walked in. "How was the party?" he asked.

Risky went to the refrigerator and grabbed the milk. "It was a lot of fun. I wish I could have stayed longer."

"How did you do at managing the risks? Were you safe?"

At first, Risky shook his head. It felt weird to talk like this with his father. "I'm safe, but more importantly, I didn't take any unnecessary risks, but I certainly wanted to."

"I'm sure you did. Sounds like you're getting some balance in your decisions." His father turned off the television and came into the kitchen. "Speaking of decisions, I spoke with your mother about your flying lessons."

"What did you say? Or more importantly, what did she say?"

"She's concerned. Quite honestly, she doesn't want you to keep flying. She said she worries about losing you to an accident."

Risky nodded. He was afraid she wouldn't let him continue flying. "Do I have to go to Ohio? Why can't I stay with you?"

"That wouldn't be fair to your mother. Cincinnati is a nice place." He started putting the dirty dishes from the sink into the dishwasher. "Besides, I convinced her to let you continue your flying lessons there."

"You did? That's great!"

"It took some convincing, but she found an instructor nearby that she trusts." His father closed the dishwasher and smiled at his son with moist eyes. "I'm proud of your progress son. I'm going to miss you."

Risky sat down his glass of milk and gave his father a hug.

Chapter Seven: Align Resources for Success

Knowledge, Skills, and Attitude
Briefings & External Resources
Automation/Technology
Checklists & Job Aids
Policies, Procedures, Flows, & Techniques

"Good luck is when opportunity meets preparation, while bad luck is when lack of preparation meets reality."
—*Eliyahu Goldratt*

Key Concepts
- Combining the ABCD process with the Resource blocks accomplishes the four principles of risk management.
- **The colored Resource blocks represent Resources** that can be used to improve performance, reduce risk, and manage a time-constrained situation. Using multiple blocks is effective at stopping an error chain.
- **Policies, Procedures, Flows, and Techniques**—Policies, procedures, flows and techniques create predictability and consistency. Predictability and consistency are important at both a personal and operational level. This block creates two distinct advantages: it reduces the mental energy involved in decision making which will improve performance,

and it creates a level of predictability which improves both situation assessment and interactions with other people.
- **Checklists and Job Aids**—Checklists and other Job Aids serve as a structured means of ensuring all critical items have been properly accomplished. They reduce the reliance on memory and/or capture errors that you might make if trying to do a task strictly from memory.
- **Automation/Technology**—Automation and Technology are the integration of people and tools to accomplish a task. When properly managed they improve performance by making information more readily available, detecting deviances, or by automating tasks. Good management involves understanding the capabilities and functions, ensuring the proper inputs are made to get the needed output, and monitoring the results to ensure it makes sense. For as useful as this block is for improving performance it can also be a trap that increases risk if it creates over-reliance or is used incorrectly in the operating environment.
- **Briefings and External Resources**—Briefings are verbal communications conducted between people working together on the same goals and in the same context. Effective briefings create a shared mental model and develop a plan. External Resources are people/groups who understand and have the same goals, but are working within a different context (e.g., Air Traffic Control, Maintenance, Dispatch, Flight Service, ARINC). When working with External Resources it is important to consider that even though the goals may be the same, the External Resources may be working with different priorities, policies, and procedures.
- **Knowledge, Skills, and Attitude**—Knowledge, skills, and attitude are acquired through study, training, and experience. Knowledge is the readily recalled information that may be required or beneficial in the conduct of the flight. Skills are the mental and physical capabilities to operate the

aircraft, and also fundamental management skills (ABCD). Attitude refers to combination of past experience, training and personal value system that forms the basis for what we pay attention to and which impacts our judgement.
- The Resources provide the tools for managing risks, disruptions, and distractions. Resources counter risk factors and improve performance.

Cincinnati, Ohio a few days later

When Risky walked into the baggage claim of the Cincinnati airport, he wanted to turn around and get back on the airplane. There was his mother standing next to the baggage carousel dressed to the nines with perfect hair and long manicured nails holding a bright pink sign stating – Welcome to Cincinnati Risky Rogers! He blushed when he saw her and wanted to hide, but it was too late.

When she saw him, she shouted, "There's my boy!" And started skipping towards him with her high heels clicking against the tile floor. "Oh, I missed you so much!" She dropped the poster and squeezed him for a good ten seconds before letting go.

Risky hugged her back and felt his ears go red with embarrassment.

"How was the flight?" she asked as she picked up the poster. "Did you talk to the pilots?"

"No." He continued over to the carousel, looking for his luggage.

"I've been telling all my friends about how you want to be a pilot. One of them has a daughter about your age who loves to travel. Maybe the two of you can go on a date or something."

Risky cringed. He had been with his mother for less than five minutes, and she was already trying to set him up on a date. He didn't answer and watched for his luggage.

"I spoke with your flight instructor. His name is Greg Gunderson, but his nickname, or is it call sign? Anyway, everyone calls him 'Guns' because he used to be a fighter pilot years ago. He's retired now and has his own airplane. He says he is willing to take you on. Everyone says he's a good instructor."

Risky grabbed one of his bags. "That's nice."

"Your stepfather, Jim, helped me find him."

Risky feigned a smile as he grabbed his second piece of luggage, and they started for the car. After they loaded the luggage, his mother handed him the keys. "Why don't you drive, and I'll give you directions. That way you can get oriented."

Risky climbed behind the wheel and adjusted the seat and mirrors. He buckled up and waited for his mother to buckle up before putting it in gear. He eased out of the parking spot and followed his mother's instructions. She continued telling him about their new house and neighborhood.

After a few minutes, they got onto the interstate, and his mother stopped talking for a moment. "You really have changed," she said. "Your father told me you had grown up a lot this summer. I can tell by the way you drive that you certainly have." She put a hand on his arm. "If you're such a better driver, tell me how you got the nickname 'Risky.'"

He smiled and began telling her all about the summer, getting grounded, and taking flying lessons. By the time they arrived at her house, he was feeling better about being with his mother, but he still wasn't ready for her to set him up on any blind dates.

When they walked into the house, his mother pointed to a package sitting on the kitchen counter. "That's for you, from Jim and me."

Risky sat down his luggage and picked it up. It was a new noise-canceling headset.

"You have your father's ears," said his mother. "So, we made sure it had large earcups."

They both laughed, and he thanked her with a hug.

Risky arrived at KI67 Cincinnati West airport and found the hangar where Guns had told him to meet. He grabbed his flight bag along with his new headset from the front seat and strolled into the hangar. A green and white RV-10 filled most of the hangar. The hangar was adorned with a sitting area complete with lounge chairs, coffee table, sofa, and a kitchenette with a variety of aviation posters and memorabilia on the wall. Greg 'Guns' Gunderson was sitting in a lounge chair with a coffee cup in his hand. He was bald and sported a thick, soup-strainer mustache.

"What time does the three o'clock lesson start?" asked Greg without standing up.

Risky looked at his watch. It was 3:04. "Uh... sorry. It took me a few minutes to find the hangar."

"First rule for all my students. Be on time. Tardiness is impolite." He stood and stuck out his hand. "Greg 'Guns' Gunderson."

Risky felt like his hand was in a vice when he shook Greg's hand, and he did his best to return the firm handshake and not wince. "Luke Rogers. My friends call me Risky."

"Always give a good firm handshake. No dead fish," said Guns as he released Risky's hand and took a sip from his coffee cup. "I called your instructor in Arizona. She told me about your nickname." He furrowed his brow. "And your attempt at the aileron roll."

Risky blushed. "Well, in my defense. I was pretty new."

"I like risk takers. They get the most out of life. Where would we be if we all sat around in easy chairs afraid to venture out into the world? Bunch of naysaying, do-nothing couch potatoes." He squinted at Risky. "Just gotta learn how to manage the risks so you stay alive." He pointed at the whiteboard next to the lounge chair. "Let's go brief the lesson and fly."

The first lesson was an orientation of the area. Guns talked about the local airspace, weather patterns, and landmarks. After the briefing, they walked down the ramp to the local FBO and checked out a Cessna 172, just like the one Risky had flown in Arizona.

When they got airborne, the differences with Arizona were immediately apparent. A thin haze hung over the horizon, and there weren't any mountains to navigate from. The green rolling hills and forests seemed to stretch on forever. Risky found himself using the moving map more than before, but by the end of the lesson, he was getting used to the environment. He also noticed the absence of other air traffic. They were the only aircraft in the pattern the entire flight. Guns seemed at ease in the air, and even though he clearly expected precise performance, he was calm and affable the entire time.

During the debrief, Guns covered each maneuver in such painstaking detail that Risky wasn't sure he would take him on as a student. Finally, he erased the whiteboard and took a seat in his lounge chair. "Vicky told me you were almost ready for dual cross country," he mentioned as he sipped from his coffee cup. "Based on your performance today, I would agree."

Risky felt a wave of relief and a bit conflicted because pleasing Guns was not an easy task.

"Vicky also told me she laid the foundation of RRM, Risk and Resource Management during her lessons."

"She did. She even made me memorize the four principles for managing risk."

"After the aileron roll. She told me about that." Guns took a sip from his coffee cup. "That's good. We used RRM at the airline I just retired from. Good system." He reached into the flight bag next to his chair and pulled out a three-by-five card, and tossed it on the coffee table. "Did Vicky give you one of these?"

Risky picked up the card. It was a concise description of the RRM model and its principles, all packed into that small space. He shook his head. "No, she didn't."

"Well you've got one now." He pulled out a calendar notebook. "I think we need to do one more local flight before we start the cross-country phase. When do you want to take your next lesson?"

Risky pulled out his phone and pulled up his calendar. He noticed a text from his mother. *What time will you be home? I want you to meet that young lady I was talking about.* He ignored the text for now. "I'm free Saturday."

"Be here at 10:00." He looked directly at Risky. "Not 10:04. And study the Resource blocks on that card. During the cross-country phase, we will focus on using the Resource blocks."

Risky nodded and stood. "Do you think I will be able to get my Private Pilot Certificate before Christmas?"

"Unlike the blue skies of Arizona, we actually have weather here." He held up his coffee cup. "You come prepared, and if the weather cooperates, you might be taking your check ride before Thanksgiving."

Saturday, Rusty walked into the hangar at 9:50 and found Guns in his lounge chair, reading a book with his coffee cup in hand.

"Morning Sunshine," said Guns without even looking up from his book. "Go to the whiteboard and brief me on the Resource blocks."

"Good morning," replied Risky as he sat down his flight bag next to the coffee table. He reached into the bag and pulled out the three-by-five card.

"Without the card," admonished Guns, still staring at his book.

Risky felt a moment of panic. He had reviewed the information but hadn't committed it to memory. "Uh... okay, I'll try." He took another look at the Resource blocks and put the card on the table. He grabbed a marker and drew five squares in a row.

"Let's see. One of them is checklists. Another is briefings." He labeled two of the blocks. "Then we have automation, and policies. I can't remember the fifth one." He put down the marker and stepped back.

Guns put down his book and took a sip from his cup. "In every accident there is a chain of events. Step by step the situation unfolds. Checklists are missed. Weather forecasts are ignored. Policies are broken. Eventually there isn't a Resource left to stop the accident." He stood and went to the board with Risky.

103

"Let's put them in the right order." He erased Risky's labels. "Grab the card and start over."

Risky picked up the card and looked at the graphics. He labeled each block accordingly without comment. When he finished, he stepped back. "How's that?"

"Good." Guns picked up the marker and drew a line through the first two blocks, and stopped at the third. "That's a visual representation of breaking the accident chain using Resources. Maybe you miss an item during your flow, but when you do the checklist, you catch it. Accident chain broken. Catastrophe avoided."

Risky looked at the blocks and nodded. It made sense, but he was still trying to wrap his head around it all.

"Why do you think they're in this order?"

Risky shrugged. "I'm not sure."

"Good aviators understand the need for structure. Policies, procedures, flows, and even good techniques create a structured environment to speed up good decision making. It even allows inexperienced pilots to operate safely. Plus, you will find this helpful later on with crew coordination." He put a checkmark next to the first box.

"Checklists are memory aids for things we don't do often or to keep us from missing something important." He checked the second box. "It's easy to get distracted in our work environment. Checklists help us review our work and trap errors."

He put a checkmark in the middle of the Automation block. "Then technology came along to change all of our problems." Guns chuckled.

"It sounds like you don't like that block as much," said Risky.

Guns shot back, "Not at all! I love all the electronic charts and electronic flight bag stuff. What a relief not to schlep around a catalog case full of charts and books, but I have to admit I'm old school, and do like the ol' round dials."

Risky frowned. "Then why the sarcasm?"

Guns curled his lip and twisted his mustache in discontent. "Because too many pilots assume the automation and technology is always going to work and they stop piloting. They stop thinking, or worse yet, they never learn to think." He looked straight at Risky and raised an eyebrow. "It also tends to give kids that play video games the false impression they could handle a real aircraft just because they can handle it on the computer."

Risky rolled his eyes. "I'm never going to hear the end of it am I?"

Guns suppressed a smile and began coloring in the block. "Used correctly, automation helps decrease workload and increase situational awareness, making it possible for us to better use all the other resource. You would think that everything would be easier, but in reality, it requires proactive programming and discipline to monitor the results." He tapped the block with his marker. "Technology can be a hindrance, if you rely on it too much. Be careful."

He took a sip from his mug and continued. "Briefings allow us to prepare for future risks. When you are flying the 'big-rigs' as part of a crew, the airline mandates standardized briefings prior to critical phases of flight, but flying GA, we need to do it ourselves. It's good discipline for us risk takers."

"What briefing do I give to myself?"

"Basically, you pause to consider four things: What are we going to do; What can make it harder; What can go wrong; How we will handle it if it does go wrong. Briefings are essential when working with other people, but equally essential to reduce risk when flying alone."

Guns underlined External Resources. "You might be alone in the aircraft, but that doesn't mean other people are unable to help you. An external resource is defined as someone who wants the same outcome, but may be working in a different context, like air traffic control, maintenance, flight attendants, or even a passenger. Never underestimate the value of information from all sources, but as you integrate their information consider their perspective. For example, ATC wants to get you in for a landing, but they need to sequence you with everyone else. So, they may ask you to speed up, slow down or turn. Before accepting the clearance, you need to be sure it will work for you. Maintenance may want you to fly with a mechanical problem which would be acceptable in VFR weather, but you, as the captain, recognize the changing weather conditions and decide the system needs to be working." He dutifully drew another check mark.

"As you look at how the blocks line up, consider how they work together to stop a potential error chain," and as he touched each block, he explained. "If you make an error in a procedure or flow, it can be 'caught' by a checklist item, or a warning from your automation, or by another crewmember. So now let's talk about this last one. Why do you think it's the last block?"

Risky shrugged. "I don't know."

"That's a bit ironic since the last block includes knowledge." Guns rolled his eyes. "It's the last block because when you run out of other Resources all you have left is your personal preparation—knowledge and skills." He drew a line through the box. "Right now, this box is pretty thin for you. That makes all these other blocks even more important to you. You will fill it in with time and training, but be careful not to rely on that block while you are student."

"Let's add one more element to this block." Guns wrote 'Attitude' next to the block.

Risky tilted his head and frowned. "I understand the need for knowledge and skills, but why 'Attitude?'"

"A lot of folks ask that question. Attitude is what shapes your perception and impacts your judgement. It's your personal lens for viewing the world."

Risky looked at the card. "Isn't that the same as judgment?"

Guns nodded. "They are related, but attitude impacts all of the ABCD process. Let's say you're out flying and see weather ahead. If you learned to fly in the blue skies of Arizona, your past experience may not prepare you to watch for pop-up showers, which impacts your judgement. Good judgement, based on policies and procedures, would prod you to turn around and avoid the weather. However, if you have a 'the-rules-don't-apply-to-me attitude,' you might just fly into the weather, even though you aren't a qualified instrument pilot. Your attitude impacts your judgement and can either enhance or minimize the other resource blocks."

Guns handed Risky the marker and sat back down. "Okay talk me through our lesson today, and include the resource blocks in the discussion."

"Well, I checked the weather—"

"EXTERNAL RESOURCE," interjected Guns.

"And it's supposed to be VMC all day."

"POLICY."

"We will complete the walkaround inspection—"

"FLOWS."

Risky paused before continuing. "After we do our preflight FLOWS—"

"Now you're getting the hang of it."

"We will run the CHECKLIST before we taxi to the runup area and do our runup PROCEDURE. We will make a radio call, EXTERNAL RESOURCE. Then we will takeoff, SKILL, and fly below the Class Bravo, POLICY, to the practice area."

Guns clapped. "Yes folks, he can be taught! You see how you have been using these Resources all along. Now you can identify them and apply them specifically, and when something goes wrong, you can debrief to figure out which resource failed you, or you failed to employ."

Risky continued the briefing, making sure to emphasize each resource block. The flight went well, and he felt like his performance was improving. He could tell that he had done better today because the debrief with Guns didn't take as long as before.

"Looks like you grasped the concept of Resources today," said Guns as he finished up.

Risky began zipping up his flight bag. "It all seemed to pretty much make sense in the briefing, but I honestly didn't think much about them when we were flying."

"That's essentially how it works. Discipline yourself to think through things before starting the flight, then about the only time the model will come to mind is when you feel yourself drifting into the Yellow. After a while you'll almost subconsciously run through the ABCD process and adjust the use of the Resources. It's like learning to read music. At first knowing the names of the notes is important for the learning process, but eventually you can just see them and play without thinking of the letters."

"Before you go, let me give you some airfields to study for your cross country." He stood and wrote down several airfield identifiers on the board.

It was a week before the good weather and schedules coincided well enough to fly the first dual cross-country flight. During the briefing, Guns discussed everything from emergency airfields to expected frequencies trying to create the shared mental model he wanted for the flight.

Risky was impatient and thought it was a bit of overkill, and at one point, he yawned.

"Are we boring you Master Rogers?" teased Guns with a British accent.

"What? No, I'm listening. It's just that during the last week I flew to all the airfields you told me to study on my flight simulator."

Guns smirked and continued briefing.

They took off from KI67, Cincinnati West, with a high layer of cirrostratus covering the sky and turned north towards KMIE, Delaware County Regional Airport near Muncie, Indiana. They stayed at 2500 feet, below the Class Bravo surrounding the Cincinnati airport, and climbed to 4500 feet when the airspace allowed them. Risky enjoyed the view when they leveled off. The layer of clouds above them muted the green landscape, and he could see the fields changing colors as fall approached.

"Okay what would you do if your map display suddenly stopped working?" Guns covered the map display with the checklist card.

Risky froze as he stared at the checklist card wishing it would magically return to the display he relied on. He opened his mouth to speak, but nothing came out.

Guns' voice over the intercom snapped him back into action. "Drifting into the Yellow? Start the ABCD process. Assess: Are you really in Green, Yellow, or Red? Are you still flying? Do you have control of the aircraft? How much time do you have? In this case, you still have control and plenty of fuel. What are your Resources?"

"Well, I have my standby instruments," answered Risky. "I could dial up the Muncie VOR and follow the signal." He tapped on his iPad. "I have the GPS in my iPad as well."

"Good. Using your Automation resource block. What else?"

"I could ask Air Traffic Control to give me a vector."

"Yep, External Resources."

"I'm familiar enough with the area behind me that I think I could turn around and go land back at Cincinnati West."

"Knowledge and Skills!" replied Guns. "Anytime you feel yourself drifting into the Yellow, just ask yourself, 'What Resources can I use to get me back to the Green.' Also, when you do a good briefing, it makes it easier for you to use the resource blocks in flight. You won't be scrambling to figure out what to do. You'll automatically gravitate to the Resources available."

Guns removed the checklist from the screen. He leaned back and stared out the window for a moment. "This never gets old."

The rest of the flight, Guns pointed out landmarks, emergency airfields, and lectured on the importance of looking outside as much as possible for traffic. They entered the pattern at Muncie just like they had briefed and made a full-stop landing.

When the propellor stopped turning, Guns climbed out and chocked the wheel. He grabbed a rag and started cleaning a bug spot from his side of the windshield. "Debrief me on the flight before you go to the bathroom."

"It was fun to finally go somewhere instead of the practice area," answered Risky as he unbuckled and climbed out. "It's different than Arizona for sure."

Guns tossed the rag back into the plane. "That's nice but talk to me more about your flying performance. What went well? What needs improvement?"

Risky shrugged. "I thought it went okay. We found the airport."

Guns raised an eyebrow. "Setting the bar pretty low aren't we. Tell me why it went well."

"Well, everything you talked about in the briefing happened the way you said it would, except for when you covered the display with the checklist card."

"So, are you saying that it went well because we did a good briefing?"

Remembering how impatient he was during the briefing, Risky smiled sheepishly. "Yeah, I guess I am."

"Good. I'm going to the bathroom. When I come back, you can give the briefing for the return flight. Remember your Resources." With that, Guns made a beeline to the FBO.

Risky's briefing was not as thorough or polished as the briefing Guns gave. He fumbled to find the words and paused several times, trying to decide what to say. At one of the slow points, Guns yawned and stretched.

On departure, they climbed to 5500 feet and trimmed the aircraft for cruise flight. The afternoon sun was pleasant, and the high cirrus clouds had started to dissipate, leaving a view of the deep blue sky in the east. The horizon stretched out ahead like a patchwork of colors.

Guns leaned forward in his seat for a better view. "Turn left ten degrees," he commanded.

Risky glanced at him and then turned the aircraft left ten degrees on the compass rose. "Do we have to make a radio call?" he asked.

"Nope. Only if we change altitude."

"Is everything okay?"

"Peachy. We are about to pass over a very important landmark in aviation history."

"In the middle of nowhere Indiana?"

Guns wiggled the controls. "I have the aircraft."

Risky let go of the yoke. "You have the aircraft."

Guns put the aircraft into a shallow left bank. "Do you see the airplane parked down there?"

Risky searched the countryside below them. He was surprised to see a grey fighter aircraft next to an old farmhouse. "Yeah."

"That young man is an F-84 fighter."

"Okay, but why is it in the middle of Indiana. Did it crash here or something?"

"Nope. You are looking at the birthplace of Wilbur Wright."

"Who?"

Guns gave him a dirty look. "Wilbur Wright, as in the Wright Brothers."

"Was that like some 80's band?"

Guns rolled out of the turn and settled back on course without answering. He shook his head. "You have the aircraft."

Risky grabbed the yoke and gave it a gentle wiggle. "I have the aircraft." He adjusted the trim and began looking at the horizon again.

Without as much as a word, Guns reached over and pulled the throttle to idle. He simultaneously keyed the microphone and made a radio call. "N1822L departing 5500."

"N1822L, Roger."

Risky squeezed the yoke and felt his heart rate increase.

Guns leaned back in his seat and nonchalantly offered. "Your engine just quit."

This wasn't part of the briefing. Risky froze for a moment. *ABCD. Remember your Resources. Maintain aircraft control.* He trimmed the aircraft for best glide. *Where's the best place to land? How much time?*

He could see an airfield on the map display only about eight miles ahead and off to the right. He checked his altitude and did some mental math. *I can make it.* He turned toward the airfield.

"Okay, I see the airfield on the display, but I can't find it."

Guns put his hands behind his head. "The Wright Brothers were not an 80's heavy metal band. They were a couple of midwestern farm boys born in the late 1800s who changed the world."

Risky felt his palms sweating. "Should I check the fuel selector?"

"Good thinking! Are you nervous Risky?" asked Guns. "I thought you liked risk."

Risky continued to search for the airfield right in front of him, but everything seemed to run together. "I do. I do. But I can't find the airfield."

Guns folded his arms. "Wilbur Wright didn't need an airfield."

Risky checked his altitude. They were descending through 4000 feet. He looked down at the display and could see that the airfield should be right in front of them, just four or five miles away. *Where are you?*

"You really don't know who the Wright Brothers are?" asked Guns.

Risky shook his head. "No! No, I don't!"

"Someone's drifting into the Yellow."

"Okay! Okay! Who were the Wright Brothers?"

"On December 17, 1903, Orville and Wilbur Wright travelled from Dayton, Ohio, to Kitty Hawk, North Carolina."

Risky continued to search for the airfield in vain, wondering why Guns was giving him a history lecture at a time like this.

"That day, Orville Wright made the first successful powered flight in the history of mankind while his brother, Wilbur Wright, looked on. They went on to develop the Wright Flyer, the world's first powered airplane."

Risky frantically searched for the airfield as the aircraft approached 3000 feet.

"Nothing? That story doesn't even register with you at all?"

Risky shook his head. "I should have paid more attention in history class, but history isn't going to help me right now!"

Guns replied in a thick British accent. "Ah, Master Rogers has forgotten his Resource blocks."

"I've used my Automation. I've used my Skills and Knowledge. I've followed the Procedure. Is there a Checklist I should be using? What am I missing?"

Guns keyed the microphone. "Can you give N1822L a vector to the nearest airfield?"

The controller responded. "Sure. N1822L turn right five degrees and Newcastle is only about two miles away."

"Roger. Thanks." Guns reached over and slowly pushed the throttle to full. "Let's head back on course. I'll get us clearance to stay at 3500 feet."

Guns sat in his favorite easy chair, stroking his mustache like he was trying to make a difficult decision during the debrief. "Pull out that card I gave you and talk to me about the Resource blocks you used when you drifted into the Yellow."

Risky pulled out the card. "Well, I followed the Procedure for engine out. I used my Automation by looking at the display for the nearest airfield. I used my Knowledge and Skill by establishing the best glide and trimming the airplane."

"What Resource blocks did you not use?"

"Obviously, I didn't use External Resources."

Guns nodded. "Why didn't you?"

"I don't know. I didn't think of it."

"Why didn't you think of it?"

"I guess I was little freaked about not seeing the airport."

"Why were you 'freaked out'?"

Risky shook his head and threw his hands up in the air. "I've never been in that situation before."

"On the way up to Muncie, do you remember all the emergency airfields I pointed out?" asked Guns.

"I remember you talking about them, but I was so focused on finding Muncie that I guess I really didn't pay attention."

"Which Resource block would have helped you while we were still at the FBO in Muncie?"

Risky stared at the card again, but nothing jumped out at him.

"Our Briefing could have been a bit more thorough and included enroute airfields. Don't you think?" interjected Guns.

Risky just nodded. He felt a knot in his stomach. This wasn't the way he wanted his first cross-country to go. He fiddled with the card but didn't say anything.

"Part of being a professional pilot is learning from our mistakes. Don't beat yourself up," said Guns.

"One more thing, when you were focusing on trying to find the airport, were you distracted by anything else? "

"Yes! You! It was a strange time for a history lesson."

"So why did you not ask me to stop the history lesson and help look for the airport."

"Well," Risky paused, "You sort of outrank me! And I figure you knew better. I mean, I figured you knew what you were doing."

Guns smiled and replied, "Risky, when you're part of a crew and think things might be going south, you need to speak up, regardless of rank."

He stood and walked over to the bookshelf against the wall. He grabbed a book and held it up. "Take home this book about the Wright Brothers and read it. They knew a lot about managing risks and learning from mistakes." He found a page. "In fact, here's a quote from Wilbur Wright himself. 'The man who wishes to keep at the problem long enough to really learn anything positively must not take dangerous risks. Carelessness and overconfidence are usually more dangerous than deliberately accepted risks.'" He plopped it on the coffee table in front of Risky. "Take this home with you and read it in your spare time."

Risky nodded but didn't say anything. He stood and let out a heavy sigh and wondered if he would get his Private Pilot Certificate before Christmas as he had hoped.

Guns sat back down in his easy chair and grabbed his coffee mug. "Why so glum? You did good today."

"Then why does it feel like I failed?"

"That's the funny thing about learning. It doesn't happen without making mistakes." He held up his mug. "Here's to making mistakes and learning. Go home and read about the Wright Brothers. And remember to use your Resources!"

Hindsight is 20/20. It's easy to see the accident chain develop when we read the accident report. We can clearly see the event unfold—the missed checklist, the incomplete briefing, and the failure to apply policy or procedure. We can easily identify where the ABCD process broke down. We can recognize the unused Resources that would have trapped errors before they developed into an undesired aircraft state. We all learn from our own successes and failures, but to be as successful as possible, we need to learn from the success and failures of others. (This is one reason the D in the ABCD is so important.) This is also how we learn to identify and apply the Resources.

When you find yourself (or your operation) drifting into the Yellow, or even the Red, use the resource blocks to move back into the Green. Each block is designed to improve performance and reduce risk, especially in stressful situations. They create consistency in our habit patterns and standardize our performance. The content of each block will vary for a given aircraft and/or flight operation, but the principle remains the same. As a professional pilot, fill each block completely and employ them consistently.

Airlines devote a trained workforce to collect operational data and analyze the risks. These Safety Management Systems use a similar color-coding system to rank the level of risk in multiple dimensions: risk of accidents and incidents; risk of non-compliance with regulations; risk of financial loss; even risk of not meeting customer-driven metrics. They typically refer to additive conditions as 'hazards' and refer to Resources as the 'controls' to deal with the risk. Operational personnel work with the Safety Management Systems, aircraft manufacturers, and even the FAA to provide the Resources needed to avoid and trap risks before they become consequential.

General Aviation flight schools put similar effort into the design of the Resources provided to student pilots, but when you are flying solo, it will be up to you to develop your own set of Resources and to utilize them when needed.

The design of the Resources is based on Human Factors principles that have evolved over many years of training observations, analysis of operational data, and research. In aviation, we have given specific titles to the blocks to align with the common titles of operational documents (as you have seen in the graphics), but they can be more generalized as:

- *Consistency: Policies, Procedures, Flows, and Techniques*
- *Memory Aids: Checklists and Job Aids*
- *Technology: Automation*
- *Other People: Briefings and External Resources*
- *Personal Preparation: Knowledge, Skills, and Attitude*

When working on your own, you need to design and commit to them yourself. So, how do we put them together?

Building a firm foundation with the brick-colored block

(Philosophy), Policies, Procedures, Flows, and Techniques: Although it looks like we added a bit to our first block here, in reality we just revealed a bit more about the design of consistency in a complex operating environment. Consistency is the best friend of anyone that works in a time-sensitive or time-critical environment. In addition to reducing cognitive workload (i.e., not having to think as hard about what needs to be done) consistency is critical to people being able to work well together.

On the other hand, it is incredibly important to avoid rigidity, which can be a hazard in itself. The ideal way to integrate consistency in a complex environment is to layer the guidance.

- ***Techniques*** are simply your personal way of getting things done. They can be learned from other people, but there is little need for any formal documentation. Techniques should accomplish the desired outcome, within the framework of Policies and Procedures, and should not interfere with the expectations of other crewmembers.
- ***Flows*** are most useful in a very predictable environment when there is a short sequence of well-defined tasks that need to be done in a limited amount of time. Flows must follow the same pattern each time in order to become efficient. Airlines and flight schools will often design and teach preflight flows to help crewmembers prepare an aircraft for flight. In general, a flow is good if it is linear, repeatable, and does not miss anything. (Technique—if your flow gets interrupted it is best to start back at the beginning to ensure you don't miss anything.)
- ***Procedures*** are clearly defined steps that must be accomplished at prescribed times and can include specific callouts. They are the most restrictive method to create consistency. In addition to reducing the cognitive workload required to accomplish a task, procedures produce a standard outcome and help improve crew coordination. The level of consistency in a procedure is particularly important when working with other people in high risk, time-critical situations. The caveat is that procedures are only effective in predictable environments since variable conditions can make it impossible to complete the procedure as written. Procedures are powerful, if you follow them.
- ***Policies*** are a deliberate system of guidelines with broad application intended to achieve a predictable outcome. They serve multiple purposes in complex or variable situations. First, they reduce conflict by making us more predictable to each other. They also establish the boundaries for acceptable risk. Airlines and flight schools establish policies to address the risk of operations based on their own operational priorities. Policies are particularly useful in time-sensitive or

time-critical situations. You can reduce risk and improve performance at a personal level by creating policies to prevent mistakes or poor decisions. Some can be simple—like always putting your car keys in the same spot. Others can be more serious—like always landing with at least one hour of fuel on solo cross-country flights. Good policies can help keep you from making a poor decision when under stress. Never change a policy when you are under stress. Policies protect you during those moments of vulnerability.

- **Philosophy** *refers to the underlying system of values and priorities. All of the policies, procedures, and flows are designed to achieve, and be consistent with, an underlying philosophy. Then, in the absence of any specific guidance, a stated philosophy can be a great aid in decision making. A philosophy is more effective when it is simple. For example: "Safety, Service, and Efficiency." Safety: Follow the four principles of risk management; Service: Take care of people while working to achieve your goal; Efficiency: Be a good steward of money and time. Then, when it comes time to make a decision, the priorities are clear.*

This brick-colored block is the foundation for safety of flight and often referred to as simply SOPs (Standard Operating Procedures). Remember, many policies and procedures are written in blood. Don't ignore them or think of them as restrictions. Instead, see them as the framework for managing risks and achieving safety and success in a given environment. By understanding how they layer together, you can better understand how they control risk, and apply them in your own life.

Improving success with the Green Block

Checklists were born of necessity. As aircraft became more complex, the risk of errors, or simply missing important items, increased. Checklists were developed to trap any errors or missed items critical to flight before they became consequential, and

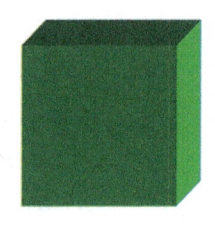

keep you from depending on unreliable memory, especially in moments of high stress. Checklists can generally be categorized in two types: Normal and Non-normal and employ a variety of techniques for completion.

The Normal Checklist is designed to ensure all critical items and tasks in a flow or procedure have been accomplished during normal operations as a layer of verification. The redundancy may seem unnecessary, until it saves you from a critical mistake. Be smart from the start. Don't marginalize checklists by cursory completion. Read and verify each step.

The Non-normal Checklist is designed to walk crewmembers through the necessary steps during non-normal, or emergency situations. This checklist is usually accomplished step-by-step as it is read to ensure each item is completed in the correct order. As part of your personal training, it is good to review the non-normal checklists periodically to test your familiarity. In addition to decreasing reliance on memory, it also decreases the level of effort required in training.

Keeping your head above water with the AQUA block

Technology includes our interactions with any automation, devices, or software provided to access and use information, or to spread out our workload. First, ensure you understand the capabilities and limitations of the technology you employ. Second, ensure you have prepared the technology before you need it. Third, and most importantly, continually monitor the aircraft's flight path and energy state and be prepared to intervene as necessary.

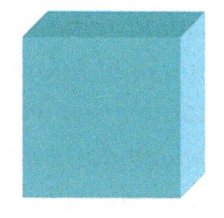

Automation technology is increasingly significant in aviation. In addition to providing timely, easy to interpret information, automation can completely fly the aircraft IF it has been properly programmed and employed. Automation is applied in levels based on the environment and the proficiency of the crewmember. At low levels of automation crewmembers interact in real-time, hand fly the aircraft and use the automation to improve situation awareness. At higher

levels, information is pre-programmed and the automation takes flight-path control. High levels of automation spread out the workload when flying in a predictable environment. On the other hand, when responding to changes in a variable, time-sensitive environment, lower levels of automation are generally more advantageous. The predictability of the operating environment influences the choice of Resources.

Automation is an effective tool, BUT the professional pilot understands how overusing automation can lead to complacency and skill degradation. Turn off the automation from time to time to maintain the necessary flying and cognitive skills. Additionally, the use of automation requires you develop the skill for intentional attention—being able to pay attention even though you know it is unlikely anything will go wrong.

Understand the capabilities of your aircraft's automation so that it doesn't become a distraction. Learn about the aircraft's automation and any supporting technology on the flight deck, like the iPad or other approved devices. Flying by automation is a skill just as important as flying without automation. Proper use of automation should reduce fatigue and workload allowing you to broaden your intake of information and improve your situational awareness. But automation will only be a benefit if you understand what it can and cannot do; you practice using it; and you maintain your skills to takeover when needed.

Working with other people with the GOLD block

Working with other people includes working as part of a crew with people who have the same goals and the same context, or working with people outside of your current context. We use Briefings to communicate in both scenarios and we classify anyone outside of our context as External Resources.

Briefings can help you avoid those moments of confusion during a critical phase of flight. A briefing is concise communication of information and/or a plan intended to create a shared mental of model. Prior to conducting a briefing you need to clearly understand the goal and any conditions that could impact success or increase risk. It also includes your contingency plan if things don't go according to the original plan of action.

Briefings are also effective when you are working alone. Brief yourself by thinking through what you need to accomplish. What is your plan? What will you do if your plan is disrupted? What is your contingency plan? If you are flying solo, brief your instructor or a peer to help you think through the phases of the flight.

External Resources are the people that provide additional information and guidance. This includes Air Traffic Control, maintenance, aircraft dispatchers, even your peers. Reach out to External Resources during your preflight and in all phases of flight. The FAA has created a structure of support to help you with everything from weather briefings to finding the nearest airfield in an emergency. Additionally, most air operations have some sort of dispatch or operational control center with qualified people waiting to assist. Don't let your pride keep you from reaching out to those valuable Resources. As you consider information provided by External Resources, be sure you understand the context of their information and guidance and compare it to your own information, operational priorities, and goals. Also consider that if you're in the Red, their situational assessment could be more encompassing than your own.

Cementing the foundation with the Grey Block

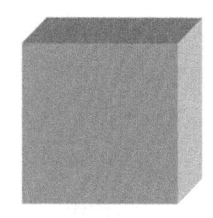

Knowledge is recallable information used to solve problems and accomplish desired outcomes. It can include aircraft systems, regulatory guidance, weather, and other general knowledge. The amount of information you will study as a pilot can be overwhelming so it is useful to think of it in terms of what needs to be memorized for quick recall, what needs to be well understood for application, or what needs to be understood but can be referenced in a timely manner.

A good working knowledge of your aircraft limitations, systems, immediate-action items, and regulatory guidance can save your life. For example, as good as emergency checklists are, they cannot provide guidance in every situation, particularly when there are multiple conditions to consider. The combined knowledge you acquire through study and experience can provide you with the solution to a problem when nothing else seems to work. Additionally, a good working knowledge can keep you from burying your head in the books during a critical phase of flight. Knowledge is the foundation for all the other Resource blocks.

Skills are different than knowledge. Skill is the ability to perform an activity or action. Knowing the procedure for landing an aircraft and actually making the correct decisions and landing the aircraft are not the same thing. Skills require practice. For training purposes, Skills are often divided into two categories: Motor Skills, which involve manipulation of the technology, and Cognitive Skills which involve the integration of knowledge within the context of what you are attempting to accomplish. You can practice skills with mental practice (chair fly) to improve cognitive skills and utilize simulation at various levels to hone specific skills. Fly the aircraft at every opportunity. Develop your skills with practice and keep them polished with consistent experience.

Attitude is the personal equivalent of an organization's operational priorities. Attitude not only shapes the decisions we make, but it also determines what information we pay attention to and how we weigh the consequences of actions or inactions. In short, your past experiences and training shape a personal value system that impacts situation assessment, decision making, and communications. Much of your success will depend on developing an attitude toward professionalism.

In the end, each of the Resource blocks improves your performance and mitigates risks. Maximize their effectiveness and employ them. Utilizing the Resources outlined within RRM can help you manage risks, achieve safety, and expedite expertise.

Chapter Eight: Recognize Risk Factors

"Our ability to manage our attention is our most important defense against a world that is constantly conspiring to steal it."

—Maura Thomas

Key Concepts
- Risk factors are anything that increase risk and decrease performance. These can be categorized into one of three categories—Task Loading, Additive Conditions, and Crew Factors.
- **Task Loading**—The amount of time needed to accomplish tasks vs the time available to accomplish tasks. Crew Members should remain vigilant of high task loading—high number of tasks in short amount of time, and low task loading—low number of tasks with an abundance of time. High task loading increases stress and decreases performance. Low task loading can lead to inattention or complacency which also increases risk.

Task Loading

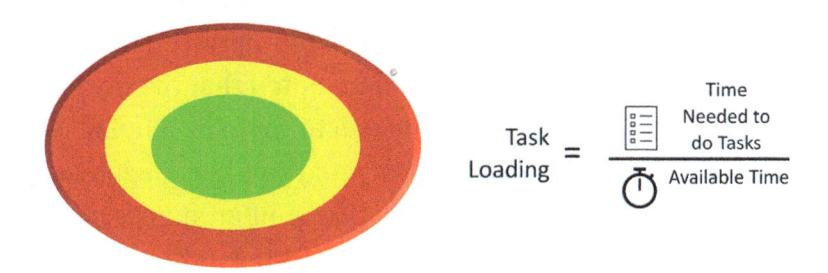

$$\text{Task Loading} = \frac{\text{Time Needed to do Tasks}}{\text{Available Time}}$$

- **Additive Conditions**—Any factor that adds to task loading or causes a distraction or disruption (e.g., the environment, equipment problems, operational problems, organizational influences). Unpredictable situations or lack of information are additive conditions that can increase risk. Additive conditions are sometimes referred to as threats due to the increased risk they can bring, but in most cases moving into the Yellow or Red is caused by a combination of conditions and not just a single threat. Crew Members should beware of focused attention and/or tunnel vision from themselves and others.

Additive Conditions:
Competing for Your Attention

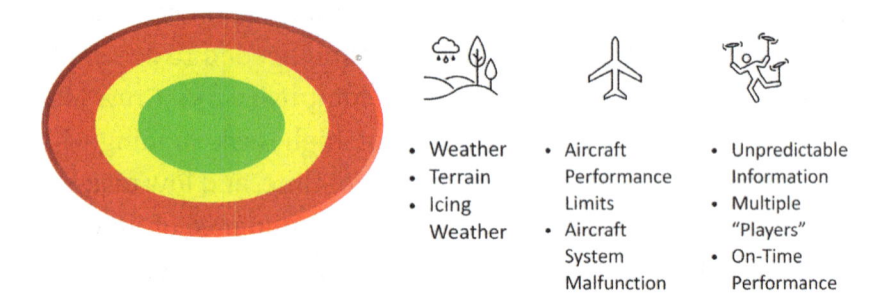

- Weather
- Terrain
- Icing Weather

- Aircraft Performance Limits
- Aircraft System Malfunction

- Unpredictable Information
- Multiple "Players"
- On-Time Performance

- **Crew Factors**—The physiological elements of Crew Members that negatively impact operational effectiveness and safety (e.g., fatigue, stress, fear, illness, experience). Additionally, group mindsets and attitudes, such as "press on regardless," can negatively impact the performance of an individual or Crew. It must also be noted that the normally positive aspect of having an instructor or expert flying with you (CFI, Check Pilot, Evaluator, etc.) can be a negative aspect if that expert makes a mistake and an inexperienced student or crewmember hesitates to bring it up. The expert should brief beforehand and insist that if a mistake is seen, it must be verbalized, regardless of status. If in the Green, be diplomatic, but if in the Yellow or Red, disregard rank and be more directive in communications.

Crew Factors:
Factors Impacting the Individual, Crew, or Team

- Level of Training
- Experience
- Currency
- Attitudes
- Psychological Factors
- Personality
- Impact of the Organization

- Recognizing the factors that increase risk can help you manage them.

Risky parked in front of the hangar and checked his watch. He was 45 minutes early, just like he wanted to be. Today he was going on his first solo cross country, and he wanted to stay ahead of everything. He grabbed his flight bag and locked his car before strolling towards the FBO, whistling to himself. He was happy his mother had allowed him to continue his training here in Cincinnati. If the weather held up, he would take his check ride around the middle of November.

His phone vibrated, and he pulled it out to check the message. It was from his new girlfriend, Sarah, the girl his mother introduced him to a few weeks back. *Good luck Luke! I think it's pretty cool you're going to go solo cross country on my birthday.* He stopped and read the message again, and a cold sweat broke out on his forehead. He was no longer whistling. They had only been dating a few weeks, and he had forgotten it was her birthday. He hadn't made any plans or bought her a gift. He could hear Vicky's voice in his head—*Unmet expectations are a major cause of people entering the Red.* He had never dealt with a girlfriend in the Red and was not looking forward to that experience. He hurried into the building in a panic.

Good thing I'm early. Maybe I can order something for her that can be delivered today. He hurried past the front desk into the briefing room without greeting anyone and pulled his iPad from his flight bag. *What was it she said she wanted?* Nothing came to him. He scrolled through pictures of moon lamps, scented candles, and boxes of chocolates, looking for anything that could be delivered by the end of the day. He settled on the combination bedside night light/alarm clock/and Bluetooth speaker in what he hoped was her favorite color, green. When the email confirmation came through, he breathed a sigh of relief and texted her. *Your gift is coming this afternoon. We can go to dinner after I get back. Where do you want to go?*

Feeling a little more at ease, he began flight planning on his iPad, hoping to have everything ready by the time Guns walked down from his hangar. The plan they had discussed had him flying from KI67, near Cincinnati, down to KJVY, near Louisville, and back. Guns wanted him to use KSER, in Seymour, Indiana, as a backup. He pulled up the weather for both locations and took a look. The weather forecast called for mostly clear skies all over northern Kentucky and southern Indiana during his time of flight, but it did include the possibility of rain showers in the vicinity of Louisville an hour after he was scheduled to depart there. He checked the NOTAMS and loaded his route.

He had everything ready when Guns walked into the room. Sarah's birthday gift still worried him, but that would have to wait. He silenced his phone and put it away so he could focus.

Guns took a seat and sat his coffee cup on the table. "So, what's your plan? How are you going to get to Jefferson City and back in one piece?"

Risky turned the iPad where they both could see it. "My plan is to takeoff from here and head southwest below the Class Bravo at 4500 feet making sure I'm outside the fifteen-mile ring and continue that direction using these fixes in the G-1000 to get me there."

"What landmarks are you going to use if you lose the GPS?"

"I can use the Ohio River. If I go south and follow it, it will take me there."

Guns nodded. "What's the weather forecast?"

Risky pulled up the weather information. "It's supposed to stay clear most of the day. They are forecasting a chance of rain showers, but not until an hour after I am scheduled to leave Jefferson City."

"And if the forecast is wrong and the showers come earlier?"

"I can turn north, descend down to 3500 feet to stay below the Military Operating Area, and go to Seymour, Indiana. The forecast there is good all day."

Guns continued trying to poke holes in Risky's plan. He asked about other alternates, Flight Following, and lost communication procedures. They discussed what he should do if he got lost, or as Guns was prone to call it—temporarily disoriented. They planned the fuel burn and how to refuel the aircraft if needed. With each question, Risky felt confident that he was prepared.

"One last question, what will you do if you accidentally fly into a cloud?" asked Guns.

"Just what you have told me a hundred times—Trust my instruments and make a shallow 180 degree turn out of the weather."

"Can't be too careful with a new pilot that trained mostly in the clear blue skies of Arizona. Good. But don't accept any unnecessary risk by flying into the cloud. Turn around before you get into any weather." Guns reached for Risky's iPad. "I don't know if I'm ever going to get used to using electronic logbooks. Okay, let me input my endorsement and you will be ready for your first solo cross country."

Risky arrived at the aircraft and tossed his flight bag into the right seat. Before starting the walkaround, he checked his cell phone. Two missed calls from Sarah. A pit formed in his stomach as he called her back.

She answered right away, "Finally!"

"I'm sorry. I was in the briefing with my instructor. What's up?"

"You forgot my birthday, didn't you?"

Risky closed his eyes and tried to think quickly. "I bought you a present and I'm taking you to dinner after I get back."

"Yeah, but you didn't call or text me this morning before your flight. You didn't post anything either."

Risky could feel the knot in his stomach getting tighter by the second. "Cut me a little slack! I've just been focused on this flight. I promise I'll make it up to you."

"So, you did forget."

Risky rubbed his forehead, searching for an answer. "Look, if it will make you feel better, I will post something before I take off. And I promise to make it a special birthday as soon as I get back."

She sighed. "Okay, it's just that sometimes I feel like you're more interested in flying than me."

"That's not true. It's just that flying takes a lot of focus to be safe, and you want me to be safe, don't you?"

"Of course."

"Then I need to stay focused so I always come home to you."

There was a long pause before she answered. "Okay, Luke. Stay focused and we can celebrate tonight."

When he hung up, Risky still wasn't sure if she believed his answers. He opened his photos and found a picture of the two of them together from a few nights back and posted it with a long, sappy happy-birthday tribute. When he finished, he checked his watch. He was twenty minutes behind schedule.

He hurried through the walkaround, hoping that the birthday present he ordered would get there on time and that she would like it. He decided some flowers were in order as well and wondered where he could get some roses on the way to her apartment. When he climbed into the seat and started buckling up, he saw Guns approaching the airplane with his coffee cup and a frown.

"Forgetting something?" asked Guns.

Risky wracked his brain, trying to remember the details of the walkaround, but all he remembered was his internal conversation about roses. "I don't think so," he answered, trying to sound confident.

Guns reached down and pulled the chocks away from the wheels and handed them to him. "If you remove these, it makes it a lot easier to taxi."

Risky turned white. He had never forgotten them before. He sighed and put them on the floorboard behind him. "Thanks, I guess I missed them."

"Why did you miss them? What distracted you?"

Risky let out a heavy sigh. "I guess I'm nervous."

"I noticed you were on a phone call for a while. Is everything okay?"

Risky stared out the windscreen and shook his head. "I forgot today was my girlfriend's birthday. I was trying to patch things up with her before I took off."

"Remember that target we talked about? The Green-Yellow-Red target?"

"Yeah, I remember."

"On a personal level, where do you think you are in the target?"

"I don't know. Maybe in the Yellow?" he answered, trying to sound convincing.

"How do you feel at this moment? Be honest."

He reflected before answering. "Honestly, my stomach is in knots and I'm worried about what's going to happen tonight with Sarah."

"Do you think that distracted you during your walkaround?"

"Probably."

"Which caused you to forget the chocks?"

He just nodded. The confidence he felt during the briefing had left him.

"Don't dwell on the mistake. This is a good lesson in human factors. Now you know how to recognize when you are personally drifting into the Yellow, or Red. More importantly, what Resource block can you use to help you get back into the Green?"

Risky chuckled. "Obviously, my instructor, but you won't be with me in the airplane."

"No, but if you had done your FLOW of checking for chains and chocks right before climbing into the airplane, like you've been taught, do you think you would have noticed the chocks?"

Risky realized that he had skipped that step. "I guess so."

"What Resources will you have in the airplane with you today?"

Risky glanced at his flight bag. "My iPad, the checklist, ATC."

Guns nodded. "If at any time today you feel like you are drifting into the Yellow or Red, remember those Resources to get you back into the Green." He put a hand on Risky's shoulder. "Is there anything you can do about forgetting Sarah's birthday right now?"

"Not really. I ordered a gift. I plan on getting flowers and a card on my way to her apartment."

"So, now you can set that all aside and go fly. The most important thing for you to do right now is focus on this flight so you can get home to her safe and sound. You can't celebrate her birthday with her if you're a smokin' hole in the ground."

He nodded.

"Why don't you redo your walkaround and that will put you back into the Green." Guns started walking away. "I'll head back inside and let you refocus. Oh, and turn off your cell phone."

Risky got out of the airplane and did another walk around, trying to put his mistake and Sarah's birthday out of his mind. He walked to the front of the airplane and stopped for a moment. "No chains. No chocks," he said to himself. He took a deep breath in and held it for a moment before releasing it. Then, he took out his cell phone and turned it off.

The departure was uneventful, and soon he was out of Class Bravo and cruising at 4500 feet on his way to KJVY. He followed the Ohio River and passed one of his emergency airfields, KIMS, along the way. The sky was mostly clear, but he could see a line of clouds building off in the distance. The drone of the engine pulled him along, and he relished the fact that he was alone in the air, charting his own course. He smiled when he thought about the party in Arizona that had led to this moment, but he didn't give himself much time for reflection.

He checked his route and compared the actual winds to the forecast winds. They were a little stronger, but not enough to negatively affect his fuel planning. He dialed up the ATIS and listened to the current weather and was surprised. It included showers on the field. He looked at the time. He was about thirty minutes later than he originally planned, probably because of the phone call with Sarah and having to do a second walkaround, but the forecast didn't call for showers until an hour after he was supposed to depart the airfield.

He looked at the horizon ahead. Sure enough, he could see a line of showers off in the distance. *No worries. I planned for this contingency.* He keyed the microphone. "N1822L request a change to destination due to weather."

"N1822L, what will be your new destination?"

"Kilo Sierra Echo Romeo."

"Roger. Cleared own navigation to Seymour airfield."

Risky turned the aircraft towards the north and began to plug the information into the G1000 for navigation. Before he finished, he looked up and found himself in a slight left turn. It took him a moment to recalibrate his eyes and brain to the attitude of the aircraft, but he focused on the horizon and returned the aircraft to level flight. When he glanced back down at the display, he was disoriented. He looked outside for landmarks, but without the river to follow, everything looked like Indiana farmland in the fall. He thought he would see a major highway, but the roads looked more like country roads.

He felt a moment of panic. *I'm lost, or temporarily disoriented.* He quickly assessed everything. He was flying straight and level on a 290-degree heading. He had enough fuel for several hours of flight. He relaxed a bit. He looked at the map display and could see that his heading had drifted, and he was heading more westerly than he needed. He turned back to the right until KSER was at the top of the display. He looked outside for recognizable landmarks and thought he saw a major highway. Then, he heard Gun's voice in his head—*Use your Resources.*

"Flight Following this is N1822L. Can you give me a good heading for KSER?"

"N1822L looks like about a 350 heading will work but be advised the upper MOA, Juliet Papa Golf-Bravo, is active. You should be below it at your altitude."

"Roger." He turned to heading 350 and took a moment to stabilize. He pulled up the VFR map on his iPad and compared the landmarks on the map with what he saw outside the airplane. Things began to coincide. He plugged some data into the G1000, being careful not to enter into another shallow bank. According to the display and the VFR map on the iPad, at this altitude, he would be below the upper MOA.

The remainder of the flight was largely uneventful. He was able to use the interstate highway and other ground references, backed up by his map display in the aircraft and on his iPad, to find the airfield. Based on the ATIS information, he planned for runway 23. He remembered his radio calls and announced his entry to the downwind on the CTAF, but no one else was in the pattern. He made a full-stop landing and taxied to the ramp in front of the blue and white hangar. The sign across the top read, "FREEMAN FIELD, Seymour Indiana, Elevation 583."

He checked the fuel before shutting down and setting the parking brake. *Over a half a tank left. That's more than enough.* When he put the flight into his logbook, he realized he was an hour behind his original schedule. *I need to hurry if I want to make it back in time to take Sarah out for her birthday.* He turned on his phone and took a selfie in front of the hangar before checking his messages. She had texted him five times to check on him. He sent her the picture and hurried into the FBO.

After filing his flight plan and checking the weather for his return flight, he hurried back out to the aircraft and did a quick walkaround, remembering to check for the chocks. Before he turned off his cell phone, he checked the status of the gift he had ordered Sarah and was happy to see it had arrived. *If I take off now, everything will work out.*

When he flipped the master switch and checked the instruments, he noticed the fuel quantity read zero. *I know I have enough fuel. I landed with both tanks over half full.* He flipped off the master switch and switched it back again, but the display remained the same. In the back of his mind, he knew he should call Guns, but he also realized that might ground him, and he would miss Sarah's birthday. *I know I have enough gas to make it home.*

He started the motor and took off.

Once he departed the pattern, Risky called for flight following. "N1822L is airborne off of Freeman Municipal headed to Cincinnati West climbing to 5500 feet. Request flight following."

"N1822L squawk 6254 and ident."

Risky put in the code and sent the signal.

"N1822L radar contact. Are you going direct to Cincinnati West?"

"Affirmative," answered Risky, trying to sound confident over the radio.

"Are you aware that Restricted Areas 3403 Alpha and Bravo are active?"

Risky wracked his brain, trying to remember where those restricted areas were. He looked at the map display and zoomed in. They were directly in his flight path. When he changed destinations, he must have missed them in his planning.

"Roger, I see that now."

"Recommend you fly heading zero three zero to go north around them."

"Roger. Heading zero three zero." He turned to the heading. A knot formed in his stomach. *How much extra fuel is this going to take?*

He began trying to check distances and do the math, but every time he focused on that, he would look up and find himself in a shallow bank and have to correct. After a couple of tries, he decided to wait until he got to altitude and trimmed the aircraft for cruise.

I know both tanks were at least half full when I landed in Seymour. He checked his new routing and calculated it would only take him about thirty minutes to get back to Cincinnati West with this new routing. *I should have plenty of gas.* He had an uneasy feeling, but pressed on.

He pulled out the emergency checklist to see if it offered any help but didn't see anything that applied. Calling Guns at this point wasn't an option either. He remembered that he had the aircraft handbook on his iPad and thought about looking for information there, but he was worried about aircraft control. *What do I know about the fuel system?* He remembered the aircraft had about 40 gallons of usable fuel, and it used about nine gallons an hour. With a bit of mental math, he calculated that he would land with at least ten gallons in the tanks when he landed. He checked the fuel selector and made sure that both tanks were selected.

With the fuel issue mostly settled in his head, Risky focused on the remaining flight. He could see on the map display that he would clear the restricted area in a few miles, and then he could turn towards KI67. Other than a few high clouds, the horizon showed no signs of weather. The aircraft hummed along, responding to his commands. It was a great day to fly.

With the help of flight following, he descended below the Class Bravo airspace and made an uneventful landing. When he pulled into the ramp, Guns came strolling up with his coffee cup and a stern look on his face.

"Is your cell phone broken? Why didn't you call me before you took off?" asked Guns as soon as Risky opened the door.

Risky grabbed his flight bag and climbed out. "I guess I was in a hurry."

"Did you text your girlfriend?"

Risky pretended to adjust the seatbelts in the airplane to avoid eye contact. "Yeah, I sent her a picture."

"But nothing for your flight instructor who put his ticket on the line?" He took a sip from his coffee cup. "Meet me in the hangar to debrief." He turned and started for his hangar.

Risky checked his watch and sighed. He only had about thirty minutes to debrief and still pick up Sarah on time. After Guns' reception, he was certain he would need more time. He texted his girlfriend that he was safely back and told her he was running about thirty minutes late and hoped she would understand.

Risky started the debrief with an apology. "I'm sorry I didn't call you, or at least text you, from Seymour. I was just trying to get back."

Guns took a deep breath but didn't say anything. "So, tell me how it went?"

Risky sat down. "The first leg went well, after I got airborne, but there were showers over Jeffersonville, and I had to divert to Seymour."

"That explains why no one had seen you when I called the FBO in Jeffersonville."

Risky blushed. "Yeah... sorry about that."

Guns stroked his mustache. "Tell me what Resources you used when you diverted to Seymour."

"Well, we briefed that as a possibility before I took off. I spoke with Flight Following. I used my map display and my iPad when I got lost."

Guns raised an eyebrow. "When you got lost?"

"Well, more like disoriented. But I remembered what you taught me—remember the Resource blocks. It worked."

"Okay, what else?"

Risky hesitated and, for a moment, wondered how much information he should offer up about the second leg. He didn't want to get into any more trouble with Guns, but he knew it would be worse if he tried to hide it. "On the second leg, the fuel gauge stopped working."

"Oh? When did it stop working?"

Risky stared at the floor. "When I turned on the master switch."

Guns nodded and steepled his fingers like a psychiatrist in session. "So, the fuel gauge stopped working before you took off?"

"Yeah, but I knew that both tanks showed over half full when I shut down and I didn't want to miss my girlfriend's birthday. I did some quick calculations and figured I would land with plenty of gas. Sure enough, it worked out."

"Okay, what Resource did you use to determine that you had enough fuel?"

"I remembered that the tanks have about forty gallons of usable fuel. The airplane uses about nine gallons an hour. The flight was only about forty minutes, total. Based on the tanks being at least half full when I shut down, I calculated I would land with at least ten gallons."

"Okay, you relied on your Knowledge. Did you check with anyone at the FBO? Did you look at the tanks to make sure they had fuel?" He pursed his lips. "Did you call your instructor?"

Risky sighed. "No, I didn't do anything of those things."

"Why not?"

"I guess I was in a hurry to get back."

"Pull out that card I gave you on RRM."

Risky dug it out of his flight bag.

"See the section that says 'Factors Increasing Risk'?"

Risky turned over the card and nodded.

"I know I haven't trained you on this yet, but which one of those factors pushed you into the Yellow today?"

Risky looked over the card for an awkward minute as Guns waited in silence. "I would say Crew Factors."

"I agree. Your girlfriend's birthday, and her texts, distracted you during your walkaround and you forgot the chocks. It sounds like you also felt pressure to get back home on time, or get-home-itis. Did you make any mistakes because you were trying to do too much at one time?"

"Yeah, I think that's how I got lost... temporarily disoriented."

"Did the fuel gauge problem distract you any?"

Risky nodded. "I forgot about those restricted areas on the way home. Luckily Flight Following helped me out."

"Oh! Master Rogers remembered to use his Resource blocks." Guns held up his coffee cup and then took a drink. "Most of the distractions that increase risk and decrease safety can be categorized as Task Loading, Additive Conditions, or Crew Factors. Sounds like you dealt with all of them today, BUT you used your Resources to keep you in the Green." He scowled. "Except for calling your flight instructor!"

Guns stood up. "There's one more thing we need to do before you go pick up your girlfriend for her birthday. Follow me." He started walking towards the FBO.

Guns grabbed a ladder and a yardstick from the FBO and opened the ladder next to the wing of the Cessna. "If you had called me, or spoken with someone from the FBO in Seymour, we could have helped you measure the fuel before takeoff." He climbed up and opened the fuel cap. He dipped the yardstick into the tank and showed it to Risky. "Roughly every inch is three gallons of fuel, for this aircraft. You landed with..." He eyeballed the yardstick. "Maybe six gallons, if the other tank is the same."

Risky nodded but didn't say anything. His face turned white when he realized how far off his calculations were.

Guns climbed down, folded the ladder, and returned it to the FBO while Risky just waited by the wing.

"Yep. You survived today partly because of luck. Luck is not a Resource. You can't depend on it." He put a hand on Risky's shoulder. "You get good airmanship by having bad airmanship and living to tell about it. Next time, have enough good airmanship to manage those factors that increase risk by using all the other Resource blocks. That way, you won't need to rely on luck."

Risky nodded but didn't say anything.

Guns looked at his watch. "Don't you have a birthday party to get to?"

Risky drove methodically from the airport to his house. He made a quick change and grabbed the package he had ordered. His mother insisted that he use one of her gift bags and gave him a nice yellow one. He shoved the gift into the bag and grabbed a bouquet of red roses on his way to pick up Sarah. He feigned excitement when she got into the car, but his mind was still stuck on today's flight.

After they ordered dinner, Sarah opened the gift. "How did you know green was my favorite color?" she asked.

"What? Oh, I think you mentioned it once." He felt relieved that he had guessed correctly.

Sarah leaned over and gave him a kiss on the cheek. "Thank you! I'm just glad you remembered my birthday and made it home safely." Risky smiled politely. He looked at the items on the table—a green speaker, a yellow gift bag, and red roses. A big smile broke out over his face, and he laughed to himself. *Green, Yellow, Red. Even in my relationships, when factors increase my risk, I just gotta use my Resources to stay in the Green.*

Have you ever been in an emotional conversation and didn't hear an alarm or buzzer go off? You were in the Red, or at least the Yellow. Several factors can drive you and your performance out of the Green. The RRM model categorizes them into three categories: Task Loading, Additive Conditions, and Crew Factors.

Task Loading *is the amount of time needed vs the time available to accomplish tasks. You experience high task loading when you have numerous tasks to complete in a limited amount of time. You experience low task loading when you find yourself with little or nothing to do for long periods of time. Both can increase risk and decrease performance.*

High task loading decreases performance by causing you to prioritize tasks incorrectly, like analyzing a caution light over flying the aircraft. It can lead to channelized attention, focusing on a single task at the expense of all other tasks, like focusing on holding a heading as the aircraft approaches a stall. It can also cause inaction or action paralysis in a critical moment, like not responding to a fire warning bell because you are completely overwhelmed.

Low task loading also decreases performance and increases risk. It can cause complacency, like glossing over a critical briefing item because you are no longer mentally engaged. It can lead to inattention or distraction, like missing a descent checklist because your mind is elsewhere after a long time at cruise altitude. It can create mental lethargy, like forgetting to perform required fuel checks during a long cruise segment.

Task loading is impacted by proficiency, priorities, preparation, and perception.

A proficient pilot who can perform required tasks quickly and correctly is capable of handling more tasks in a given amount of time, whereas a pilot who is not proficient will not have the same capacity. Improving proficiency through practice and training will enable you to reduce the amount of time needed to perform the given tasks, thus reducing the impact of high task loading.

A proficient pilot can also intuitively prioritize what deserves the most attention and can use available Resources efficiently. A clear understanding of operational priorities will speed up the judgment needed to make decisions when prioritizing tasks or changing plans. Prioritizing tasks, like choosing to fly the aircraft before completing a checklist or choosing to complete a checklist before making a radio call, will help keep you in the Green.

Preparing for a flight, or flight segment, will reduce the impact of both high and low task loading. Reviewing the weather, route, and navigation for a given flight beforehand will reduce both the number of tasks and the time needed to perform the tasks once in flight. Additionally, using times of low task loading to review changing weather conditions, routing, and approaches will help keep you mentally alert and engaged.

Your perception of the time available and time required can also become distorted during high and low task loading. The stress of a *time-critical moment may cause you to perceive that you have limited time, when in reality, ample time is available. Rushing and taking shortcuts can cause errors and actually increase the time required. Augustus, the founder of the Roman Empire, is attributed with saying "Festina Lente," which translates as, "Make haste, slowly." In aviation it's more commonly expressed as, "Slow down to go fast." On the other hand, you may perceive you have an abundance of time during low task loading, when in reality, time is limited. This can create complacency and mental lethargy.*

How do we adjust task loading during flight? Change the time available or change the time required using the ABCD process

A: The first step is recognition. Some of the symptoms are making small errors you usually don't make, difficulty communicating, struggling to find solutions to problems, or feeling general anxiety. When you sense the effects of task loading, take a momentary pause to properly Assess the time available.

B: Balance time available, resources, and priorities.

You can adjust the time available if you have enough fuel. Fuel is the equivalent of time in the tanks. Create more time by accepting a delayed departure, abandoning an approach and going around, or entering a holding pattern.

Balance the load by using Resources. Is there a Checklist, Procedure, or External Resource that can help you manage the tasks? If possible, distribute the workload by offloading tasks to others, or to Automation.

Adjust priorities and offload lower priority tasks in the moment. Modify your current plans or goals for the sake of a higher priority goal, like diverting to an alternate instead of shooting an approach at an airport below your personal minimums.

C: Promote open communication allowing for direct communication with other crewmembers or External Resources during high or low task loading. Good communication will help you distribute the workload, prioritize tasks, and trap errors. Effective briefings mitigate the impact of high task loading by prioritizing or delegating tasks before they become overwhelming, and help reengage you after a long period of low task loading.

D: Develop consistency of performance and execution. Make the situation more predictable with improved skills training that reduces the amount of time needed to perform a task. Get good at performing the required tasks to minimize the time required.

Finally, when task loading is low, develop a habit of scanning and checking the state of the aircraft during long intervals of inactivity. Checking fuel, winds, engine readings, and navigation at regular intervals can keep you engaged in the flight.

Additive Conditions are any conditions that can distract you or detract from your performance. We use the term "additive" because they are not singular in nature, but often layer one on top of the another adding complexity to the situation. It can be anything from a distracting radio call to a thunderstorm. Weather, particularly conditions not forecast, can degrade your performance and the performance of your aircraft. Use Automation (weather display tools) and External Resources (ATC) to mitigate those risks. Briefings and proper fuel planning can provide you with options and alleviate stress in rapidly changing conditions.

An aircraft malfunction, no matter how minor, will require your attention. This can be a dangerous distraction and can lead to channelized attention—focusing on environmental factors or tasks at the expense of all others.

Situations that differ significantly from expectations can push a person or crew into the Yellow in a number of ways. Our brains are hard-wired to see what we expect to see, so it requires some intentional attention to notice changes. In addition, it requires adaptability and flexibility to respond, particularly if it is necessary to change previous plans. When time is short or prior expectations are high, it is possible to end up in the Red. Constantly assessing and reassessing changing conditions and balancing priorities with the help of the principles of risk management can keep you in the Green.

Consistently employing the ABCD process with emphasis on available Resources will help mitigate the impact of Additive Conditions.

Crew Factors *deal specifically with any performance-decreasing factor that originates with a crew member. Any time you feel stress, fear, or fatigue, your risk increases. It can manifest itself in a 'can-do attitude' that pushes you to take risks you would not normally take. You may suffer from 'get-home-itis' and ignore policies or procedures because you just want to get home on time. When you feel any of these conditions creeping into your performance, slow down. Make sure you are utilizing all the Resources available to you, and if necessary, ground yourself until the condition is resolved.*

Failing to recognize these factors can be deadly. Sometimes it is hard to accurately judge your physical, emotional, and mental state. Ask yourself, "Am I pushing too hard and taking shortcuts around Policies or Procedures? Am I making mental errors I don't normally make? Am I finding it hard to concentrate because of something going on in my personal life?" Rarely is everything perfect, but learning to make good self-assessments and continually applying all available resources will prevent unnecessary risk taking.

Because it is typically easier to recognize when someone else is slipping into the Yellow or Red, External Resources are perhaps the most valuable in recognizing and mitigating the factors that increase risk. Seek competent peers and mentors. Create layers of accountability within your flying operation. Speak up when you see someone else dealing with any of these factors. You may be the Resource that helps someone else get back into the Green.

Chapter Nine: Choose a Strategy

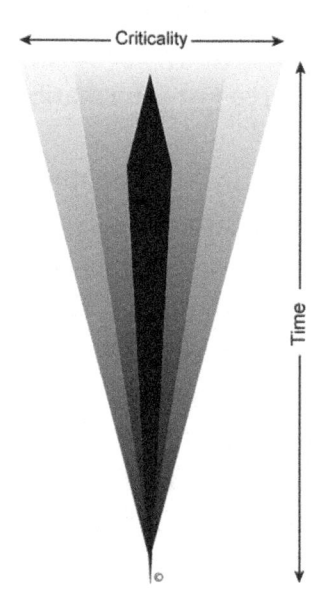

Making good decisions is a crucial skill at every level.
—Peter F. Drucker

Key Concepts
- The cone of time illustrates decision-making strategies and the types of Resources, including other people, that work best in different parts of the cone. Understanding the cone of time can help us determine the priority and type of decision we face.
- The vertical axis of the cone represents the product of time and the criticality of a decision.
- The narrow tip represents a scenario where there is very little time to make the right decision in a high-risk environment.

- The top represents the situation where there is very little time pressure and time to correct the course of action if a mistake is made.
- Risk increases as we move closer to the time-critical (narrow tip) area of the cone of time.
- The optimal decision-making strategy is impacted by: Available time, criticality of the decision, available tools, Resources, & sources of information, and the roles of the people involved
- Preparation, while time is available, improves performance during time-critical situations.
- Analytical decision making is used when it is important to get the BEST answer. It often requires the use of technology and data to examine past performance and trends. It's used to establish long-term goals, conduct in-depth planning, and create the Resources needed for action-based decisions. Analytical decision making is most successful in the Green, particularly if other people are involved. Analytical decision making is possible in the Yellow when well supported by references and technology that has been prepared in advance. Depending on Analytical decision-making when in the Red is nearly impossible.
- Knowledge-based decision making applies to situations where a GOOD decision is needed, particularly when it requires cooperation with other people. This could be a complex situation where there are no pre-defined tools or Resources that fit the need or when the inclusion of other people's insights, ideas, and cooperation will improve the outcome. Knowledge-based decision making uses easily-recalled

knowledge that can be applied using skill and past experience. Knowledge-based decisions are best made when in the Green. They will be more difficult in the Yellow, and very challenging in the Red (particularly if other people are involved.)
- Action-oriented decision making applies to situations where a QUICK decision is advantageous, such as in time-critical operations or when there is low risk and time to correct a decision. Because action-based decisions are often based on intuition, it's important to prepare and use pre-defined priorities, tools and Resources to ensure actions and decisions are accurate and predictable in high-risk environments, or working with other people. With proper preparation, action-based decisions can be successful in the Green, Yellow, and Red.
- A single decision can bounce between strategies.
- The ABCD process is impacted by the amount of available time between two or more events. Assessing what is occurring now and how it will affect a future outcome helps to accurately determine the time sensitivity of a task and avoid time misperceptions.
- Time is often misperceived by Crew Members in the Yellow or Red.
- Debriefs of past performance help prepare for future time-critical situations.

The Examiner handed Risky his temporary Private Pilot Certificate. "Congratulations! You now have a license to learn."

Risky shook the Examiner's hand and smiled. He had done it. He was now a Private Pilot, and he had finished before Christmas.

He stopped by the hangar to tell Guns the good news and found him sitting in his easy chair reading a book. "I passed," he said.

Guns raised his coffee cup and smiled. "Of course you passed. You were prepared."

Risky chuckled to himself. It was the exact reaction he expected from Guns. "And he didn't ask me any questions about the Wright Brothers."

"Did he ask you about weight and balance? Or stalls?"

"Of course."

Guns raised his coffee cup. "Then he asked you about the Wright Brothers."

Risky grinned and shook his head. "I think I want to continue. I think I want to be a commercial pilot."

Guns stroked his mustache. "You might want to talk with your mother about that."

"What?"

"Let's just say she picked me in hopes that my instructional demeanor might dissuade you from wanting to continue in aviation."

Risky gave him a surprised look. "I guess that plan backfired."

Sarah was waiting on the front porch when Risky got home. She clapped and shouted, "Way to go! Good job!" They hugged and celebrated with a kiss.

His mother was in the kitchen. "Congratulations! You're a pilot now."

"Thanks," offered Risky, trying not to seem too excited.

"Tell us about it," said Sarah. "Was the examiner tough?"

"Not nearly as tough as Guns." Risky looked at his mother, and she looked at the floor. "It went well. No surprises."

"Does that mean you can take me for a flight now?" asked Sarah.

"Yes," Risky smiled. "Yes, it does."

His mother cleared her throat. "And how about your mother?"

"You can both go, provided there aren't any issues with weight and balance."

His mother pointed at him with one of her manicured nails. "Never ask a woman about her weight and balance." They all laughed.

After they had a piece of cake to celebrate, Risky made the announcement. "I think I want to be a commercial pilot."

Sarah clapped. "Does that mean we can fly for free?"

"Yeah, if I get hired by an airline."

His mother stood up and started collecting the dishes without saying anything.

Risky seized the opportunity. "Mom, did you really pick Guns as my instructor because you thought he would be so difficult I would give up?"

His mother turned on the faucet and began rinsing dishes and putting them in the dishwasher. "I just wanted to be sure you weren't doing this just because your father wanted to be a pilot when he was young."

Risky stood and walked over to her. "Thank you, that was a good decision. After this experience, I've realized that I want to be a pilot for myself, not because Dad wanted to be a pilot."

His mother looked up at him and smiled. "Do I get free flights too?"

One Year Later

Luke drove onto the airport and parked in front of a hangar with a big sign on the wall—Sweet Aerial Inspections. Between finishing high school and earning money to pay for his flying lessons, it had taken him a year to get his commercial license. He had hoped to become a Certified Flight Instructor, but Guns had suggested he take a job flying as a pipeline inspector to build time faster, and put in a good word to help him get the job. He grabbed his flight bag and went through the front door.

A tall, Black man stood with his back to the door looking at a large map that covered most of the wall. "If y'all are here looking for a job, I already hired someone."

"Well," replied Luke. "I hope I'm the guy you hired."

He turned around and gave him a once over. "You must be the young man Guns sent me. Nice to finally meet you." He stuck out his hand. "Alan Sweet, president of Sweet Aerial Inspections, but you can call me Sweet Tea."

He returned the smile and gave him a firm handshake. "Luke Rogers."

Sweet Tea chuckled. "Luke? Guns told me you went by Risky. He told me a little about your nickname. I see he also lectured you on firm handshakes."

Luke shook his head. "Guns lectured me about a lot of things."

"Yeah, he's pretty good at lecturing." Sweet Tea sat down and offered Luke a chair across from him. "Sit down and take a load off. You need a bottle of water?"

"No thank you." He sat down and tried to relax. He had been offered the job, but this still felt a lot like an interview. "How do you know Guns?"

"Guns was my first squadron commander years ago," he answered. "It seems like another lifetime ago. He said you were trying to build your hours and go fly for the airlines."

"Yes sir."

"Let me see your logbook."

Luke dug out his iPad and pulled up his electronic logbook before handing it to him. "I've got almost three hundred hours."

Sweet Tea scrolled through the entries and handed it back. "Well, before we go fly, do you want to be called name or your nickname? Luke or Risky?"

Luke blushed a bit. "I think it might be better if I use my name. Somehow, I don't think the nickname 'Risky' is going to help my professional pilot career."

Sweet Tea laughed and stood up. "Well Luke let's see if you can fly." He motioned for him to follow. A few minutes later they were airborne in a Cessna 182.

After a couple of patterns, Sweet Tea took the controls. "Okay, you can handle pattern work. Let me show how we fly this airplane." They exited the pattern and descended to three hundred above the ground. Once he trimmed the aircraft and stabilized it, he continued. "This is where we fly. It doesn't give you much room for error. Notice that I'm not looking at you when I talk. My eyes are constantly looking out. My hands are always on the controls." He looked over at Luke. "If I do have to look inside, I start an internal timer—one thousand one, one thousand two, one thousand three." He looked back outside. "Never let your attention stay inside for longer than three seconds. You don't have a lot of time to react at this altitude." He shook the controls. "You take the aircraft."

Luke focused on the ground rushing by much closer than he was comfortable. He took the controls and responded, "I have the aircraft." At first, he gripped the yoke with a death grip, but then forced himself to relax and loosen his grip.

"Keep your eyes on the horizon and scan from side to side—10, 12, and 2. Just follow this pipeline."

Luke let his eyes scan from side to side and soon began to feel more comfortable. "This is kind of fun."

"Yeah, try doing it at four hundred knots. Which brings up a good point. Keep a few extra knots down here. They can buy you some time."

Luke nodded his head, but he didn't understand, and he didn't want to ask a question at the moment.

"If anything happens, remember the phrase—climb to cope. Let me show you." Sweet Tea shook the controls. "I have the aircraft."

Luke released the controls and put his hands in his lap.

"Let's say you are flying along and suddenly your engine quits." Sweet Tea pulled the throttle to idle. "The first thing you do is start a climb." He raised the nose gently and the aircraft began to climb. "This will give you a few extra seconds to cope with the problem." The aircraft climbed to almost eight hundred feet above the ground before it reached the optimum glide speed and began to descend again. "See how high we were able to climb before we ran out of energy? We traded airspeed for altitude, which will give us more time to work on a solution. That's why it's important to keep up your speed when you're down in the dirt."

Luke nodded, but this time he really did understand.

"Okay, you take the aircraft and try it."

Luke took control, pushed up the power, and descended back down to three hundred feet. After he stabilized the aircraft and picked up speed, Sweet Tea reached over and pulled the throttle to idle and said, "Your engine just quit."

Luke mimicked the maneuver he had just seen. When the aircraft began to descend again at optimum glide speed, he was almost eight hundred feet above the ground as well. He checked the ignition and fuel, and began looking for a place to land.

"Nice! But remember that it doesn't have to be anything as drastic as losing an engine. Any distraction at low altitude can kill you. If anything distracts you, climb to cope."

Sweet Tea pushed in the throttle. "Flying, particularly low-level flying like this, requires intentional attention. You discipline your mind to pay attention to the important details. Believe it or not, flying pipeline can begin to feel routine, so your mind can wander and boom! There goes your situational awareness, which can be followed by a bigger BOOM!" He smacked the dash for effect and startled Luke.

Sweet Tea chuckled and shook the controls. "I have the aircraft. Let me show you the pattern entry." He turned back to the airfield. "This job requires you to fly at the pointy-end of the spear. The risks are high if we don't constantly pay attention, have good reflexes, and follow procedures. You seem to have the right reflexes. That's good. And I don't see any risky behavior." He grinned. "So, we'll call you Luke, unless you do something to change my mind.

They flew back and landed. Luke was excited to land his first flying job. As they were walking back to the hangar office, Sweet Tea asked, "Did Guns ever lecture you about the cone of time?"

"He lectured me on handshakes, the Wright Brothers, and how to measure fuel with a yard stick, but I don't remember him mentioning the cone of time."

"He must be slipping in his old age. C'mon, let me explain it to you." Sweet Tea moved to a conference room with a whiteboard. "Take a seat," he directed.

Luke sat down where he could see the board.

Sweet Tea drew a vertical cone on the board with the narrow point at the bottom. As he was drawing, he continued to talk: "This is the cone of time. It's a bit more abstract than the RRM Model, but it really helps you understand the decision-making strategies available to you."

He drew a vertical arrow beside the cone. "The height is a combination of how much time is needed and the criticality of the decision." He tapped the narrow tip at the bottom with his marker. "Down here, at the pointy end, you have to make the right decisions quickly because it's both time-critical AND high risk, like flying 300 feet above the ground.

"It's really weird, but people will actually develop a decision-making bias based on their experiences. Pilots, police officers, firefighters, anyone that has to make snap decisions on a regular basis, are good at time-critical decision making and usually comfortable giving a quick answer, even if it's just an estimate. They intuitively use the ABCD loop and know they can make a correction before anything adverse happens."

He tapped the wide end of the top of the cone. "But up here you have a lot of time and the decision isn't as critical. So, you can take as much time as needed to make a decision. People that are not used to using predefined Resources or working in a time-critical environment—like researchers, analysts, government workers—work up here and may want to talk through a problem to get to a solution." He chuckled. "People like that can drive pilots crazy."

"Oh. My. Goodness." Said Luke.

"What?" asked Sweet Tea, surprised by the interruption.

"I finally understand why I get annoyed with my mother. She has no routines and talks through every decision like we have all the time in the world." He shook his head. "It drives me nuts! It takes forever for her to get ready to go anywhere. She constantly loses her keys. The simplest decision takes f-o-r-e-v-e-r."

Sweet Tea laughed. "Yeah, I know the type. They're afraid of being wrong for some reason. Painful for people like you and me to live with at times, but it's a great decision bias if you are a civil engineer building bridges."

He wrote out ABCD beside the cone. "The ABCD process is impacted by the amount of time available. You don't want to sit around and analyze a problem ad nauseum if you just lost an engine at three hundred feet. You need to act. That's why this middle black part is called 'Action Oriented.' If you're down here at this pointy end, the only Resources you have are the ones you prepared before you got there. That's why there are some maneuvers you practice so that you can do them almost instinctively when needed and why you study some knowledge until you know it as well as you know your own name."

"Like 'climb to cope,'" said Luke.

"Exactly. And by the way I was impressed how you went straight to the fuel selector and ignition during the simulated engine failure."

Luke smiled.

"You've heard the term CRM? Crew Resource Management?" Sweet Tea asked.

"Of course."

"Well, those Resources and the ABCD Process are foundational to good CRM. However, your Resources are also limited by time. You probably won't have time to figure out new solutions or look up system schematic or procedure. Long conversations with crew members or dispatch aren't an option. You might not even get done with all the checklists you normally accomplish." He drew an arrow moving from the narrow portion of the cone to the wide portion. "Unless you can create more time by putting the aircraft back into a safe flying position, your options are limited to what has been pre-planned."

"Got it."

"Now let's say you are flying up at five thousand feet and your engine quits. How is that different?"

"I would be a little more relaxed at five thousand feet because I have some time to figure out my course of action."

"Exactly! We have moved up the cone to this area." He pointed to the middle of the cone. "We need to take action to maintain aircraft control and stabilize the situation, but we have some time to run through the ABCD process multiple times. It's time sensitive, but not time critical. We also have more time to use more of our Resources like Procedures and Checklists. Because we have more time, the ABCD process and our Resources can have more impact."

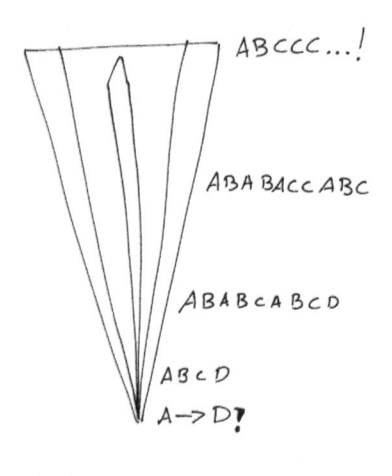

Sweet Tea stepped back and crossed his arms. "What if we are analyzing a new pipeline route for a customer? Where would you put that on this cone?"

Luke shrugged. "Up in the wide part, out on the edge?"

"Right! We have time to get things right. As long as we are not going to crash and burn, we can take all the time needed to get the best answers. We're in the same spot during pre-flight planning. We can sit around and talk about the hazards and risks along the route—terrain, traffic, weather. We have enough time to really dig into the information and even do some research. It isn't time sensitive. We can assess and reassess, balance risks with Resources, communicate multiple possibilities and use of Resources long before we have to actually fly the route for the first time—Do and debrief." He put the marker down.

"One more thing, if you need the cooperation of other people to get something done, it's good to include them in the discussions during the planning process." He shook his head. "I've found in business if you let folks be part of solution, they're more likely to go along with the final plans. Sometimes this requires some patience, but you never really know where the next great idea may come from, or if you may be missing an important detail."

Luke nodded. "Seems simple enough."

"It is simple, but when we get under stress, we often distort the time available. Sometimes we want to analyze when we should act, or vice versa. The key is constantly assessing and asking yourself, 'What's new? What's different now?' The second thing we forget is that we can often buy ourselves some time through good preparation and like you saw in the airplane today, *climb to cope*."

Luke nodded. "So, when can I start?"

Sweet Tea checked his watch. "Everyone should be back around four o'clock. If you want to hang around here for a couple of hours, you can meet everyone and get started tomorrow." He stuck out his hand. "Welcome to the team!"

Luke stood and gave him a firm handshake. "Thanks! Do you mind if I ask you a question?"

"Sure."

"Why didn't you do like Guns and go to the airlines when you left the Air Force?"

Sweet Tea smiled. "After twenty years of punching the clock, I wanted to be the master of my own time, and I enjoy having different challenges every day." He chuckled under his breath. "Owning a business sure does bring its variety of challenges." He shrugged. "This operation was for sale and I had some connections to make it grow. So, I took a chance." He grinned. "Besides, who wants to drive a bus in the air?"

Time is a finite resource that must be managed well.

Decision making falls into one of three categories: Action-oriented, Knowledge based, and Analytical. Even when there is more time available, an action-based decision is an efficient way to get started, and there is time to take corrective action if needed. At the narrow end of the cone of time, both operational effectiveness and safety are improved by using pre-defined Resources. When pre-defined Resources do not address a situation, or it is advantageous to think through a situation, knowledge-based decisions are appropriate. When the risk of an incorrect response is high, analytical decision-making is called for.

When you find yourself in the Yellow or Red, your perception of time can get distorted. You may think you have more time than you actually do, or you may think that immediate action is required when you actually have more time to analyze the problem before acting. If you have ever been in an accident, you may have even experienced temporal distortion, where the brain perceives time differently—things appear to happen in slow motion or blend into an indiscernible blur. The decisions and actions you take must be relevant to the time available.

Because flying is action-oriented, you will feel the urge to do something when a problem arises, but in reality, you may have more time than you feel like you do. One technique to keep yourself from moving too quickly is to "wind the clock." This comes from the old manual clocks in cockpits, but it is a good way to force yourself to use the resource of time appropriately. Take a beat, and slow things down. Very few things require immediate action in the aircraft. This will help keep you in the Green and ensure that the ABCD process remains intact and isn't shorted.

The ABCD process is impacted by the time available.

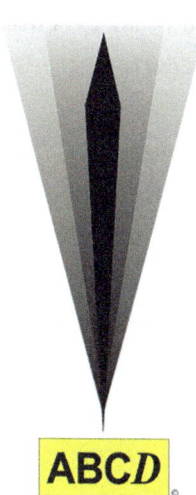

A: Time available impacts situation Assessment because it impacts our perception. During high task loading, we can fall prey to channelized attention and miss important cues. With low task loading, we can become complacent and not perceive changing conditions. Both conditions require intentional attention. Intentional attention refers to using self-discipline to maintain situation assessment. In periods of high task loading, we must pay attention to the important issues, not the distractions, and continue to absorb new information. In periods of low task loading, particularly *in routine operations or working as the monitoring crewmember, we must proactively look for changing conditions and their impact on desired outcomes.*

B: *Time available has a significant impact on the Balance of Resources and distribution of workload. Routine operations depend heavily on the design and use of the pre-defined Resources to manage tasks and risks with predetermined actions. In unpredictable or complex situations, other decision-making strategies are needed. Knowledge-based or Action-oriented decisions may be necessary to return us to a position to utilize predetermined Resources.*

C: *Time available has a significant impact on Communications. When time is limited, communications must become more direct. Green to Green communication is easy, but as individuals move into the Yellow and Red, limited perceptions and decreased ability to think through issues have a significant impact on communications. Standardized communications, such as callouts, proper radio communication, and prescribed checklist language, reduce confusion in time-sensitive and time-critical situations. When time is not sensitive, communication can be more indirect and exploratory.*

D: *Time available impacts how we execute and carry out our plan. When time is available, we can execute our plan and take corrective action multiple times. When time is sensitive, we can execute and make minor corrections. When time is critical, we must execute correctly, or almost correctly, to achieve success or return to a less time-critical state.*

Debriefs should be performed only when the time for open discussion is available. Avoid laundry lists of mistakes or failures and allow for an open discussion of what went well and what could have been improved.

Understanding the cone of time will help you prioritize action, keep you in the Green, and help you manage the risks.

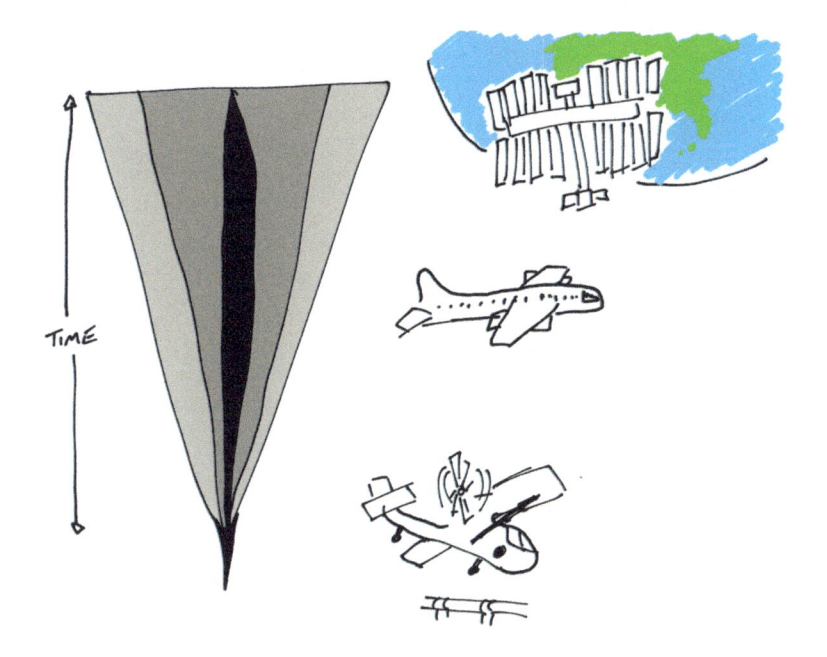

ALTITUDE CAN GIVE YOU MORE
TIME TO MAKE DECISIONS

Chapter Ten: Cultivate Resilience

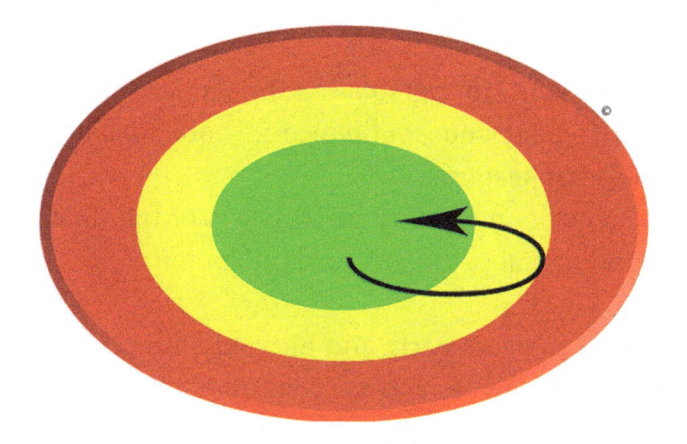

"Success is not final; failure is not fatal: It is the courage to continue that counts."
—Winston S. Churchill

Key Concepts
- The arrow in the target represents the ability to return to the Green after getting into the Yellow or Red.
- Resilience is future oriented, learns from experience, and avoids excessive focus on past mistakes to be able to concentrate on what must be accomplished.
- Resilience allows you to recover from adversity and unexpected or difficult circumstances and return to the original, or improved, state.
- Resilience at times requires acceptance that the original plans or goals may need to be modified.
- Resilience includes the ability to regulate emotions and reactions.

- Personal resilience grows through consistent effort, disciplined execution, and a commitment to continuous improvement.
- Confidence in the Resources and the ABC*D* process helps regulate emotions in high stress situations.
- Recognition of Green-Yellow-Red status and the risk factors contributing to the status decrease sense of personal failure.
- Commitment to personal debriefs leads to continuous improvement and confidence in both management skills and use of Resources.
- Resilience is necessary at all levels of the operation from the individual to the entire organization.

Luke got to the gate early and hurried down the jetway dragging his new roller bag. He was nervous about starting his first trip after training at the regional airline and wanted to give himself some extra time. The aircraft was cold and dark when he walked down the jetway. After checking the logbook, he switched on the electrical power and brought the aircraft to life. The hum of the systems powering up made him smile.

He stowed his bag and began his preflight flows like he had been trained. Things were going smoothly until he got to the Flight Management Computer (FMC), and he couldn't remember which screen he needed. He sat there with his fingers hovering over the keyboard, feeling out of his element.

"You look like a pig staring at wrist watch. Must be another new guy."

Luke turned to see his Captain stowing his bag. He had salt and pepper hair and looked old enough to be his father. "Yeah, fresh out of training." He stuck out his hand. "Luke Rogers. Nice to meet you."

The Captain let out a sigh and shook Luke's hand. "How did I get so lucky to have another new guy this week? Captain Mark Redding." He climbed into his seat and began unpacking his flight bag. "Well Sport, I hope you don't make us late like my FO last week, and let's not do anything that requires any extra paperwork. Do you think you can figure out how to program the FMC?"

Wanting to avoid eye contact, Luke stared down at the screen. "I think I can. I'm just brain-farting at the moment."

The Captain shook his head. "Have you done the walkaround?"

"Not yet."

"Tell you what. You go do the walkaround and I'll program the FMC. You do know how do the walkaround don't you?" He began programming the FMC.

Embarrassed, Luke dug his flashlight out of his flight bag and got out of his seat. "Yeah, I know how to do the walkaround." He went out onto the tarmac and began his exterior preflight inspection gritting his teeth. *What a jerk! This is going to be a long trip.* When he got to the tail cone of the aircraft, he realized he hadn't checked the brakes because he was so distracted by his reaction to the Captain's comments.

He remembered his first solo cross country and Gun's voice echoed in his head. *If, at any time today, you feel like you are drifting into the Yellow or Red, remember those Resources to get you back into the Green.* He took a deep breath, then he walked back to the front of the aircraft and began the exterior preflight inspection again. *FLOW. Just like Guns taught me. If you get distracted in the middle of a flow, start over again. Gotta get myself back into the Green and not let this Captain push me into the Yellow again.* He focused on the exterior inspection and checked every item thoroughly. When he got to the top of the jetway stairs, he paused a moment and took a deep breath before opening the door.

Luke climbed back into the first officer's seat. "Everything looks good outside, Captain."

Captain Redding was texting on his cell phone with one foot on the dash. "Took you long enough, Sport. Remember, we're just flying it, not buying it."

Luke ignored the dig and reviewed the flight plan. "Yeah, I'm new. I'll get faster." He took a look at the FMC programming. "Hey

Captain, can you teach me your techniques for getting the FMC ready to go?"

The Captain stopped texting and checked his watch. "Yeah, I guess we have a few minutes. I know in training they do it differently, but here's how I do it." He began to explain his techniques for programming the FMC. Luke made a mental note to crosscheck the manuals and make sure the techniques were in compliance, but he listened and took notes without interrupting and thanked him for the advice.

"What did you fly before you came here?" asked the Captain.

"I flew pipeline patrol to build hours and then managed to land a job flying a King Air for about a year."

The Captain smirked and nodded. "I'll fly the first leg and you can see how I fly the jet." With that, he began briefing. As they ran the checklist, his altimeters were not set correctly. "That's why we run the checklist," he commented as he corrected the setting. "There goes the perfect flight."

Luke was glad they pushed on time, but he had hoped he would feel a little more ahead of the airplane for his first trip after training. Instead, he felt like he was hanging on by the tail for most of the flight. He did notice how efficiently Captain Redding flew the aircraft and also how he greased the landing.

"That's how you do it," commented the Captain as they cleared the runway.

When they got to the gate and opened the door, the Flight Attendant said with a chuckle, "I'm sure that wasn't the First Officer's landing." Several passengers also complimented him on the landing as they deplaned, and Luke felt the pressure to perform well on his leg ratcheting up.

The departure procedure for the next leg required a turn shortly after takeoff to intercept a course. Wanting to impress his Captain, Luke decided to hand fly the aircraft on the procedure.

On takeoff, he pulled back on the yoke, and the aircraft lifted off. He turned to the required heading and continued climbing. He checked the intercept and prepared to make the turn.

Right about then, the Tower called over the radio, "Regional 214 contact departure."

Captain Redding answered, "Switching. Good day." He changed the radio frequency.

Luke expected to hear the Captain make the radio call, but instead, he heard him command, "Turn. Turn now!"

He looked down and could see he was about to overshoot the course intercept. He banked the aircraft sharply to maximum bank.

"Level off. Level off now!" barked the Captain.

Again, he responded with abrupt control movements and began leveling off to avoid going through the assigned altitude. The aircraft overshot the course and the altitude, and he had to correct back, but the deviations were within acceptable limits.

"Hey Sport, the airline purchased the autopilot for this airplane. You should probably use it," teased the Captain.

Embarrassed, Luke engaged the autopilot and monitored its performance. "Sorry, I wanted to hand fly and improve my proficiency."

The Captain ignored him and made a radio call. Once they leveled off at altitude, he said, "Okay, I'm glad you want to be a better pilot, but until you catch up to the airplane, use the automation as a resource. There's no shame in using your Resources."

Luke nodded and let out a sigh. "Thanks for keeping me on track."

"Remember. I don't want to do any extra paperwork."

The remainder of the flight went better, but Luke's landing was much firmer than the Captain's. When they opened the flight deck door at the gate, the Flight Attendant said with a laugh, "I'm guessing that was the new guy's landing."

He just smiled and nodded. He was a little frustrated with himself, but he was glad the Captain had helped him get back into the Green.

Once again, they pushed on time, and Luke was beginning to feel like he was keeping up with the pace. During the climb out, the airspeed crept up to 265 knots below ten thousand feet. Luke called out, "Airspeed," as required by procedure.

"Okay Sport, I have more time on path and glideslope than you have total time." He rolled his eyes. "Correcting." He raised the nose and returned to normal airspeed. "Happy?"

"Just making the required callout."

"Yeah, yeah, whatever."

Luke wasn't sure how to respond but decided to let it go. He had followed procedure, and it wasn't meant as a personal affront. Getting into an argument would only add tension to the situation. He decided to try humor instead.

"My favorite captain told me the airline bought the autopilot with the airplane," he said with a smile.

At first, the Captain scowled at him, but then he busted out laughing. "True that Sport. True that."

For the rest of the leg, the Captain opened up and began talking about his life. At first, the conversation centered on flying, but it soon turned to a discussion about why he had stayed at the regional airline. He had a daughter who suffered from a medical disability, and he didn't want to give up his seniority and quality of life. He had made career sacrifices to be there for his family. As they descended below ten thousand feet, Luke wanted to stop the conversation but wasn't exactly sure how. Before he knew it, they were approaching the airfield, still high and fast, and the Captain was still talking.

"Hey Captain," interrupted Luke. "Sorry to interrupt this engaging conversation, but there's the airfield."

The Captain looked out the front windshield. "I guess I better shut up and start flying. Gear down."

"Gear down," Luke repeated and extended the landing gear. The aircraft began to slow with the drag, and they extended the flaps. With the aircraft in the landing configuration, he thought they were still too high to make a stable approach, but he wasn't sure.

"I know I'm new, but this looks doesn't look good," advised Luke.

"I've been in worse spots," answered the Captain. He kept his eyes fixed on the runway threshold. He keyed the radio microphone and asked, "Can we get an S-turn?"

"S-turn approved," answered the Tower.

The Captain made a sharp turn to the left and kept the nose of the aircraft buried, trying to get down. After a few seconds, he turned back to the runway, still fixed on the runway numbers like he was a missile locked on a target.

Luke felt a knot in his stomach. *We're in the Yellow, and I'm not sure what to do about it. How do I get us back in the Green? What resource do I have? How do I get the Captain to reassess? How do I communicate in this situation?* He checked the fuel and realized they had plenty of fuel to go around and make another approach. They were only if the Yellow if they continued a bad approach. He decided to create more time.

"Hey Captain, we have plenty of gas. Why don't we just go around and do another approach?"

The Captain never took his eyes off the runway. "We got this Sport."

Luke reassessed again. He felt certain they would not meet the stabilized approach criteria spelled out in the company policy by the time they reached one thousand feet, but he decided to wait until the approach was clearly out of parameters. He was confident the Captain would not violate company policy if it was pointed out to him. For now, he would be quiet and let the approach continue.

It was quiet on the flight deck for several seconds, but when the aircraft approached one thousand feet above the runway, the airspeed was twenty knots above target airspeed, it was one and a half dots above the glideslope, and the sink rate was almost two thousand feet per minute. It was clear to Luke that the approach did not meet the stabilized approach criteria specified by company policy and procedure.

"Go around," he directed.

The Captain didn't respond and continued the approach.

Luke tried again. "We're out of stabilized approach criteria. Go around!"

The Captain continued.

The ground was only five hundred feet below them, and he knew he needed to act quickly. He reached over and put a hand on the Captain's shoulder. "Mark. Go around!"

Captain Redding broke his lock on the runway, glanced at him, and initiated a go-around. The aircraft climbed away from the ground. It was quiet on the flight deck during the pattern and approach, except for required conversation. Luke was worried about the ensuing debrief once they got on the ground, but at least everyone would be safe on the ground to have the conversation.

When they got to the gate, and the Captain shut down the engines, he slid his seat back and looked at Luke. "I really thought I could salvage the approach. I guess I got channelized attention. Thanks for telling me to go around."

"No problem. I don't want to do any extra paperwork either."

"I should have listened to you when you first questioned the approach, but I thought I could show you how to salvage a bad approach. We had plenty of gas and time. I should have abandoned the approach at that point instead of pushing it."

Luke nodded. "I was willing to let it continue, until we didn't meet the stabilized approach criteria. Since I'm so new, I wondered if you might actually be able to salvage it."

"Obviously not. Glad you didn't let your inexperience keep you from intervening. Thanks!"

"No problem, but can you do me a favor?"

"Sure. What?"

Luke smiled. "Tell the Flight Attendant that it was your approach."

The Captain laughed. "No way Sport. I'm gonna put it all on the new guy."

History doesn't repeat... Like the ABCDs, it loops

Perfection is a worthy goal but rarely attainable. As humans, we make mistakes. Things break or don't work as advertised. The weather changes. Our best-laid plans and intentions don't work out as we expected or hoped for. However, while perfection is rarely attained, consistent adequate performance is attainable if we develop resiliency through habits, processes, and the use of Resources.

Sir Ernest Shackleton never made it to the South Pole as he intended to do when he set out, but he did manage to bring his entire crew safely home in spite of extreme environmental conditions, dwindling resources, and the limits of isolation. We remember him for his resilience in those difficult circumstances. We think of the arrow in the RRM Model as the "Shackleton Maneuver" in honor of him. How do we develop similar resiliency using the RRM model?

Keep the ABCD process working. When faced with disruptions, distractions, or deviations, make sure that the ABCD process does not break down. Ask yourself, "What has changed? What is different?" Don't stop assessing and reassessing. Balance changing priorities. When Shackleton realized that his original goal of crossing the Antarctic was impossible, he changed his priority to keeping his entire crew alive. Communicate changing intentions. To combat the psychological impact of their dire situation, Shackleton kept hope alive by "... encouraging and cajoling the men into believing they would escape." Additionally, he spoke with his men one-on-one to encourage them. (Contributor 2021) Do. Focus on the execution of the task in front of you in order to emotionally let go of the emotions of unmet expectations.

Focus on the use of Resources. When we realize that we have drifted, or been pushed into, the Yellow or Red, we can respond with resilience by utilizing a Resource. Shackleton kept his crew focused by keeping them focused on Resources when it seemed like they had none. They utilized everything from the trapped ship they could carry and eventually utilized lifeboats to seek better shelter and assistance. Resources, such as Procedures or Checklists, provide us with an anchor point to pull ourselves back into the Green. By shifting our focus from the disruption or distraction to the Resource, we mentally and emotionally center ourselves in the Green again.

Perhaps the most important tool for developing resiliency is the Debrief. We've all been there: disappointed in our performance, regretting we didn't use our Resources well, or letting the ABCD process break down because of distraction or inattention. These events, and others like them, can be turned into a positive learning experience and help us build personal resilience.

There are three parts to the debrief: Identification, Release, and Commitment to improvement.

In order to improve performance, we first need to identify poor performance. This requires an environment conducive to learning (sometimes referred to as a "Just Culture") where we can debrief performance without fear of punitive action for honest mistakes. Most often, we can self-assess and determine the reasons (Task Loading,

Additive Conditions, or Crew Factors) for our performance, but sometimes we need the help of a peer, instructor, or evaluator to help us. Part of being a professional is learning to actively listen to the feedback of others. In order to identify the root cause of our performance, we need to ask why multiple times and dig deeper than the initial identification. Identifying areas for improvement and their root causes is the first step.

It is important to release the emotion of unmet expectations. What's done is done, and no amount of emotional energy is going to change it. More than one aircraft accident has been caused by pilots who allowed an error earlier in the flight to cause so much emotional distraction that they could no longer focus on the task at hand. Like Shackleton who abandoned his original goal, we can focus our debrief on how we will improve future performance because of what we have experienced instead of beating ourselves up and decreasing our ability to perform in the future.

Most importantly, the debrief should produce a commitment to continuously improve. Perfection is a worthy goal, and although it may never be reached, we can continuously make strides toward achieving it. As the old adage goes, "Amateurs practice until they get it right. Professionals practice until they can't get it wrong." As professional pilots, we should be committed to continuous improvement. Don't wait until the next check ride or training event to improve performance. Take a few moments to debrief your personal performance and make improvements every time you fly.

Resiliency is a personal leadership characteristic. However, the RRM model provides several tools that will help you develop and maintain resiliency as a professional.

Chapter Eleven: Put It All Together

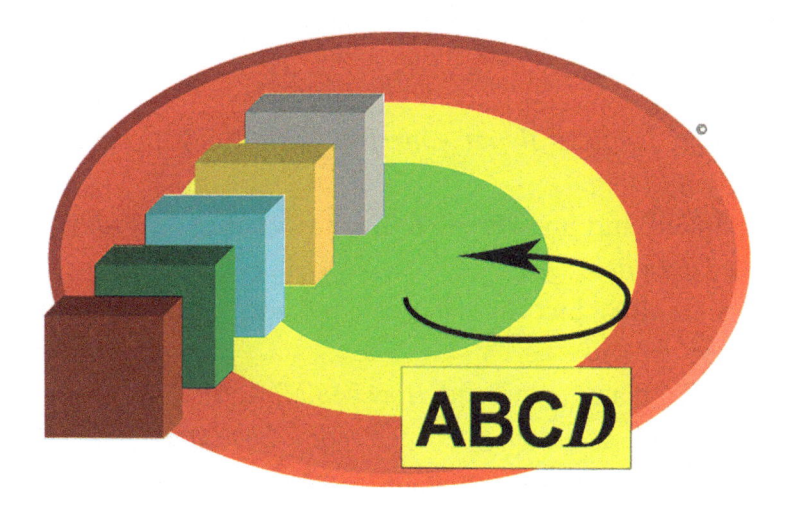

*"Amateurs practice until they get it right;
Professionals practice until it cannot be done any better."*
—Unknown

Key Concepts
- The RRM model is a concise, actionable model that produces safe outcome in your personal flying, your flight operation, and your entire organization.
- The RRM model is intuitive (easy to use) and robust (provides tools for analyzing complex tasks) at the same time.
- The language and concepts of RRM are equally effective for individual use, crew coordination, or throughout an organization.
- Successful pilots have been using the concepts of RRM since the dawn of aviation, and continue to use them today.

Three years later

Luke pulled into the employee parking lot at Hartsfield-Jackson Atlanta airport thirty minutes earlier than normal. He tilted the rearview mirror and checked his uniform before getting out of the car. It was his first day as an airline Captain, and he was proud of the four stripes on his epaulets.

His phone buzzed, and he checked the message. It was from his wife, Sarah.

So excited you're flying your first Captain trip on my birthday! Love you!

He smiled and answered. *Thanks! I promise I'll make it up to you when I get home.*

She sent him a picture of a green bedside speaker/alarm clock. *Remember this?*

He laughed and answered. *How can I forget?*

She replied, *Keep it in the Green today. Love you!*

He sent her a kissing emoji and got out of the car. Within a few minutes, he was walking through the terminal, pulling his roller bag past the hustle and bustle of travelers, wondering if anyone noticed the four stripes on his shoulders. It had taken him a lot of hard work and sacrifice, but he had made it.

He was the first one to arrive at the gate, and the aircraft was sitting there powered down and waiting to start the day. He spoke with the operations personnel and got his paperwork before heading down the jetway to start his preflight. After stowing his bag, he brought on the ground power and energized the aircraft. Then he sat in the Captain's seat and looked over the dispatch paperwork.

The first flight was from KATL (Atlanta) to KBNA (Nashville), about an hour flight. *We're going to be busy.* The fuel load included the required reserves and extra fuel for an alternate and holding. He looked at the weather and could see why. There was a cold front pushing through the area and a line of rain between Atlanta and Nashville along the route. *We'll probably have to deviate around those cells. What is the forecast for Nashville?*

The forecast called for low ceilings and cooler temperatures at their arrival time, signaling that the cold front, and the rain, should be past the airfield when they landed. The dispatcher had given them KBWG (Bowling Green, Kentucky) as an alternate. He checked the weather to make sure it met the required forecast weather minimums. He thought back to his first cross country with Guns and realized he had automatically used multiple Resources (Policies, Procedures, External Resources, Knowledge) as he was Assessing the flight. It had been automatic, almost subconscious like Vicky had told him it would be.

The First Officer arrived and interrupted his musings. "Hey Skipper, didn't expect you to beat me to the airplane." He punctuated the sentence with a soft chuckle.

Luke turned to see his First Officer. He looked like a bodybuilder in a pilot uniform, sporting a grin from ear to ear. Luke stuck out his hand. "Morning! Luke Rogers."

The First Officer gave a bone-crushing handshake. "Jason Murphy."

After the handshake, Jason stowed his luggage and began unpacking his flight bag and 'making his nest' for the flight. "So, I have to tell you, this is my first trip in almost a month. I've been on vacation." The grin never stopped, and the soft chuckle seemed integrated into his vocabulary.

Luke smiled and shook his head. "Well, I'm the newest Captain at the airline. I just finished my training and this is literally my first Captain trip." *Crew Factors. This should be interesting.* "Where did you fly before getting hired here?"

"Well, I was in the Marine Corps for six years after high school, and when I got out, I used the GI Bill to get my ratings. Then I flight-instructed for almost three years to build my hours and got hired." Although it seemed impossible, the grin got bigger. "It's a lot easier than being a Marine, but then again, just about any job would be easier than being a Marine." He chuckled and pulled out a shaker bottle full of a green concoction, and took a swig. "How about you?"

"I've been flying about six years, all civilian. I flew pipeline patrol and a little over a year in the King Air to build my hours. I've been here three years." He grabbed the dispatch paperwork off the dash. "I was looking at the route for the first leg. There's a line of weather between us and Nashville. We have an alternate and extra gas. I think I'm going to give dispatch a call before we leave."

"Okay Skipper." The First Officer pulled himself out of the seat. "I'm going outside to do the walkaround."

Luke picked up his phone and dialed the number for his dispatcher. *Using External Resources to Assess. Guns would be proud.*

After getting through the menu, the dispatcher answered. "This is Monica in Dispatch."

"Hey this is, um, Captain Rogers on flight 265 from Atlanta to Nashville. I have a question about that line of weather."

"Captain Rogers? Do they call you "Jolly Rogers?" she said with a chuckle. "Sorry, I couldn't resist."

Luke smiled. "No, I earned the nickname of Risky Rogers from my father years ago."

"Ooooh! I like that better. It has a dangerous sound to it, but you might not want to tell the passengers." She laughed again. "Anyway, enough with the jocularity, you wanted to know about that line of weather. It looks like your route of flight will take you mostly to the west of it. You'll probably have to deviate some, but everyone is getting through. We have had some reports of moderate turbulence in the vicinity as well."

"What altitude are the tops?" he asked.

"Right now, radar echoes put the tops around FL370."

He looked at the dispatch release and saw the cruising altitude at FL340. *Balance. We will have to deviate, which means we need plenty of extra gas.* "I see you added fuel for deviating, and we have an alternate. Can we add any more?"

"No. We're pushing our max landing weight based on a wet runway in Nashville."

"Speaking of Nashville, the forecast looks good. Is it starting to clear?"

"Latest weather shows it at seven hundred overcast, five miles, and mist. The front is pushing through, and it should continue to improve."

"And the alternate?" he asked.

"Bowling Green is currently one thousand overcast and ten miles visibility. Looking good."

Luke felt satisfied that he had used this External Resource to Assess the situation and Balance priorities and Resources. "Okay, thanks for the information."

Monica answered, "Before you go, Captain Rogers, you have to tell me how you got the nickname Risky."

Luke groaned and wished he hadn't said anything about his nickname. "Well, when I was a teenager..." Jason, the First Officer, slid into the seat next to him. "My father told me I took too many risks while driving and dubbed me "Risky Rogers." He even grounded me from driving, but during that time, he also put me into flying lessons to help me learn about managing risks. The nickname stuck, but I think my risk management skills have significantly improved since then."

Monica laughed. "I should hope so. Based on our conversation, I would even say so. Have a safe flight! I mean stay in the Green!"

Luke ended the call and shook his head. *A safe flight? Accept no unnecessary risks. Mitigate risk by planning. Accept risk when the benefits outweigh the costs. Make risk decisions at the right level. That should produce a safe outcome.*

Jason spoke up. "Everything looks good outside. Not that I was eavesdropping, but did you say your dad called you Risky?"

Luke shook his head. "Yeah, and I guess I'll never get rid of it."

Jason began programming the Flight Management Computer (FMC). "Well that's not as bad as my callsign in the Corps."

"Oh yeah?"

Jason grinned. "Chuckles. They called me Chuckles."

Luke nodded. "Of course they did. Welcome aboard ladies and gentlemen! This is Captain Risky and First Officer Chuckles."

Jason continued to grin. "Doesn't exactly instill confidence does it?"

Just then, the Flight Attendant stuck his head into the flight deck. "Hey, guys! I'm Kelly. What's so funny?"

Luke blushed. "Just making fun of ourselves." He stuck out his hand. "I'm Luke and this is Jason."

Kelly shook his hand. "Nice to meet you both. Can I get you anything?"

Jason held up his shaker bottle. "Nope. I'm good."

Luke shook his head. "I'm fine as well." He grabbed his iPad. "I was just talking with Dispatch about our first leg." He showed him the weather radar picture. "This line of weather is creating some turbulence along our route of flight, and we will probably have to deviate some. It may limit your time to serve."

"Well, I'll get started early. Just give me enough time to secure my galley."

"Will do. We have Bowling Green as our alternate, but the weather is improving in Nashville. I think we are flying together all day. If you need anything, don't hesitate to ask."

With the call to dispatch and the flight attendant briefing out of the way, Luke finished his flows and preparation. Each time he touched a switch, he remembered the aircraft system behind it. He applied the Procedures to set up his navigation radios and autopilot. He remembered and applied company Policies and FAA regulations as he looked over the taxi chart and Standard Instrument Departure (SID). He plugged in his headset and adjusted the rudder pedals per his technique. When he was all done, he took a deep breath and looked around the flight deck. It amazed him how much difference sitting on the other side of the flight deck made, but he was starting to feel more comfortable.

He looked at his watch. It was still twenty minutes until push time. He had felt rushed, but in reality, he had plenty of time. *Just like*

Sweet Tea told me. When we're stressed, we tend to distort time. He looked over at Jason and saw that he had finished his preparations and was looking at his phone with one foot propped up on the dash.

"I know it's a little soon, but do you mind if we get the briefing out of the way?" asked Luke.

Jason put down his phone. "Yeah, sure."

Luke followed company guidelines and briefed the entire flight from start to finish. He talked about everything he could think of. When he finished, he noticed that Jason was nodding but not saying anything.

"Did I miss anything?"

"Nope, you were very thorough." He uttered his signature chuckle and picked back up his phone.

Crew Factors. I don't think we really have the shared mental model I was hoping for. "Okay, I'm going to walk up top for a minute." Luke got out of his seat and walked up the jetway and into the terminal. The last few passengers were already trickling down. He checked his watch. They still had fifteen minutes until the scheduled push time.

He looked up and saw a gentleman in a suit stopped in the jetway. "Are you the captain?" asked the man.

Luke smiled. "I am the captain."

"You don't look old enough to drive a car, let alone fly an airplane. How do I know you'll get us there safely?"

"Believe it or not, I already have over two thousand hours of flying time." Risky grinned. "And, thanks to some excellent instructors, I'm well-trained at managing the risks of flying."

The gentleman nodded. "Let's hope so." He continued down the jetway to the airplane.

Luke just shook his head. When he got to the top of the jetway, the agent was inputting information into the computer.

"Hey Captain, do you mind if we push a few minutes early? Everyone is on board and we have an aircraft holding out for this gate," asked the agent without looking up from his work.

"Um... yeah, sure."

The agent continued, "Well, they let us push five minutes early if we have everyone, but would you mind if we push ten minutes early?" He handed Luke the final paperwork. "We have everyone on board and all the bags. I want to get that airplane holding out on a gate as soon as possible."

Make risk decisions at the right level. Luke took the paperwork. "Let me call dispatch and see it that works for them." He started back down the jetway as he dialed dispatch.

"Did you miss me?" answered Monica, the dispatcher.

"No, I was hoping to hear that music you play while I'm hold, but you answered too soon. Hey, the agent wants me to push ten minutes early. Will I get in trouble if I do that?"

"You should be okay. Let me clear it with the operations supervisor." She got off the line, and the silence filled with soft music for a few moments. "He says you're good to push whenever you want."

"Okay, we'll be off the gate in a few minutes."

Luke ended the conversation and entered the aircraft. The First Officer and the Flight Attendant were both standing in the galley talking. "We're going to push early. They have an aircraft holding out for a gate."

Jason nodded and hurried back into the flight deck. The Flight Attendant gave a thumbs-up and started preparing the galley. Luke slipped into the captain's seat and finished his final preparations for pushback. He was excited to fly his first captain trip.

"Uh oh. Looks like I can't get the APU generator online," said Jason, still grinning in spite of the inconvenience.

Just then, the agent stuck his head in the door. "Hey, Captain, thanks for pushing early. Have a good flight!"

Luke twisted in his seat so he could look at the agent. "Hang on a minute. We're having trouble with the APU generator."

The agent let out a heavy sigh. "Can we push back and have you deal with it off the gate?"

Balance. We have to call dispatch and maintenance. We have to fill out the logbook. I'm going to need some time. "No, it's going to take a few minutes at the gate to handle the situation."

The agent frowned and stepped back into the galley.

Luke looked over at Jason. "It's not coming online?"

Jason flipped the switch. "Nope. Nothing."

"Okay we will have to start one engine at the gate. You coordinate with ground ops while I call dispatch." *Balance the workload.* He pulled out the Minimum Equipment List and read what to do if the APU generator wasn't working. *Procedures.* He pulled out the logbook and then dialed the dispatcher again.

"Wow you really do like elevator music, don't you," said Monica when she answered.

"You didn't leave me on hold long enough to acquire a taste for it, but that's okay. Hey our APU generator won't come online. I need to put it in the logbook and get it deferred."

In a few minutes, he put the fault in the logbook and coordinated with maintenance and dispatch to continue the flight under the MEL guidance. The flight could continue as long as they started one engine at the gate and landed at the nearest airfield if one of the engine generators also quit working. *Accept the risks if the benefits outweigh the costs.* Once he finished documenting everything, he noticed that a worker from the ramp was standing in the flight deck door.

"The first officer tells me you have to start an engine at the gate," said the worker.

"Yeah, our APU generator isn't working. We need to stay hooked up to gate electrics until we get an engine started. Can we do that?" asked Luke.

"No problem. Just let me get the jetway out of the way after we disconnect." With that, he headed back down to the ramp area.

Luke held up the logbook for Jason to see. "Okay Jason, we put the fault in the book and got the MEL to operate without the generator. Have you ever started an engine at the gate?"

"A couple of times, but it's been a while," answered Jason.

Luke stowed the logbook and opened his operating manual. "It's been a while for me also. So, let's look it up." He opened the procedure and gave it a quick review. "Okay, we spoke with the ramp already. Any questions about the procedure?"

"I think I got it, Skipper." He buckled his seatbelt and put on his headset. "Ready when you are."

Luke got out of his seat and stepped into the galley. The agent was standing in the door. "Okay, we're ready to go. We will have to start one engine at the gate using ground power. Then we can push back and start the second engine, but I'll tell the ramp to push us back far enough to let the next aircraft in."

The agent began closing the aircraft door. "Thanks Captain!"

Luke slid back into the captain's seat as the flight attendant closed the flight deck door behind him. *Feeling rushed. Slow down.* He paused for a moment and took a deep breath. Before he strapped in, he picked up the hand microphone and made a quick announcement to the passengers, explaining the need to start one engine at the gate. Then he fastened his seatbelt and shoulder harness. *In the Green now.* He looked over at his first officer. "You ready?"

Jason simply nodded and pulled out the checklist.

"Checklist please," ordered Luke. They ran the checklist and confirmed all the items on it together. Jason's voice took on a more serious tone when they started the checklist.

With the checklist complete and everything ready to go, he put on his headset and spoke with the ground crew. "Flight deck to ground?"

The ramper answered, "Hey Captain, safety zone is clear. Ready for push."

"Roger. We're ready to start the first engine at the gate as briefed. Is the area behind us clear?"

"All clear captain."

"Starting number one."

Luke looked over at Jason. "Okay, we're clear to start number one at the gate, as briefed."

"Starting number one," answered Jason as he began the engine start procedure.

They both watched the jet engine spin up and come to life when the fuel ignited. When it stabilized, Jason announced, "Looks like a good start. Do you want me to call for pushback now?"

Luke nodded. "Call for pushback." He keyed his intercom switch. "Hey ramp, we have a good engine and the generator is on-line. Cleared to disconnect the electrical power."

"Roger, Captain. Disconnecting" The sound of the engine bled through the headset and muffled the voice.

He looked over at Jason. "Cleared to push?"

His first officer nodded. "Cleared to push."

Luke keyed the intercom microphone. "Brakes released. Cleared to push. If you can, push back far enough to let company onto the gate."

"Roger that," answered the ramp. The jet began to move backward.

As the jet continued backward under control of the tug driver, Luke took another look at the procedure to make sure he didn't miss anything. *Checklist. Procedures. External Resources. Knowledge. Using my Resources.*

"Pushback complete captain. Please set your brakes," informed the tug driver over the intercom.

"Brakes are set. Thanks for your help. Cleared to disconnect." He waved at the pushback crew as they disconnected and shuffled back to the gate to marshal in the waiting aircraft. "Okay, the pushback crew is all clear. I forgot to brief it, but let's taxi out on one engine to save fuel. Is that okay?"

"Roger that, Skipper," answered Jason. He began his after-start flow.

When they both finished their flows and ran the checklist, Jason called for taxi.

"Taxi to Runway 26L via Foxtrot 5 and Echo," instructed the Ground Controller.

Luke released the brakes and pushed the thrust lever forward. *First flight as an airline captain. Here we go!*

When they got out of the ramp area, they could see a long line of aircraft waiting to take off. They taxied into their spot in line and stopped. Luke checked the fuel and calculated that they had enough fuel to delay the takeoff by about twenty minutes if they held off on starting the other engine until they were close. He pulled up the weather on his iPad and checked the routing again. They would have to deviate, but it would work. "Looks like if we wait to start the second engine until we get close to taking off and we get airborne in the next twenty minutes, we should be okay on fuel." *ABCD.*

"Sounds like a plan, Skipper."

The line of aircraft inched forward and Luke watched the airplanes takeoff as they waited their turn. Jason interrupted the silence. "Fly Delta Jets. How long has Delta Airlines been in business? Are you hoping to go to Delta eventually?"

Luke shrugged. "I'm not sure where I want to end up."

"I hear Southwest is a fun place to work, but they don't have any widebody aircraft. I think I'm going to try for United. I've got family in the Houston area. Do you know anybody at American?"

He started to answer and continue the conversation, but he remembered the policy against idle chatter below ten thousand feet. *Make risk decisions at the right level.* "Once we get above ten thousand feet, we'll talk more about it." With that, Luke had set the tone and expectation.

Jason nodded, and then it was quiet on the flight deck again.

The line moved better than Luke anticipated, and he calculated that they would have plenty of fuel. "We should be good on fuel and the line's moving pretty good. Start the other engine please."

The First Officer sprang into action, and a few moments later, the second engine was humming along as well.

"Before Takeoff Checklist."

Jason pulled out the checklist and began reading the items as Luke responded. After they completed the second item, they were interrupted by a radio call from the Tower. "Regional 2301 can you takeoff from Echo 13? The two aircraft in front of you are on the same routing and I have to build some spacing."

Jason looked over at Luke for an answer, and it felt like the entire airport was waiting for him to make a decision. *It's a long runway, but did we run the performance numbers? We'll have to reload the FMC. How long will that take? It would save us fuel.* He needed a moment. *Consider our priorities: Safety, Service, Efficiency.* He keyed the microphone and answered, "Standby one."

He looked at Jason. "Do we have the numbers for the intersection?"

Jason grinned. Of course, we do, Skipper. I can load them in the FMC in a few seconds."

Balance. Accept the risk when the benefits outweigh the cost. We're following procedure. He keyed the microphone. "We'll need a minute to load the numbers, but we can accept a takeoff at Echo 13."

"Regional 2103, hold short of 26L at Echo 13. Load the numbers and let me know when you're ready," answered the Tower Controller.

Luke echoed back the clearance as Jason began entering the takeoff numbers in the FMC. After waiting in line for several minutes, he suddenly felt rushed. He taxied up to the hold short line at the assigned intersection and set the parking brake.

"All loaded Skipper."

"Tell them we're ready," he replied, but then he remembered they had been interrupted while doing the checklist and hadn't finished. "Wait! We need to finish the checklist."

Jason pulled out the checklist. "Good catch."

They ran the checklist again, uninterrupted. "Okay, tell tower we're ready now."

"Regional 2103 is ready at Echo 13."

"Regional 2103, winds 240 at 6, Runway 26L at Echo 13, cleared for takeoff."

Luke released the parking brake and taxied onto the runway. He pushed the thrust levers forward and guided the aircraft as it accelerated down the runway.

Jason called out, "V1, Rotate."

He pulled back on the yoke, and the aircraft lifted off the runway. His first trip as a fully-qualified captain was airborne. He focused on flying the airplane smoothly and following the departure procedure. After a few minutes, he reached up and engaged the autopilot to reduce his workload and allow him the opportunity to evaluate the weather ahead. He turned on the radar and began adjusting the tilt for a clearer picture. The line of weather that dispatch had briefed him about was dead ahead. He could see the tops of the clouds, but it didn't look like they would be able to top them.

"There's the line of weather dispatch told us about," said Luke. He pointed at the radar picture. "I don't think we can top it. I think we'll have to deviate to the west. What do you think?"

Jason looked down at the radar picture. "Sounds good to me."

"Tell the controller we want to deviate to the left for about 80 miles."

Jason keyed the microphone. "Atlanta Center, Regional 2103 needs to deviate to the left for that line of weather ahead."

"Regional 2130, cleared to deviate to the left. Direct to SWFFT when able."

"Cleared to deviate to the left. Direct SWFFT when able, Regional 2103."

Luke selected heading mode on the autopilot and announced, "Heading selected."

"Selected." Jason announced as he verified the setting.

Luke subconsciously recited VVMI—verbalize, verify, monitor, intervene. Maybe Jason was not as rusty as he had first thought.

The aircraft turned to the left and rolled out on the selected heading. He checked the radar picture again. "That should keep us clear of the storm."

"I don't have a lot of experience with the weather radar. How do you know what tilt to select, or do you just leave it AUTO all the time?" asked Jason.

Luke spent a few minutes explaining his techniques with the weather radar as they deviated away from the weather along the route. When he was finished, he checked the fuel again. Even with the deviations, they would arrive with enough fuel to divert to their alternate if necessary. He pulled up the most recent ATIS from Nashville: 400 overcast and five miles of visibility.

"It looks like we'll have to shoot an approach into Nashville. I'm thinking the ILS to runway 2R. What do you think?" asked Luke.

"Sounds good to me, Skipper. I'll get us some landing numbers." Jason began typing in the FMC.

Luke checked the heading. They were about to clear the west end of the line of weather. They would be in the clouds, but the line of storms would be behind them on the arrival. He checked the fuel again. Still good. He selected SWFFT on the FMC routing. "Hey I think we can head direct to SWFFT now. How does it look to you?"

The first officer glanced up at the map display. "Looks good to me."

Luke executed the command, and the aircraft returned to the programmed routing into Nashville. He checked the fuel one more time now that the computer had a clear routing. *Still going to land with more than divert and reserve fuel. Good.*

"Hey Jason, as soon as you're ready, I can brief the ILS to 2R." *Anticipate and manage risk by planning. Briefings.*

Jason pulled up the approach procedure on his iPad. "Ready."

Luke briefed the arrival and approach procedure, meticulously pointing out each waypoint, altitude, and frequency. He discussed the weather requirements and airport lightning. He rehearsed the missed approach procedure in case they were unable to see the runway at the decision altitude. Lastly, he talked about how they would taxi to the gate once they landed. This time, Jason seemed a little more engaged and followed along. *I think we have a shared mental model now.*

"Anything I missed in the briefing?" asked Luke as he finished up.

Jason shook his head. "No, I can tell you're fresh out of training. Very thorough briefing. A lot of captains get lazy with their briefings."

ATC interrupted their conversation. "Regional 2103, descend and maintain FL230."

"Descend and maintain FL230, Regional 2103," answered Jason.

"FL230," announced Luke. He selected the altitude on the autopilot and changed to a descent mode. Just as the aircraft began to respond to the command, a Master Caution light illuminated. He looked up and saw that the #1 engine-driven generator had dropped offline.

"Master Caution. Looks like the #1 engine-driven generator quit working," said Luke. "Pull out the QRH for generator failure. I'll fly the airplane and handle the radios."

The first officer pulled out the Quick Reference Handbook and fumbled through the pages.

Luke's internal monologue kicked into high gear while he was waiting for Jason to find the correct checklist. *That only leaves us with one generator. If that one quits, we are down to only standby power. Do we want to go into Nashville with the weather that bad? I wonder if there's another airport nearby with better weather? I wonder if we can get the generator back online?*

Jason interrupted his thoughts. "Ready with the checklist."

They went through the checklist step by step. It instructed them to try bringing the generator back online, but the attempt didn't work. The checklist directed them to use the APU generator, but that was broken. When they finished the checklist, they both realized they only had one generator working.

"We need to land at the nearest suitable airport," said Luke. He looked down at the map display. Nashville was the closest airport, but with the low ceilings and only one generator, he was concerned it wasn't suitable.

"If that last generator quits working, we'll only be left with standby power," said Jason. "Are you sure you want to shoot your first approach as a captain in this airplane using standby instruments?"

"Good point." Luke looked down at the map display. "What's the weather like at our alternate?"

Jason quickly checked. "A little better than Nashville. One thousand overcast and ten miles visibility," he said. "What do you want to do Captain?"

Luke looked at the map display. Nashville was only one hundred miles ahead of them, and they were on the arrival already. The alternate was only slightly better. Behind them, Atlanta was clear, but they would have to deviate around the weather again, prolonging their time in the air. He checked the time. If they continued on the arrival and approach into Nashville, they would be on the ground in less than thirty minutes. He just finished practicing an approach on standby power during his simulator training a couple of weeks ago and felt comfortable with it. He smiled to himself. *Use your Resources. Keep it the Green. ABCD.*

"Let's continue into Nashville. The weather is improving, and it's above CAT I minimums. We have enough fuel to divert, even after a missed approach. We're going to be on the ground in less than thirty minutes. Since I just did a standby power approach in the simulator, I'll fly the approach. Are you okay with that?"

"Sounds good to me Skipper. Do you want to declare an emergency?"

"Yes. You take the radios back and declare the emergency. I'm going to focus on flying the airplane. Tell ATC we want direct to the FAF for runway 2R."

Jason keyed the microphone. "Atlanta Center, Regional 2103 is declaring an emergency at this time."

Confident that his first officer could handle the radio work, Luke focused on flying the airplane. ATC cleared them direct to the FAF, as requested. He did some quick mental math to plan the descent using the techniques he had been taught. Everything was all set up for the approach, but he double-checked it all. He mentally rehearsed what he would do if he had to rely on standby power.

"Jason, can you tell Kelly, our flight attendant, what's going on? I don't think we need to tell the passengers, but let's give Kelly a heads up in case that last generator quits on us."

"Got it. You have the radios for a minute." He flipped a switch on his communication panel and began talking with the flight attendant.

ABCD. Is there anything I'm missing? I don't think so. Time to execute. Do and then Debrief when we get to the gate. Comfortable that he had made a good decision, he focused on flying the airplane.

The arrival and approach seemed almost anticlimactic. The remaining generator continued working and picked up the load as designed. The ride was smooth, and because they had declared an emergency, they got traffic priority. They entered the clouds around fifteen thousand feet, and Luke double-checked the instruments. In spite of the generator failure, all the instruments and indicators were working normally. Except for passengers on board, he almost felt like he was back in the simulator practicing his instrument flying.

Luke slowed the aircraft, and they began configuring as they approached the final approach fix. They intercepted the localizer and the glideslope on approach speed and fully configured. He glanced out the window, but all he could see was white.

Jason called the Tower. "Nashville tower, Regional 2103 approaching SKAGS for runway two right, emergency aircraft."

"Regional 2103, winds 030 @ 8, runway two right, cleared to land."

"Runway two right, Cleared to land, Regional 2103."

They were on course, on glideslope, fully configured, with a clearance to land. Luke checked the fuel one more time. They still had enough to go missed approach and make it to their alternate with a comfortable margin. He focused on flying the approach precisely and procedurally correct, expecting to break out of the clouds before they got to the decision altitude. As forecasted, at around four hundred feet, they descended below the cloud layer and saw runway two right in front of them.

He hoped for a smooth landing, but it was a little firmer than he wanted it to be. He transitioned from flying the aircraft to taxiing it, and they exited the runway.

"Nice job Skipper! Glad that generator kept working."

"Me too. I guess they'll ground this airplane now."

"I don't know. With a nickname like Risky, they might send you out to fly with only one generator." The signature chuckle punctuated his comment.

He laughed. "Not with first officer nicknamed Chuckles."

When they parked at the gate and finished the parking checklist, Luke turned to Jason. "So that was an exciting start to my first day as a captain. What feedback do you have?"

"I appreciate how well you communicated everything. I wasn't sure if we should divert to somewhere with better weather, but when we discussed it and briefed everything, it gave me confidence in the decision."

"Nice job helping me balance the workload. I wish the landing would have been a little better."

"Yeah, we dodged storms, handled an emergency, flew a precision approach in marginal weather, and all that people will remember is that the landing was a bit firm. Can't win."

Luke stood in the galley to say goodbye to the passengers. The gentleman in the suit stopped and stuck out his hand. "Thanks for the safe flight."

Luke gave him a firm handshake and smiled. "You're welcome, but I was thinking mostly of me."

At first, the gentleman gave him a puzzled look, but then he laughed and exited the aircraft.

James Clear said, "You do not rise to the level of your goals. You fall to the level of your systems." (Clear 2018) Perhaps instead of seeking perfection, we should create a system to encourage consistent performance. What would that system look like? It must provide a framework to compensate for human error. Sound risk management principles and a defined process for processing changing risks need to be included. Our system should help us recognize increasing risk and provide the Resources to mitigate or decrease risk. It should create resiliency in the individual operator and the operation. We need a system that can be employed by the individual and the entire operation at the same time using a common language. An effective system must facilitate and expect continuous improvement from the individual, the crew, and the leadership.

RRM provides the framework for building that system.

Luke "Risky" Rogers' journey took him from a novice risk manager to a professional one. Along the way he learned about the inherent risks of living. Instead of avoiding risk, he embarked on a journey to better understand and manage risk. He maximized all his opportunities and learned the value of a system for achieving his goals. His journey from novice to expert took less time and effort because of a systematic approach he learned step-by-step. RRM helped him manage risks, achieve safety, and expedite his journey to expertise. Risk and Resource Management will help you manage risks, achieve safety, and expedite expertise.

> "It's not all about talent. It's about dependability, consistency, and being able to improve. If you work hard and you're coachable, and you understand what you need to do, you can improve."
> —Bill Belichick

Four years later

Luke sat in the briefing room waiting for the two crew members he had just evaluated to return from the simulator. Through the window, he could see the simulators, like large elevated shipping containers, moving back and forth on their mechanical stilts. He mused on the series of events that had brought him to the flight training center as a Check Pilot and was surprised how much he enjoyed helping others improve their flying skills and mentoring them along in their career.

The crew had done a good job flying a difficult scenario for the last few hours, but he could see the apprehension on their faces as they entered the briefing room. Luke remembered his own experiences and the anxiety of his first Line Operational Evaluation. Empathetic to how they were probably feeling at the moment, he smiled at them to put them at ease.

"First of all, nice job today. This will be a facilitated debrief, which means I need your participation. How do you think it went today?" Luke asked.

The pilots glanced at each other, and after a moment of hesitation, the First Officer spoke up. "Fine, I guess."

The Captain nodded in agreement. "Yeah, it went okay."

Luke leaned back in his chair. "Well, something that's really important to me, and to the airline, is that you are able to identify your own mistakes, determine what led to the errors, and then consider how you can improve future performance." He glanced up at the RRM poster on the wall. "So let me ask the question a different way. Did you two ever get into the Yellow, or Red, today?"

The pilots glanced at each other before the Captain responded, "Yeah, I was a bit in the Yellow during that missed approach. I guess I wasn't expecting it."

"Why did it catch you by surprise?" asked Luke.

The Captain shrugged. "I guess I was so focused on flying the approach."

"What Resource could have helped minimize the surprise, or at least prepared you for it?"

The Captain looked up at the poster. "My approach briefing could have been a little better."

Luke looked at the First Officer. "Did his briefing create a shared mental model? Did you know what to expect during the missed approach?"

"Well, he covered all the correct items," answered the First Officer.

"Okay, then why wasn't the briefing effective?"

The First Officer gave him a blank stare.

Luke realized the debrief might take a bit longer than he expected. He thought of his instructors and what they might say. Great risk management, great mentorship. *Thanks Vicky, Guns, and Sweet Tea!* He grabbed a marker and stood next to the whiteboard. "Let's go over some points that will help."

Conclusion

Risky's journey from teenage driver to airline pilot is not unique. The knowledge, skills, and judgment he learned on his journey molded him into a successful risk manager and pilot. You can take that same journey, no matter what your chosen field of endeavor.

The RRM model provides the framework for learning how to understand risk, the skills to manage risk, and the judgment to mitigate risk at all levels of an operation. The tools from the model can be used on a personal level, by a flight crew, or by an entire airline. They are intended to be easy to remember, actionable, and applicable in a multitude of situations. They apply to any situation that involves risk and decision-making.

Risk management is the process for achieving a safe outcome. It involves recognizing the hazards and associated risks, mitigating and managing those risks, and achieving a safe outcome in spite of the possibility of experiencing harm or loss. It is the methodology we employ when we strive to be safe.

Additionally, these same principles can improve performance, whether it be on-time performance or financial performance. We learn risk management through experience, but understanding and applying the principles and tools of RRM will expedite your risk-management expertise. The model provides a common language to communicate risk and the Resources to mitigate risk, enabling an inexperienced pilot to manage risks as well as an experienced pilot.

If you take the time to understand and internalize the principles and tools of the RRM model, you will be more successful at managing the risks in your life. You will be more standardized and consequently more resilient in a changing environment. Like Risky, you will achieve a safe outcome through effective risk management.

Risk. Safety. Expertise. We hope this book will help you manage risks, achieve safety, and expedite expertise by using the Risk and Resource Management model.

For more information about employing RRM in your organization, visit www.volantsystems.com.

Acknowledgements

Brock Booher

This journey started several years ago as KD and I worked closely together to develop ab initio pilot training. The RRM model had captured my attention as a line pilot and Check Pilot, and I knew how powerful the concepts and principles could be in the hands of new pilots. I knew that RRM could help new pilots think like experienced pilots and wanted to include RRM instruction early in the training program.

One day during our discussions, I asked KD, "Why haven't you published a book on RRM?" I consider RRM to be the gold standard in aviation risk management, and I couldn't understand why she hadn't written a book.

She explained that she had a technical writing background, but she was open to the idea. From there, we began to discuss the idea of writing a book together. She could provide technical and intellectual expertise, and I could provide my aviation expertise and writing skills. I was excited to help her promote the model.

Then the COVID pandemic hit. The world ground to a halt. The idea sat on the shelf until things began to return to a semblance of normal. Without invitation, I wrote the outline, the introduction, and the first chapter and sent them to her. That was the spark we needed to pull the idea off the shelf and give it life.

This entire book is built on the intellectual property developed by KD VanDrie and her coworkers over the last 20 years. Concept by concept, she built the RRM model and tested it in training centers and flight operations. Her ability to observe, dissect, and teach optimal performance helped her create the framework of RRM. She fine-tuned the concepts and language that make RRM actionable at the personal level, the operational level, and the organizational level. She spent countless hours educating pilots, instructors, and evaluators on how to use Resources, the ABC*D* process, and keep things in the Green. She helped leaders learn to apply RRM to achieve operational goals and manage risks at every level. She provided software tools to Instructional System Designers, AQP managers, and Training Leadership that helped them construct effective training. Through all these difficult tasks, she has remained curious, generous, and passionate about her intellectual property. Always with a smile on her face, she has developed an intellectual model that is the gold standard in the worldwide aviation industry.

LX Van Drie was a sounding board for the book concepts from the beginning. Because of her, we chose the fictional format in an effort to make the book more readable and relatable. Additionally, she kept us focused on the market we wanted to serve.

The book is dedicated to the hard-working men and women of the Southwest Airlines Standards Department. I spent almost five years working side-by-side with them. They are my brothers and sisters, and although I will not name them all, they have all made me a better pilot, evaluator, and person.

Greg Bland and I were connected at the hip on a project for over a year. We spent so much time together that we began to finish each other's sentences. He is an old soul, gentleman, and consummate professional. If I make enough money on this book, I promise to buy him a new cardigan sweater. His contributions to this work are too numerous to mention.

Mark Damiens and I spent several hours discussing RRM and how it can apply to so many situations. His no-nonsense approach helped me shape the prose and the exposition of the book. He taught me to be a better evaluator and to be a better human being.

Always the gentleman and professional, Mark Arriola took the early manuscript and provided much-needed critical feedback. He took nothing at face value and dug into the concepts presented in an effort to make the book better. His passion for the topic and his eye for detail improved the work tremendously.

Gary Perkins approached me as I was finishing the project and asked for a copy of the manuscript. His passion for the topic helped me stay focused on finishing strong after many months of effort. He is an RRM advocate everywhere he goes.

Marcus North read the manuscript right before accepting a position as a Check Pilot. He was able to provide feedback as a line pilot but then had more feedback after he learned to use RRM as an evaluator. His friendship and encouragement made the journey easier.

Because of Dave Retnam, I was offered an opportunity to work with curriculum development with new pilots and incorporate these concepts at that level. Dave has always been passionate about doing the right thing, even if it costs a little more and takes more time. He offered valuable feedback on the pacing and structure of the book.

Nick Ruddell represents the target market for this book. He is a new CFI at the beginning of a long career. I asked him to read the manuscript. When he told me that he read it in one sitting, I knew we had hit the mark. Nick helped us focus on the up-and-coming generation that will need these tools.

My family members always suffer through my projects with me. My wife, Britt, has endured long lectures on mitigating risks and using Resources. I'm surprised she didn't create a family policy forbidding me from discussing RRM in our home. My son Rian, also a pilot, engaged me in long discussions about human factors and RRM. My daughter, Rylee, a Flight Attendant, asked me about using RRM in the aircraft cabin. My son, Carson, who works in an entirely different field, sharpened my instructional skills.

This book would not be possible without Southwest Airlines and its leadership. They believed in me over twenty-three years ago and have provided me with a stable and fun place to work. They encouraged me to follow my passion.

Lastly, I want to acknowledge the line pilots of SWA who have suffered through my briefings and debriefings. I have learned something from each of you that makes me a better pilot today.

KD VanDrie

This is a lengthy but very important list of acknowledgements. There are many professional contacts throughout the last three decades who have contributed their knowledge and critiques to the Volant RRM model. Since so many people contributed to its development and implementation there truly is a need to recognize all, but they are so numerous that to remember all of you is difficult. If I forget to mention your contributions, I apologize in advance.

I have always considered myself as the integrator and perhaps curator of the Volant RRM Model, not the sole inventor. If you take the number of detailed acknowledgements listed below and multiplied it by their number of years as professionals, you will have a truly astounding number. It is easily over 1000 years of aviation experience.

To continue the acknowledgements, my first thank you is to the Standards Check Airmen, Training Departments, and Safety Department at Southwest Airlines. The integration of RRM into the culture, training, and the Safety Management System have moved it to the current level of maturity. A significant culture change is necessary to transform an organization, and through the years Southwest took on the culture challenge and made RRM their own. So to start, thank you in particular to Tim Speak and Greg Bowen for dragging me back into working with the airlines after the years of focusing on military training. And of course a thank you to Bob Owsley for the vision and tenacity to get RRM into the Southwest culture, Steve Vaught for the leadership needed to make it a standardized practice, and Dave Hunt for the vision of integration with the Safety Management System and expansion to other work groups.

To Mark Boots (a founding member of Volant Systems, LLC) whose decades long friendship and collaboration aided in implementation and sustainment in both the airline industry and military.

Matt Currin was the RRM evangelist during the introduction of RRM to VMMT-204, the USMC MV-22 training squadron. His tenacity and application to the mission of VMMT-204 was critical to its acceptance and success. After retiring from the Marine Corps he continued work in the field, working with Gary Klien to train the concept of Naturalistic decision making. Many, many discussions with Matt further refined the RRM approach to time-critical decision making.

Thank you to Jack Eggspuehler, Chairman of Department of Aviation at Ohio State University and President of the National Association of Flight Instructors. Jack was my first mentor and inspired my love for training and Instructional System Design (ISD) in the design, development, implementation, and evaluation of AOPA Weekend Ground Schools. As a result of that experience, I saw the advantage of ISD and how it could be applied to airline training.

To Ron Schilling, who, as Director of Training at USAirways was the first to understand and support the vision with my first contract to document a fleet-wide task analysis with the help of five very talented SMEs: John Hope (Airbus), Kent Ernsberger (Foker F-100), Paul Morrel (Boeing 757/767), John Furneaux (Airbus 320), Paul Eddy (Boeing 737-200/300/400) and Bill Dunbar (DC-9/MD-80). We spent 3 months locked in a small conference room in the USAirways bunker/simulator building to create a standardized, fleet-wide task analysis that eventually became the foundation for both the RRM model and the USAirways Advanced Qualification Program (AQP).

The next layer of the foundation was established with the insight of Doug Farrow (who has been a career long mentor for both Instructional System Design and "KD you need to write a book"). Doug provided so many opportunities, one of which was to conduct a survey of AQP Best Practices during which I observed both the strengths and weaknesses of training data, and the other was working on the Flight Operating Quality Assurance (FOQA) implementation team, which provided additional insight into the potential of using data to improve training and operations.

Finally the real birth of RRM began after Jim Gibbs, who initiated the concept of Green, Yellow, and Red by coining the term "Additive Conditions" in describing the limitations for FOQA data in 'grading' flight crews. Jim drew the first target on a paper napkin on the way home from a Safety Conference as he described that the FOQA data was quite accurate in recording WHAT had occurred, but was lacking was information about the additive conditions that may have contributed to the event.

A thank you needs to go to the folks at NASA Ames that have contributed incredible publications in support of Aviation Safety and Operational Effectiveness.

In particular, the publications by Asaf Degani, Earl Weinger and Immual Barshi contributed to the development of the "Consistency" block (Priorities, Policies, Procedures and Flows) In addition, Barb Kanki's research, papers and consulting at USAirways informed the initial development of the Job Aids (Checklist) Block. Key Dismukes' research and writings informed SO much of Instructional Design, Instructor/Evaluator Training, and Human Factors. Key was an incredible intellect and gentle soul. He made it seem easy to bridge the gap between research and practical applications which is the sole purpose of the RRM Model.

There were so many individuals from USAirways whose comments and insights added to the explanation of the RRM Model. One of my favorite episodes was when Paul Morrel pointed out the need to include "Crew Factors" as one of the additive conditions. Then, to reduce the complexity of the subject George Elliott, suggested that we explain it as the "Seven Dwarf Syndrome." According to George that day, if a pilot could identify with one of the seven dwarves (Dopey, Happy, Grumpy, Sneezy, Bashful, Sleepy, or Doc) they would have a higher potential for error. When I questioned him about how

Doc (the know-it-all, proficient dwarf) would increase the potential for error, he replied that Doc's demeanor could prevent others from pointing out his mistakes. After some consideration for pilot sensibilities (and copyrights) we renamed the Seven-dwarf syndrome as "Crew Factors" George was also one of the three founding members of Volant Systems, LLC.

Ron Thomas and Robert Sumwalt, contributed to the integration of James Reason's Swiss Cheese concept in displaying the Resource Blocks. Ron was also integral to the initial development of the original "ABC's". One afternoon, Ron Schilling, who was then the Director of Training, held Ron Thomas, John Ross, and myself captive in a conference until we could agree on the "CRM approach." The original ABCs were born that day. In the original model this stood for Assess, Use your Barriers to prevent Error, Communicate, Follow SOPS, and Make sure it makes sense.

To Ted Wirginis, Risk Manager, Naval Safety Center. Ted introduced himself to me at a Safety Conference after I had completed a presentation of RRM. He was enthusiastic about the application of RRM to System Safety. We had an engaging conversation about the difference between actual risk and the impact of the perception of risk on human performance. In the airline work done to that point I had observed the impact of the perception of high risk on human performance but had not really thought to include a situation where continuous work in a high-risk environment, then returning to a moderate risk environment could also be detrimental.

Years later when I, as Volant Systems CEO, was working with the Marine Corps MV-22 flight training program, I ran into Ted again and we explored integrating RRM as a strategy for Time Critical Risk Management in the Navy. It was of great value to our project that the Navy included significant portions of the Volant RRM model into their time critical portion of OPNAV INSTRUCTION 3500.39C dated 02 JUL 2010.

In addition to being a great friend and mentor, Ted's contribution included helping to expand the description of the "Cone of

Time" to address decision making bias and in generally driving me crazy with his questions. OK, truthfully he asked great questions that overall improved many of the technical publications.

Ted also introduced me to the work of Mica Endsley, the former Chief Scientist of the Air Force and President/CEO of SA Technologies. Mica is a prolific writer and presenter on the topics of Situation Assessment and Human Factors. A simplified version of her three stages of situation assessment are integrated into the "A" and "B" of the ABCD process.

Major Vince Martinez, USMC, was instrumental in helping to design the presentation that put additional emphasis on the use of the ABCD as a continuous PROCESS, and not simply an Acronym.

> *"The value of an idea lies in using it."*
> *-Thomas Edison*

To John Ross, who has been one of the most enthusiastic evangelists of RRM since I have known him: as the US Airways 737 Fleet Captain during the first implementation of an AQP based on the RRM framework, a SME, Instructor, and leader as we introduced RRM in the Marine Corps, as a Ground School Instructor and AQP Manager at Southwest Airlines. John has a way of truly connecting with his audience and has been a champion communicating the concepts to upper management and in using the RRM model across departments in the airline to improve communication and coordination.

To Jim Owsley at Southwest who shared the vision for integrating RRM into the framework of the Advanced Qualification Program and has contributed his intellect and creativity to take it to new heights.

To Len Nemeth who has been the sounding board for more RRM concepts than I can count for over two decades. His wise counsel kept the presentations focused and pragmatic. His insistence on using a facilitative approach to train RRM propelled implementation to success. His tenacity in pushing me beyond self-imposed limits kept me on track.

To Richard "Pops" Preble who was the Commanding Officer of VMMT-204 during the MV-22's Return to Service (RTS). Pops was the first to point out the similarity between the use of the RRM ABCD process and John Boyd's OODA loop.

To Jim Levin who was a doctor, friend and neighbor with whom I had many conversations about the application of RRM into the field of medicine. Jim was fascinated with how we used a layered approach to establish Priorities, Policies, Procedures, and Flows to create standardization without hindering Operational Effectiveness. He introduced me to the concept of designing for complexity to help us further explain the type of Resource that is available for each operating environment.

"When all the dust has settled, and all the crowds are gone, the things that matter are faith, family and friends."
-Barbara Bush

Wow ... where do I start. Gary, my most treasured friend, counselor, editor, instructor, partner-in-mischief, and husband has seen me through 40 plus years of transition. He was the first to hear about (and critique) the RRM Model and has been instrumental in its development and implementation from the start to the finish as we are about to turn the reins over to the next generation. He has been an indispensable source of information and expertise from his experience as a former USAF pilot, Captain at US Airways/American, Check Airman, B737 and APD.

Although his best look is as an airline Captain (well ... maybe it was the USAF flight suit ...) he has truly shined as an instructor. He has that rare ability to provide just the right learning environment and then let mistakes go just long enough for learning to occur. In addition, he has had the incredible patience to put up with all of the mistakes and mis-steps throughout the years as I was laser focused on the RRM development. And now, he has the incredible patience to fix everything I break on the farm and put up with dogs, horses, chickens, and goats.

To LX Van Drie, our oldest daughter who grew up with an intuitive knowledge of Green-Yellow-Red. It is absolutely impossible to document all the insights and education she has provided, both in the past and even now as she has contributed to the illustrations and editing of this book. But I CAN tell you the favorite insight she provided. One day, when she was about 14, we were rushing to leave the house and she asked "Do know how you can tell when you're in the Red?"

"No," I replied.

"The cat's in the Red."

Yep. Red is contagious. She had made her point.

To Christine Van Drie who was right there by my side instilling the confidence needed to get through the tough times. As with LX she has also contributed more than I could possibly document. One of the major contributions was in the expanding the RRM concepts beyond-aviation as it has been integrated in our own lives. Christy's insights were instrumental in developing the caretaking routines we needed for people with dementia and cognitive disabilities. She pointed out what should have been obvious: the basic human factors to handle stress in an airplane were equally applicable to us as caretakers and the people we're caring for. She has also applied the RRM to her own profession as a sound engineer for live events and raising a toddler.

As I stated above, there are many throughout the years who have contributed their knowledge and critiques to the Volant RRM model. They are so numerous that to remember all is difficult. If I forgot to mention your contributions, I apologize in advance.

Appendix

Trifold card for cutout

Risk and Resource Management (RRM)

ABCD ®

Assess (Situational Awareness)
What is different now?
Task Loading, Additive Conditions, Crew Factors
How will it impact me?
How will it impact the future?
Are we in the Green-Yellow-Red?
Moving into Yellow and Red -
Situational Awareness will decrease.

Balance (Decision Making)
Balance time, priorities, workload
What are our options?
How should we use them?
How much time do we really have?
Moving into Yellow and Red -
Creative decision making becomes more difficult.

Communicate
Who has more information?
Who needs to know?
Who can help?
Who can provide back-up?
Moving into Yellow and Red -
Communications must become more directive.

Do & Debrief (Active Learning)
Take action.
Carry out the plan.
Were we successful?
Were expectations met?
Debrief improves future performance and develops resilience

Four principles of Risk Management improve the odds of reaching your goals:
• Accept no unnecessary risk.
• Anticipate and manage risk by planning.
• Accept risk when benefits outweigh the cost.
• Make risk decisions at the right level.

Using RRM daily improves effectiveness, increases leadership skills and trains the brain to continue to think, even under duress.

• The **Green-Yellow-Red** Target
 = Potential for error
• The colorful blocks
 = **Resources** to improve performance, reduce risk and manage a time-constrained situation
• **ABC***D* = Fast, continuous process to improve performance and minimize risk

Learning by using the RRM framework:

1. Recognize the 'symptoms' Green-Yellow-Red (G-Y-R) status for yourself and others
2. Communicate in appropriate style for the G-Y-R status (in yourself and others)
3. Practice **ABC***D* until it is a subconscious habit when
 • Sensing a change in G-Y-R status
 • Changing a phase of operation or task
 • Recognizing a new or changing risk factor
4. Consistently review performance to strengthen resources and improve resilience
5. Recognize when it is time for a "Shackleton Maneuver"; changing the current goal to enable long-term success

VOLANT SYSTEMS

Assessing Risk

⇨ **The Green** — Proactive management anticipates problems and minimizes errors
- Good Situational Awareness
- Resources in place to catch errors before they have an impact

⇨ **The Yellow** — Higher chance of errors "escaping"
- Situational awareness could be decreasing
- Higher task loading, additive conditions and/or crew factors
- Resources may not be in place to enhance performance or catch errors
- Decision Making may be impacted by increased stress

⇨ **The Red** — High chance of serious error or operational failure
- Tunnel vision may occur as stress increases
- Resources not effective to achieve goals or catch errors
- Requires a "recovery"
- Communications must become more directive

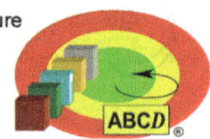

Factors Increasing Risk / Decreasing Performance

Task Loading
- Task overload / underload
  → Task loading = Time Required/Time Available

Additive Conditions
- Degraded or distracting conditions: *Equipment, Environment, Expectations*
- Be aware of channelized attention
- Unpredictable situations or flow of information

Crew Factors
- Factors that impact the performance of individual, crew or team, such as:
  → Fatigue / Stress / Fear / Experience
  → Expectation Bias
  → Group mindset
  → "Press on Regardless" attitude

Use Resources to Improve Performance and Reduce Risk

■ **Policies, Procedures, Flows, & Techniques**
increase the speed of actions and decisions. They also improve the ability to work with others and/or work under duress.
(Use ABCD to recognize unique situations and avoid complacency.)

USE THE RESOURCES TO CREATE BARRIERS TO CONSEQUENTIAL ERRORS

■ **Checklists & Job Aids** reduce reliance on memory.
(Reduce training required and decrease risk by providing back-up for critical times.)

■ **Automation/Technology** provide more accessible information, spread-out workload, automate routine tasks.
(Use ABCD to determine right level of automation and set it up before you need it.)

■ **Briefings & External Resources** provide the crew/team with common strategy and a different perspective. *(Standardization improves information transfer.)*

■ **Knowledge, Skills, and Attitude** -Knowledge and targeted experience improve overall performance and decreases impact of crew factors.
(Use ABCD to enhance coordination and improve future performance.)

Bibliography

Andino, Gabe. 2014. "United Flight 232: Surviving the Unthinkable - NYCAviationNYCAviation." NYCAviation. July 18, 2014. https://www.nycaviation.com/2014/07/disaster-miracle-united-flight-232/34639.

Clear, James. 2018. *Atomic Habits*. Penguin.

Contributor, Shackleton. 2021. "Shackleton's Imperial Trans-Antarctic Expedition." Shackleton. Shackleton. August 9, 2021. https://shackleton.com/en-us/blogs/articles/shackleton-imperial-trans-antarctic-expedition.

Dictionary.com. 2023. "Safe Definition & Meaning | Dictionary.Com." Www.Dictionary.Com. January 1, 2023. https://www.dictionary.com/browse/safe.

FAA. 2006. "AC 120-54A - Advanced Qualification Program - (Change 1)." Federal Aviation Administration. FAA. June 23, 2006. https://www.faa.gov/regulations_policies/advisory_circulars/index.cfm/go/document.information/documentid/23190.

Groom, Winston. 2015. *The Aviators*. National Geographic Books.

IATA. 2022. "IATA - IATA Releases 2021 Airline Safety Performance." IATA - Home. March 2, 2022. https://www.iata.org/en/pressroom/2022-releases/2022-03-02-01/.

Kolker, Robert. 2019. "Why US Airways Pilot Chesley Sullenberger III May Be the Last of His Kind -- New York Magazine - Nymag." New York Magazine. https://www.facebook.com/NewYorkMag. April 11, 2019. https://nymag.com/news/features/53788/.

McCullough, David. 2016a. *The Wright Brothers*. Simon and Schuster.

———. 2016b. *The Wright Brothers*. Simon and Schuster.

Merritt, Ph.D, Ashleigh, and James Klinect, Ph.D. 2021. "Threat and Error Management (TEM) | SKYbrary Aviation Safety." SKYbrary Aviation Safety. 2021. https://skybrary.aero/articles/threat-and-error-management-tem.

NTSB. 2009. "Accident Report NTSB/AAR-10/03 ." *Loss of Thrust in Both Engines After Encountering a Flock of Birds and Subsequent Ditching on the Hudson River US Airways Flight 1549 Airbus A320-214, N106US*, January.

NTSB. 2018. "NTSB Docket - Docket Management System." Ntsb.Gov. NTSB. November 14, 2018. https://data.ntsb.gov/Docket/?NTSB-Number=DCA16FA217.

NTSB. 2019. "Left Engine Failure and Subsequent Depressurization Southwest Airlines Flight 1380 Boeing 737-7H4, N772SW Philadelphia, Pennsylvania April 17, 2018." *NTSB/AAR-19/03 PB2019-101439*, November.

———. 2023. "Survivability of Accidents Involving Part 121 US Air Carrier Operations: 2020 Update." Home. March 30, 2023. https://www.ntsb.gov/safety/data/Pages/Part121Accident Survivability.aspx.

Ranter, Harro. 2023. "Aviation Safety Network > Statistics." Aviation Safety Network. 2023. https://aviation-safety.net/statistics/.

Reason, James. 2021. "James Reason HF Model | SKYbrary Aviation Safety." SKYbrary Aviation Safety. SKYbrary Aviation. 2021. https://skybrary.aero/articles/james-reason-hf-model.

Scott, Richard G. 2013. *21 Principles*. Deseret Book.

US DOT. 2004. "AC 120-51B." *Crew Resource Management Training*, January.

Made in the USA
Monee, IL
29 July 2023